PIECES
OF MY SELF

MIROLAND IMPRINT 43

Canada Council   Conseil des Arts
for the Arts   du Canada

ONTARIO ARTS COUNCIL
CONSEIL DES ARTS DE L'ONTARIO

an Ontario government agency
un organisme du gouvernement de l'Ontario

Canadä

Guernica Editions Inc. acknowledges the support of the Canada Council
for the Arts and the Ontario Arts Council. The Ontario Arts Council
is an agency of the Government of Ontario.

We acknowledge the financial support of the Government of Canada.

PIECES
OF MY SELF

KEITH GAREBIAN
Fragments of an Autobiography

MIROLAND (GUERNICA)
TORONTO • CHICAGO • BUFFALO • LANCASTER (U.K.)
2023

Guernica Founder:
Antonio D'Alfonso

Connie McParland, Michael Mirolla, series editors
Michael Mirolla, editor
David Moratto, cover design and interior design
Guernica Editions Inc.
287 Templemead Drive, Hamilton, ON L8W 2W4
2250 Military Road, Tonawanda, N.Y. 14150-6000 U.S.A.
www.guernicaeditions.com

Distributors:
Independent Publishers Group (IPG)
600 North Pulaski Road, Chicago IL 60624
University of Toronto Press Distribution (UTP)
5201 Dufferin Street, Toronto (ON), Canada M3H 5T8
Gazelle Book Services
White Cross Mills, High Town, Lancaster LA1 4XS U.K.

First edition.
Printed in Canada.

Legal Deposit—First Quarter
Library of Congress Catalog Card Number: 2022944752
Library and Archives Canada Cataloguing in Publication
Title: Pieces of my self : fragments of an autobiography / Keith Garebian.
Names: Garebian, Keith, author.
Description: First edition.
Identifiers: Canadiana (print) 20220410372 | Canadiana (ebook) 20220410380
| ISBN 9781771838009 (softcover) | ISBN 9781771838016 (EPUB)
Subjects: LCSH: Garebian, Keith. | CSH: Poets, Canadian (English)—Biography.
| LCSH: Theater critics—Canada—Biography. | LCSH: Critics—Canada
—Biography. | LCGFT: Autobiographies.
Classification: LCC PS8563.A645 Z46 2023 | DDC C811/.6—dc23

"The truth is rarely pure and never simple."
(**Oscar Wilde**, *The Importance of Being Earnest*)

"There is no end of things in the heart."
(**Ezra Pound**, "Exile's Letter")

"Grace/to be born and live as variously as possible"
(**Frank O'Hara**, "In Memory of My Feelings")

"A self that goes on changing is a self that goes on living"
(**Virginia Woolf**, "The Humane Art" in
The Death of the Moth and Other Essays)

*In memory of my
sister Elma and my parents*

CONTENTS

CHAPTER ONE

MY PASSAGE TO ARARAT

H ow did it all begin? With my own history of conflict, especially one between remembering and forgetting. Maria Stepanova has written: "Memory works on behalf of separation, it prepares for the break, without which the self cannot emerge" (*In Memory of Memory*). And Anne Carson declares: "The responsibility of the living to the dead is not simple. It is we who let them go, for we do not accompany them. It is we who hold them here—deny them their nothingness—by naming their names. Out of these two wrongs come the writing of epitaphs" (*Economy of the Unlost*).

Instead of beginning in the land called childhood, I start with my Armenian father's death as an act of understanding, a purposeful attempt to find the roots of my conflicted identity in his twisted story of exile and an irrecoverable past.

Saturday, November 25, 1995: He died while asleep in Brampton Civic Hospital, unable to reach for water on the table, unable to gasp out his plague of thirst. His mouth was a black hole, caught with grotesque suddenness in *rigor mortis*.

It was a moment I had long anticipated, dreaded, and desired. A wild man had shrunk incontestably into the final truth of mortality. My sister Audrey and I embraced in grief but I could not weep. Some other force was taking over, as if there were some ineffable release, some long-expected collapse of tensions, leaving me free and yet in some sense unprepared.

How small his emaciated body seemed, as if the bones and shriv-elled skin were the relics of an ultimate abandonment. Gone were the terrible ferocity of his bitter anger, the huge appetite for sensual indulgence, the protracted agony of filling in stretches of empty old age with the habits of decrepitude and an unspoken but undeniable longing to reject death. I prayed for the repose of his soul, I prayed that the ancient bad feelings between us would die out. Had I known the Armenian word then, I would have wished him benevo-lent *hankisd* ... rest. Rest.

My father had often spoken about the miseries of old age, yet when death seemed closest, he had never spoken about last things. Even as he rasped through dry, burning lips, he wanted to face one more round of tortuous dependency on the kindness of others.

"I'm grateful," he barely whispered when two family friends, the Kulhanian sisters, had come from Vancouver to console him. Their Armenian father, an excellent jeweller, had been my father's steadfast friend in Bombay, but had died too early from cancer.

My father and I had long been spiritual adversaries—he, unable to understand my nature and sensitivities; I, unwilling to permit my sympathy for his boyhood nightmares to prevail against my anger at his wild power.

My father's conversations at parties and around the family table invariably led to arguments with me, often at the top of his voice, about anything from religion, politics, and technology to literature, movies, and social customs. Perhaps because he was so vilely de-prived of a formal education, he wanted to assert himself—to show that he knew what he spoke about. He would always claim prior knowledge, even on such trivial subjects as film. No matter how critically acclaimed a current release was, he felt that it suffered in comparison with the "original." *A Star Is Born* with Judy Garland and James Mason was fine, yes, but you should have seen the ori-ginal with Janet Gaynor and Fredric March. The most recent ver-sions of *Back Street* or *Madame X* were "not a patch" on the original black and white versions. The chariot race in *Ben-Hur* was some-thing to behold, especially when Ramon Novarro, rather than

Charlton Heston, was at the reins. And even *Gone with the Wind* with Leigh and Gable couldn't measure up to the original. "The original, before 1939?" I asked, incredulity scrawled across my face. "Oh, yes. There was one ... with I can't remember who ... and it was in black and white."

His world was one of black and white, clear-cut options and verdicts.

How could it have been otherwise?

"I was born in a region made famous by King Dekran," he proudly related to me shortly after my mother, younger than him by thirteen years, had died of emphysema in 1991. His baptismal name was Atam (for Adam). His father, Stepan, was from a family of iron manufacturers who specialized in tools and machinery for irrigation and agriculture. He was suddenly "recruited" into the Turkish army and disappeared forever in a convoy to the front.

My father's mother was named Almas or some variant of it (later incorrectly transformed on his British passport into Elma).

"What did she look like?" I asked.

"Exactly like your sister Elma." My sister, two years younger than me, who had died at 36.

My father was the second of four children, all the others being girls: Rose (Varti or one of its variants, Vartanoush, Varteni, or Vartouhi), older than him by about four years; another, whose name he could not remember; and the youngest, Arshe, who was about four years younger than him and who had beautiful curly hair.

His birthplace, Dikranagerd, became a memory of mulberries, watermelon pregnant with pink juice, flat tiled roofs covered with white cloth to keep sleep cool. In clean evening light, the city hulled baskets of bulghur, sticking to work. My father recounted how one day in April 1915 just before dusk, when Turkish *muezzins* called Muslims to prayer, Kurds drove carts of melons to the bazaar, gendarmes rode on horseback, women shouldering amphorae met at fountains to exchange gossip and scandal, old storytellers in the marketplace sucked words from ancient water pipes, outdoor cafes filled with tea-drinkers who often played cards or backgammon as vendors offered *simit*, sesame rings on sticks. Food and drink were part of daily commerce: *raki*, (like Greek *ouzo*) a strong, clear liquor that turned milky when ice or water was added; multi-coloured fresh fish on crimson tray; *shish kebab*, yogurt, and *lokum* for those with a sweet tooth. Armenians met and talked the way they always talked, excitedly, incessantly, until it was time to return to their houses with red-tiled roofs and wide eaves.

At dusk, the Muslim call to prayer was a secret semaphore, a coded message for sanctioned terror. In small villages or cities, across Anatolia, the Turks beat on every Armenian family's door, ordering the occupants to leave all their possessions just where they were. Women were dragged out of washtubs, children snatched from their beds. On the mountainsides, where poplars latticed the sky, farmers were forced to leave their ploughs and cattle and join the "deportation" or "relocation." The Turks forbade the taking of any photographs of this "deportation" on pain of death, though a few German missionaries did manage a hurried picture or two through hotel windows. As mule-carts rumbled along the route, and as the convoys of hundreds of helpless Armenians were reduced to shuffling bundles of rags, the Turks organized special bands of criminals and Kurdish tribesmen to prey on the defenceless columns. Women and children were raped, men and youth disappeared. The Turks pretended that the males were recruits for their army, but many bodies were later discovered in ditches. Kurds had a propensity for slicing off breasts and hands with scimitars and flinging babies into burning bushes. Stray dogs had a rich feast on human carrion, scattering bones.

A little more than five years of age, my father felt a wound in his side, something wrenched from him when he, his mother, and three sisters joined other Armenians on a long trek through weeds, bare stones, and sand. Starving, thirsting, many dying of hunger and a broken heart, they trudged in the dryness of exile. Time became weeks of tendons and sinews, the fitful vulnerability of flesh, death by wholesale subtraction. His young life moved in a series of halts and marches. There was no hero or heroine to save him. He was too young for absolute truth, and nobody offered an explanation that he could possibly understand.

When he died from cancer in early winter, 1995, he had lived past eight decades, but he was a man who had been unable to be a boy who could play without a gnawing hunger in his stomach, a raw taste in his mouth. He had loved to eat as if in fear of reprising the starvation of his boyhood, the hunt for wild grass and discarded scraps from tables that never called him to dinner. And even as he gorged himself on rich food in his adult years, extravagant rice dishes with meat, raisins, and almonds, buttery chicken, cool cucumber with yogurt, he could still smell the stench of rotting corpses—those flung into yawning pits or the swollen, waterlogged ones spewed out by dark rivers or the swollen sea.

His hunger was the result of nightmare, a delirium moaning like the tide or Ararat levelled by a seismic God.

My memoir *Pain: Journeys Around My Parents* and my poetry collection *Children of Ararat* were about my father's traumatic experiences in that time of unforgivable atrocities, as I memorialized in prose and poetry what he had struggled to remember. When I was young, I would observe how at tea-time in Bombay, he would seem withdrawn in reverie, his eyes speaking for his heart. He always sipped his tea noisily, "teeth braced the way he flinched/ from certain memories, no sugar cube/ to sweeten his loss, slowly re-tasting his life/ in slurps, a far-away look in his eyes/ once gold in Dikranagerd."

But it took me a long time to learn the correct spelling of his birthplace. First, I had it as Dekranagert, then Dekranagerd, and finally as Dikranagerd. There has been a long history of alterations in spelling Armenian place names, owing to historical changes—Turkish conquest, Russian annexation, Armenian independence—and for the longest time, I did not care enough to remedy my ignorance.

Perhaps he always carried a desert within himself. Perhaps its sand blew across his silence as he moved through life in spasms of grief or rage, and bursts of joy. He could not express why his kin had gone to nothing, why he had no words large enough to hold them.

The Turkish part of his history made him feel pursued by a terror of decay, disease, and death.

In the midst of his paranoia, there was sometimes fierce comedy.

Fearing that the body could be a betrayal, he was always on the alert for disease, checking regularly for skin eruptions, bowel complications, and muscle distress. As a young man, he had been muscular and possessed great stamina, but in his middle years, his muscle tone declined as he took to heavy drinking. He paid the price one evening by slipping down a winding metal staircase and breaking his fall by smashing down an elbow. This did, indeed, break his fall, but it also dislocated one of the discs in his neck, leaving him with chronic pain. He had to use a neck brace and undertake nightly therapy in a harness that was suspended to a low beam in the house. At such times, he looked like a man about to be hanged.

"Don't feel sorry for him," my mother used to say. "He'll outlive us all."

He was always reading medical reports in newspapers and magazines about new diseases. Then he would examine himself for symptoms.

"I think I have something in my stomach."

It's probably indigestion, he was told.

"No. I know indigestion. This is something else. Serious. I feel bloated. And I have pain."

But he didn't have any fever, any discoloration, any hard lumps or discharges—which didn't arrest his anxiety. He dreamed of acute suffering, creating a scenario of emergency surgery, worried about how he would recuperate.

"He's probably imagining things again," my mother remarked.

Unable to win her concern, much less her sympathy, he took himself to the family doctor. Upon his return, my mother asked: "Well, what did the doctor find?"

Sheepishly, my father admitted: "I've got chronic constipation."

In this regard, my father was made for satire.

If there was an advertised special on footwear, he would claim to know which store had the best. "Go to my closet and you'll find a nice pair I just bought at Eaton's. Genuine leather. Very comfortable." But why were there so many unused pairs in the closet? "My damned feet are swollen." Go to a doctor, he was told.

"Damn quacks," he would swear. "It's just bad circulation, they tell me, but there's something wrong. I can feel it. Maybe I should see a specialist." But, according to him, the specialists in Brampton weren't reliable; maybe he should see someone in Toronto. That would necessitate a cab, which cost too much. Maybe he should go to a specialist in Brampton, after all. A doctor was respected only if he confirmed my father's worst fears.

In all other matters, he liked to give advice—even when it was unwanted. And it was usually linked to his paranoia.

If my car had a problem, he would insist that anything my trusted mechanic said was false. "Ech, damn rogues! All of them!" he would scoff. "Don't forget, I know the business."

He would always look at the negative rather than the positive side of things.

I almost always rejected his advice ... and more. Because I harboured anger at my father for our continual disagreements and his refusal to hear me, I rejected the Armenian language. I refused to attend Armenian class, even when it became available to me.

Once I deliberately lost a beautiful, jewelled ring crafted especially for me by an Armenian family friend, Leon Sanossian. I did not want any identification with my father's tribe, even though I loved that jeweller and his plump, short wife, Baidzer, who served pastries and tea from a silver samovar, called my two sisters and me "dollinks," frequently joked, and read our tea leaves with exaggerations of our good fortunes.

My father winked at us about her fortune-telling, but beneath this apparent scepticism there lurked his belief in superstition. Armenians have a long history of superstitions, despite the fact that they were discouraged by church leaders from believing in ancient practices, rituals, and omens. Superstition helped them in times when they could have succumbed to affliction.

Hailing from a land of great masses of rock and mountain, they believed in stone because it made the earth strong. After removing stones from a field, villagers would stack them carefully in the belief that to remove the stone entirely would weaken the earth. Stone also made for fertility. A barren tree could be turned fruitful if a stone were placed in its fork. Some stones could bring milk to the sallow breasts of dry women.

Superstition sustained the people, sometimes in the most bizarre ways. In times of drought, a woman could be yoked to a plough that dug a furrow in the dry earth. This helped produce rain.

My father never mentioned these ancient practices or the one I eventually discovered in a study of Armenian peasants: the reliable method of bringing rain by cutting off the head from a Turkish corpse and throwing it into a river. In a variant version, villagers exhumed a corpse, cut off the skull, and sprinkled water on it because it was believed that the newly dead were thirsty. Let the living satisfy the dead; perhaps, God would then satisfy the living.

I remember my father's death grimace, with his mouth open in a silent, parched cry.

I remember, too, the strange feeling of carrying his ashes in a gleaming urn to the grave where my mother had been buried four years earlier. The urn was more polished than his life, as it held the ashes of a man with large passions. Grey ashes, not a colour to cherish, something which smudged like a charcoal drawing.

William Faulkner: "The past is never dead. It's not even past."

Yerevan, Armenia, July 2013: "Keith, she has called your name!" declared my newfound American-Armenian friend, Lucine Kasbarian. "What for?" I asked, baffled. I had already seen Peter Surian, a good-natured senior Armenian from New York, receive the William Saroyan Medal for the Armenian translation of one of his novels. Peter was of the first generation of American-Armenian writers, and had played an important role as a literary critic, novelist and short story writer in the United States, while supporting the Armenian-American community, and bearing witness to the "incomprehensible destiny" of Armenians. The award to Peter made eminent sense. But I was not expecting my name to be called for any special reason—other than, perhaps, a gracious acknowledgement of my 70th birthday, which had already prompted an impromptu little celebration the night before at the ornate residence used for the Fifth Conference of Writers of Armenian Origin Composing in Foreign Languages, whose central theme was Globalization and National Identity. After four days (July 11–15, 2013) at the Writers' House in Tsaghkadzor, forty kilometres northeast of Yerevan, where I was often literally lost for words because I neither speak nor read (let alone write) in my father's language, I was expecting little more than a cordial end to a conference that had, in some ways, shaken me to the core. But a more delightful shock overcame me when I realized that I was to be the first Canadian-Armenian writer to be awarded the Saroyan Medal for my work and books on behalf of the Diaspora.

As Minister Hakobyan struggled to pin the bronze medal with ribbon on my shirt (I had abandoned my cotton jacket in a conference room), I composed a short speech in my mind, entrusting Natella Lalabekian (who typified sexy glam) to serve as my translator. I expressed how deeply honoured and touched I was by the award which came from my father's land, but I was also ruefully aware that this trip would show me more of Armenia than my father could ever have known during his childhood in Diyarbekir.

I dreamed of Ararat. "You will see Ararat everywhere!" Jirair Tutunjian had promised in Toronto, as if the sightings were a psychic inevitability for people of the mountain or those who identified spiritually with it. But the sad fact was that the mountain was not in the Republic; it was held, alive in its natural massive shape, by Turkey. Masis or Mount Ararat was just one more thing that the unspeakable nation had captured in its pornographic attempt to be an exterminating demon.

Exposed to Peter Balakian's eloquent prose and poetry (particularly *Black Dog of Fate* and *June Tree)*, miscellaneous other books and articles on Armenian history, then steeping myself in Kildare Dobbs's *Anatolian Suite*, and re-reading parts of Michael Arlen's

Passage to Ararat, I felt prepared to face the shadows. I would not be able to visit Diyarbekir in eastern Turkey, and although I had a melancholy feeling about this, I knew that I must mask or camouflage emotion on this trip lest it devolve into a voyage of hysteria.

Armenia came to me in rugged chunks: rough hills and mountains; expanses of dry, non-irrigable land; pockmarked stone churches; eroding *khachkars* in rural cemeteries and churchyards, and massive sculptures. Tsaghkadzor or Tsaghgatsor (the variant spelling) came into view only past villages and towns almost forgotten by time. The name (meaning "valley of flowers" or "flower canyon") is associated with that of the nearby mountain. Tsaghkadzor, a small settlement at first, became the favourite hunting ground for Armenian kings. Its high elevation (1800 metres) made it well suited to eventually becoming a ski resort. Writers' House was an ornate refuge, high in green wilderness. Established in 1930, it had been the haunt of many famous Armenian writers, such as Yeghishe Charents, Nairi Zaryan, Vardges Petrosyan, et cetera. There were landscape oil paintings by Armenian artists hanging on one long wall, and there was a plethora of heavy sculpted wood or ceramic panels, columns, and wall decorations on the second floor, where guest rooms were generally spartan in nature, hardly a cut above what one would encounter in a low-budget rooming-house. My own room had minimal furniture, rough-hewn, depressingly dark brown, and my bathtub lacked a curtain so that using the shower (when there was sufficient hot water) exposed the washroom to sprays that dampened everything in the room. But Tsaghkadzor was devoid of mosquito hordes—unlike the hotel in a raw, rural part of Romania where I was to stay during a poetry conference in 2015, and where my room, free of air-conditioning or even a bedside fan, necessitated my leaving the patio door open to invading mosquitoes that gratefully feasted on me.

The Armenian conference became an example of cultural schizophrenia, as native Armenian writers outnumbered the Diaspora ones, not all of whom read or wrote Armenian. In fact, there was more than one instance when a Western Armenian proclaimed the imperative of speaking Armenian in order to qualify as Armenian—an attitude that raised my ire, given my unshakable belief that as a writer in English, I was reaching a far wider readership than I would have had I performed the same function in my father's native tongue. The Diaspora writers who did not write in Armenian were allotted a mere five minutes for each of their readings, leading to bitterness on the part of many. Perhaps the Conference organizers had forgotten or ignored what Sarkis Guiragossian had written in *Aztag Daily* (Lebanon) in 2005: "Armenian writers who, as a result of bitter fate, create in foreign languages are not foreigners, but faithful and dedicated ambassadors of their Armenian blood and spirit in non-Armenian surroundings."

But this problem aside, I was treated with great warmth and courtesy. I made friends with Lucine Kasbarian (a wonderfully warm, sharply intelligent, gifted storyteller, journalist, and political cartoonist from New Jersey) and tall, willowy Kinga Kali (who had buried her father only three days before arriving in Armenia via a Russian plane reeking of gasoline). Kinga, who lives in Hungary, is a fervent feminist anthropologist with wry humour. "When I have trouble with a man, I beat him," she proclaimed. But she assured me she would never do that to me, because "You have charissma!" exaggerating the word with dramatic effect. I also was treated with great dignity and generosity by Levon Ananyan (Chairman of the Writers' Union of Armenia), David Karapetyan (Deputy Minister of Diaspora), and Roza Hovhanessyan of the Ministry—their many acts of kindness catalyzed by the active mediation of Khoren Mardoyan, assistant to the Ministry in Toronto.

Three years junior to me, Levon Ananyan was evidently not an easy man for those who clashed with him politically. A graduate of Yerevan State University, Department of Philology, he had worked for a number of state journals before becoming the chief editor of *Garoun* and President of the Writer's Union of Armenia. He ran his own publishing house (Apollo), had strong political influence with the Ministry, and did not tolerate dissent. His volatile temper was notorious; he was a man of genuine passion. Levon's English was far better than that of most other Armenians from the homeland, and I noticed him studying my face over lunch, before he remarked: "You have Armenian eyes." I understood what he meant, for I have inherited more than my name from my Armenian father. I have also absorbed Armenian *galut*, really a Hebrew term for feelings of being uprooted from the homeland. An irony in my case, because not having been born and lived in Armenia, I was not actually uprooted from it. Yet, my psyche has yearned for ancestral roots and a firm identity.

It was impossible for me to be cool and detached in Armenia, first because such *sang-froid* is hardly native to my constitution, and second because I found that my psyche is marked by a fiery Armenian intensity and argumentativeness that sometimes could seem almost pathological.

Because of the extraordinary warmth of many of my colleagues, and my senior maturity (verging on anecdotage), I was brought into a direct but brief confrontation with the rigour, cruelty, generosity, frustration, and celebration of Armenian life. It was not an easy subject to jump into, but it lured me into feeling something—discomfort, charm, pleasure, or pathos—something that transcended clichés of exhausted dignity or traumatic frissons. I felt a strange sense of sadness observing (from a bus window) a woman sheep-herder, strong boned, deeply tanned, as she controlled her flock. I would publish a poem ("Sheep in Sun") years later about this experience, representing myself as an outsider or voyeuristic passerby, separated from the sheepherder and sheep, yet feeling a radical melancholy while observing her and the animals. A typically Armenian *garod* as "a sadness" fell upon me, making feel like a "wanderer, a stranger/ in any land."

After all, despite all the benevolence of my fellow writers, I could be little more than a mere tourist admiring streets and avenues in Yerevan named after great Armenian writers or when visiting imposing but partially eroded Echmiadzin Cathedral; the ancient temple at Garni near a deep canyon and a slow-crawling river; Geghard monastery with its icy fresh spring water flowing out of black rock; the eroding *khachakars* of Noratus; the Opera House (where I attended a performance of the ballet *Spartacus*, frequently interrupted by clicking cameras in the noisy audience); the Paradjanov Museum with its intriguing collages made from hairpins, dolls, ladies' hats, and religious relics; Matenadaran (the Mesrop Mashtots Institute of Ancient Manuscripts); salty Lake Sevan where hardy swimmers dared the cold water; and festive Republic Square with its musical fountains. I felt a kinship with the rocks, the soil, the scrub, the apricot trees, the exquisite illuminated manuscripts, the massive stone architecture, the Paradjanov memorabilia (particularly the drawings he made in prison), the dancing fountains, even the biting wind whipping around the lake. There was an awesome immensity to the sky and the rocks in the countryside, and Yerevan was vivid with sweat, bread and black olives, frothy scalding tea in glasses passed hand to hand, turbulent crowds, mothers and grandmothers with breasts shaking like pomegranates, men playing chess between monuments, vendors of sizzling *shashlik*, dried fruit, hard candy, and leather goods. I felt a new sense of Time, a new provocation for thought. The huge space invited larger thoughts, but of what? The endemic poverty of rural Armenia? The undeniable threats from Russia and Turkey? The ever-widening loss of native Armenians to the lures of more economically-profitable countries? The real or imagined threats of globalization to national identity? Spectres of the genocide from almost a century ago?

Believing that I had prepared myself against an overwhelming welter of feelings, I resolved to be silent because of the "remoteness" of the genocide, silent because I felt that my father and I had forgiven each other, silent because I had already written about feeling a nomadic kinship with him, silent because I had already given voice in poetry to empty work-sheds, ruined orchards, shrivelled shoes, abandoned flutes, and blue shadows. I had delivered elegies in print for my father and his murdered tribe, for Arshile Gorky, Sergei Paradjanov, and William Saroyan. I had commemorated tools for chopping cotton that had been used to gouge Armenian flesh, tattooed Armenian girls, and at least thirteen ways of looking at the Turk, especially of their coded innuendo: "Take care of the Armenians." I had wept softly in 1991 when my father tried to articulate his jumbled nightmare in his strongly accented, tainted English, so I was done with weeping. But after I had entered the memorial proper with its twelve huge vertical slabs of stone (representing districts of historical Armenia) and had joined my colleagues, each of us adding a white rose in the circle of stone surrounding the eternal flame, I felt older than my father and subject to a sudden pain that went beyond pain. I remembered in a way I had not anticipated his tearful, terrified three-year-old sister (whose name he had long forgotten) abandoned under a lonely tree as he, his older sister, and mother assured her they would return. It was, of course, a false promise because it was rooted in an impossible proposition.

I had written of that horror and others from the 1915 genocide in *Children of Ararat*, focussing on my father's traumatic tribulations, remembering how he sometimes seemed to be lost in another world. In 2021, when reading Diana der Hovanessian's "The First Morning," I came across these lines from an old Armenian folk poem, "Andouni": "'your heart like those ruined houses/ of dislodged pillars, broken beams,/ your house always not your home."

Built in 1967 on one of the three hills along the Hrazdan River that carry the name Tsitsernakaberd (literally "Swallow's fortress"), and once the site of an Iron Age fortress, the Genocide Memorial stands apart from the Museum and garden. It stands like a tall sentinel dominating the space, almost in rebuke of the peaceful garden where countless foreign dignitaries (politicians, musicians, athletes, and religious figures) have their names proudly memorialized near trees they have planted with respect for the dead and as signs of new life.

On July 15 (my birthday) our group made its solemn way to the Memorial and completed the ritual of laying a large wreath outside the entrance. Within, a large stone circle descended 1.5 metres, and at its centre burned an eternal flame. On that sun-blazing day at the mausoleum, in July's hot white light over an arrow-shaped 44-metre stele split vertically, the Genocide Museum nearby carried more than ash in glass casings, more than soil from tombs. There was a huge silence. Grief saturated stone, and walls seemed to speak names of bodies unrisen from faraway despoiled graves. Twelve tall angled tablets were *khatchkars* carved with crosses, representing twelve lost provinces. Stone and more stone, then flame that burns longer than the lives so abruptly and brutally obliterated, with many, if not most, of their names gone forever. A monumental melancholy pressed down upon me. Silence for an ancient history where the oldest had borne most, and the youngest had lived least. Silence in which I felt I would never see as much as those dead had seen and borne.

I felt a wretched pain in my throat, as my mind rehearsed a requiem, ill with carnage of a people. Hot tears spurt from me as I was quietly comforted by the embracing arms of Hermine Navasardyan (of the Armenian Writers Union) and Lucine Kasbarian. They seemed to know instinctively the reason why I was emotionally overcome.

"We are such a strong people to have survived," Lucine said. "You and I are Dikranagertsi."

Indeed, and more, I began to realize when remembering that day. We are people of the Mountain. We are the Mountain.

I never did get to see The Mountain. There was too much July haze for that, but I thought I caught a glimpse of its far-off snow-capped peaks during a bus ride.

There was no sound from The Mountain.

To see Ararat in its reality is one reason for me to return some day. Another is my refusal to forget the Armenian past, to allow it to die with my father, or to keep it only to myself.

I have sometimes stared at the Saroyan Medal, studying its geometric shape (two interlocking squares) attached to a tri-coloured fabric. The colours are symbolic: red for the blood shed by over a million genocide victims; orange for the country's courage; and blue for the Armenian sky. The bronze medal bears an image of moustachioed Saroyan on one side; the image of a long-winged crane in flight, Ararat in the background, on the other. Saroyan, the Armenian-American writer, "his heart in the highlands, on a trapeze/ or quietly crying under comedy/ for remembered bodies mummifying/ in

Bitlis"—to quote from my own poem, "Elegy for William Saroyan." He wears no smile, his thick, bristling moustache dominantly spilling over his jawline, his eyes almost daring us to remember how the world could be "a big fat falsehood, after all." As for Ararat and the slim, long-bodied crane with huge wings, they are emblems: the sacred Mountain lost to the Turks, and the crane representing something that doesn't need to be imagined because the crane follows a repeated ritual of flight and return, with necessity and instinct quivering faithfully. I wonder if I, like the Armenian crane, created my own ritual, memorializing my father's flight from his birthplace while visiting his home country.

My father and his slightly older sister Varduhi (my Aunt Rose), survived the slaughter, but no other known family member did, although I have heard rumours about relatives in Basra, Iraq. Having no real father since boyhood, he had no model to be one to me. He could not recognize my boyhood needs, and there was no bonding between us, except in times of pain and mourning. Our mutual antipathies aside (described in my memoir *Pain*), I always empathized secretly with him and his persecuted, often callously forgotten tribe. I also admired him (just as secretly) because of his strength, courage, and ability to carve out an impressive career in Bombay, where he emigrated (year unknown to me) in order to be reunited with his surviving sister, and where I was born to him and my Anglo-Indian mother in 1943. I always thought of myself as my mother's son, and sometimes had wished for a different father. He was a good provider and loved his wife and three children, but he had been a hard man to know and live with—just as I probably am—but we did draw microscopically closer as time shrank my bitterness and caused each of us to understand that we were both, in a radical sense, resident aliens—to each other, as well as to our adopted countries.

There is an inveterate irony in our family name, for it derives from a Turkish-Arabic word for "stranger" or (sometimes) "pilgrim": *garip* or *gharib*. It is a word with many radiations of meaning: comical, extraordinary, fantastic, grotesque, peculiar, quaint, queer, quirky, strange. Many of these adjectives are applicable to my own and my father's life, though I want to stress a particular meaning that carries existential significance.

My father was obviously a stranger in India (linguistically and culturally), while I also felt alien to it. India was like a second skin that I had wanted to slough off, and he had a dwindling connection with Armenia. He did speak Armenian, and read Armenian pamphlets, but his mother tongue was not deeply practised except when he met with fellow Armenians in Bombay. The result was that his Armenian wore away gradually, and as he began to lose much of his native dialect, he became a cultural urchin or orphan again. Soon after his death in 1995, I found a copy of Franz Werfel's *The Forty Days of Musa Dagh* in one of his closets, along with old jackets and leather shoes (some hardly worn). He was always offering me his shoes, once his feet became too swollen to fit them—a semiotic irony I now can recognize. Given the incredible odyssey of his childhood, I could never know what it was to walk in his shoes in any sense.

As I wrote near the end of *Pain*: "He died without ever telling me if he had retained any faith in man, but I knew instinctively that he willed for me a survival against despair. He never said aloud whether he thought a writer disappeared so much into imagination as to be absent from the real world, but I know in my bones that he wished for me to find a place in whatever world where I could bear witness to a devastation of grace." When Frontenac House in Calgary published *Children of Ararat* (2010), I was grateful for the opportunity of paying homage to him and his murdered tribe. The book was in a radical sense my argument with the world that had turned a deaf ear to the cries of over a million Armenians and their descendants. But it was more than this: a palpable struggle on my part to understand something crucial about Armenians—not just the ordinary folk, but the creative geniuses as well, such as Arshile Gorky, Sergei Paradjanov, Atom Egoyan, and William Saroyan. Perhaps, too, it was my way of identifying myself as Armenian, at least as far as my instincts and obsessions were concerned. I have inherited some of my father's passion.

I have never studied Armenian, never spoken, read, or written it. I was *odar*—though far less so than my mother and sisters had been. Armenia and Armenians existed and cast their shadows across me, and I never felt for even an instant that they were second-rate or unworthy of my attention or devotion. I never felt it confounding that my father had come from a race of merchants and traders, jewellers, and soldiers. What I had been resisting was not Armenians, *per se*, but my father's shadow, and once I realized this, I also sensed that there was a mysterious bond between me and Armenians.

Atrocity is often magnified by the scale of statistics, but what need of a million and a half bodies when a single abandoned, anonymous child can cry out for rescue under a nameless tree in an unnamed geography of terror? That barely remembered sister of my unfortunate father reminded me why I am my father's son, a stranger to his language and some of his countrymen's customs but an Armenian with eyes that sometimes have a deep-sea sadness and a soul across which the snows of Ararat blow.

"What was it that so darkened our world?" This sentence in W. G. Sebald's *Austerlitz* struck me like a bolt of lightning. We are prone to forget our beginnings, especially those that carry bad news of the world. But beginnings are not only genealogical or geographical origins; they are cause, *raison d'être*, first gesture, collective history. And I, who have learned so little of these beginnings, wish to know who and what I am, even if only through what I reveal of myself to myself. My name was given me and is outside of who I am. Armenian, English, East Indian, Canadian. I hail from a world of wounds, surmounting them, creating my own.

As a writer, I may have become what Maria Stepanova calls "the horizon point of the family line," but I am also (as she also suggests of writers) "a stranger, a teller of tales, a selector and sifter, the one who decides what part of the huge volume of the unsaid must fit in the spotlight's circle, and what part will remain outside it in the darkness."

In a dream, my parents are alive, and I am not a ghost. Perhaps we are about to share a pomegranate together, that fruit being emblematic of Armenia because it represents fertility and good fortune. Legend tells us that in Western Armenia, a bride would throw a pomegranate, causing it to break into pieces and scattering seeds, those seeds ensuring she would bear children.

It is a difficult emblem, given the true melancholy history of an ancient country.

CHAPTER TWO

GROWING UP ANGLO-INDIAN

"**B**ring on the bears!" Timothy Findley was once urged by one of his trusted literary agents who intended the Goldilocks fable to be a touchstone. In other words, it was only through conflict or tension created by something possibly sinister that a story could thrive. In my own case, the "bears" were the dark shadow of my Armenian father. There was no Goldilocks, however, no fairy tale with a sweet, happy conclusion or sense of closure. My Anglo-Indian mother was sweet, gentle, patient, diplomatic, but unable to forestall, challenge, or quell his inclination towards violence, physical or emotional. Theirs was a marriage that probably conformed to the broad contours of middle-class domesticity in a period where the wife could rule the household without being a direct threat to the husband. She had only the money he budgeted for daily living, no funds of her own. This economic dependence was a limitation with a corollary: psychological dependence. The wife could not make an existential decision on her own or sustain a life truly emancipated from the husband's authority. Nevertheless, much of her marriage was comfortable, perhaps because the only "bear" was her husband, whom she learned to cope with, secure in the knowledge that he loved her, as well as their three offspring in a land where the sea always smelled and tasted the same, and where the sun shone with predictable consistency, except in the monsoon season.

My story could have been called a tale of two cities. One was Bombay, from which my mother came. Mumbai, the vernacular derived from *Maha Amba*, Great Mother. The other city was one from which my father fled wildly, around the edges of terror and rootlessness. I could produce a clear, clean map of the first city, show you exactly where it lies in the dense tangle of a teeming subcontinent, show you how it suckles at the teat of Mother India. But I have no map of the second city, which to my father was the disappearing trick of an atrocious magus, envoy to the underworld of inhumanity. I think of the first city as an illustrious dream, not because of inherent beauty, but because it was many-fabled, often lost in a plenitude of cheap illusion. I think of the second as a defacing nightmare, ever returning, an encircling *cauchemar* of history, scattering a tribe recklessly.

I was born a divided river beneath a bizarre zodiac. My father, a traumatized survivor of this century's first acknowledged holocaust; my mother, an Anglo-Indian, tributaries of her blood flowing from two directions. Even in Bombay, as an adolescent, I was never fully of a single place.

India and Armenia lay in a strange juxtaposition in my life. The first English woman to make a voyage to India in 1617 was actually the companion of an Indian-born Armenian lady. Armenians were in India long before the British. An Armenian merchant, Thomas Cana, landed on the Malabar Coast seven centuries before Vasco de Gama. As traders, Armenians came by the overland route, through Persia, Afghanistan (once called Bactria), and Tibet. According to *Armenians in India*, by Mesrovb Jacob Seth, "It was Akbar, the Marcus Aurelius of India, who induced them to come and settle in his dominions instead of being mere sojourners in the country." A thriving community soon sprang up in Agra, where an Armenian church was erected in 1562. One of Akbar's *begums* (women of high rank) was an Armenian, as was the lady doctor of the royal Seraglio. By the 18th century, a number of wealthy Armenians made their influence felt, and there was even an Armenian version of Krupp in Lahore who cast bronze guns, one of which was immortalized as "Zamzamah," a fire-breathing "dragon" in Kipling's *Kim*.

Armenians left their mark in Delhi, Surat, Kabul, Chandernagore, Julfur, Madras, Lucknow, and, of course, the large cities of Bombay and Calcutta. The largest Armenian community was in Calcutta, which accommodated three classes of Armenians: the so-called "Calcutta Armenians," whose ancestors had settled there in the 18th and 19th centuries, and most of whom enjoyed the benefits of English education. Historical archives reveal some interesting Armenian characters. Sarmad, a merchant and Sufi poet during the reign of Emperor Shah Jehan, smoked *bhang* (mild marijuana), which he kept in an earthen pot near him always. He fell so passionately in love with a Hindu girl, and grew so distracted by her that he would go about naked in the streets. His indecent exposure finally earned him execution. Petrus Arathoon, another merchant, was employed by Lord Robert Clive in the 18th century as a confidential agent in negotiations with Mir Jaffir, commander of Bengali forces, in order to overthrow Suraj ud-Daulah, the Nawab or sovereign ruler, who had perpetrated the "Black Hole" tragedy in 1756. His services rendered, Arathoon went unrewarded and was eventually abandoned by Clive. There was the ignoble Carapiet Petrus Moorat, an importer who practised various impostures: surgeon, secretary to the Khedive's architect in Egypt, benefactor to young Armenian students (though his salary never exceeded twenty rupees a month), and scholar of the French and Armenian languages (though he spoke little French and no classical Armenian). And there was the eccentric Hripsimah Eleazar Leembruggen (the surname a result of marriage to a Dutchman in Surat), who was the soul of generosity but who was in the habit of drawing up a new will every year.

Apart from Mesrovb Seth's book, there is, however, no extensive record of the entry, domicile, or collective Indian experience of the Armenians. There is abundant information on the English in India. There is even much information on the first English ladies on the subcontinent. Many of them were bent on fishing for husbands and new status. India let them in, acting as a lure to the boredom that would stun them, brittle *memsahibs*, masters' wives, untouchable in their privileged whiteness among rats, rabid dogs, chintz-covered furniture mined by ants, and gardens wilting with decorum. Theirs was an age of gentleman-callers, and of warnings to never shake hands with an Indian because they'd never know where his hand had been. Casual racism that prompted laughter in English clubs, at polo or horse-races. India was not for dabbling. Like the salt air, it could seep into their bones.

India, of course, is at the core of my memories. Its dense web of valences was part of my growing up. But my true country was Literature. In boyhood, I collected postage stamps, silver and gold foil from cigarette packets and gift wrappings, glossy black and white photographs of movie stars, and marbles (used in competitive games). Most of these collections dwindled in time, especially when I began collecting books. In high school, I turned into a voracious reader, ignoring subjects that did not engage me, racing through homework with minimal effort, playing outdoor sports (especially cricket), going to movies, but always electing books by which to occupy my idle hours. Idle, however, is the wrong word, for reading is anything but an idle activity.

Our neighbours who lived directly below our flat at The Retreat included a retired doctor, Priscilla Soares, her widowed sister (Amelia D'Souza), and her spinster niece, Dorothy D'Souza, who had had a university education and was an inveterate reader. "Doc's" library of medical treatises, in their black or brown leather covers and binding, were thick, looked forbidding, and had the smell of age. I pored over them in my adolescence, memorizing some of the medical terminology, such as "hydrenocephalocele of the occipital region," and feeling very proud of my facility with technical terminology. I was determined to take up medicine, feeling that I had a distinct advantage over my peers. But there was the allure of other books, as well. Dorothy (nicknamed Dot) introduced me to the novels of Howard Spring, Monica Dickens (great-granddaughter of Charles Dickens), Han Suyin, Pearl S. Buck, A.J. Cronin, Neville Shute, and others. Dot, who worked in an office, ran the company's

library and sometimes brought home delisted books. I was fascinated by the books in her sturdy wood and glass cabinet.

I started collecting second-hand books (all I could afford on a
schoolboy's low budget of a few annas a week) in a stout, wooden,
blue-grey trunk, circa British India army, stencilled with the name
and rank of my godfather, Charles Ronald Williams, a large man
with an overwhelmingly jolly disposition but a core of deep sadness.
A bachelor all his life who had been jilted several times, he was
Falstaffian in humour, teaching me inadvertently that every comic
has a potentially tragic underside. The life of any party, he would
regale us all with vividly droll anecdotes and mimicry before succumbing to a maudlin melancholy from whose centre he would sing
sad Portuguese love songs. He, alas, was no reader to any significant
degree. So, I continued my fascination with books, beginning perhaps
with a sensory lust for the smell of glossy jackets, the exotic creamy
paper of hardbacks, with elegantly stitched binding around gilt-
edged pages that could be fluttered like a surprised covey of birds. I
loved the Penguin classics in their cream and orange covers. When
my hormones began to rage and sexual fantasy preoccupied my idle
hours, I could turn to the prose of the *Kama Sutra* or *The Perfumed
Garden* or *The Pillow Book* before seeking the poetic ravishment of
Edward Fitzgerald's translation of Omar Khayyam, though not in
Palgrave's staid volume. Many a tumid hour was spent in the company of the paperback edition published by Jaico Publishing House,
replete with provocative line-drawings by Gordon Ross, particularly
of naked or semi-naked women bending over delightful herbs and
tender greens or nestling in a lover's arms where "with a loaf of bread
beneath the bough,/ A flask of wine, a book of verse—and Thou" I
turned wilderness into "Paradise enow." My chum Alan Oscar once
vanished into his washroom with a copy of the unexpurgated
Rubaiyat and didn't emerge for a considerable time, though when he
did, his face was flushed as a sly smile crept over it.

The poetry we read and often memorized in school had more
than a whiff of British and American sentimentality: "The Blind Man
and the Elephant," "Old Ironsides," "Barbara Frietchie," "Horatius at

the Bridge," "The Charge of the Light Brigade," "Sea Fever," "Invictus," an excerpt from *The Lay of the Last Minstrel*, et cetera. Our school system demanded voluminous memorization, which helped expand our power to record and regurgitate material.

As a Catholic, I was fed a diet of exemplary hagiographic biographies, *Lives of the Saints* with their graphic martyrdoms which could well have been instances of soft-core pornography, especially the iconic illustrations of Saint Agnes with her virginal throat offered to a pervert's knife or of Saint Sebastian looking for all the world like a particularly handsome bodybuilder in a loin-cloth, albeit pierced with phallic arrows. Though Catholicism burned guilt into my soul, I tried to be catholic in my reading. I mixed Protestant, Jewish, Hindu, and Taoist material with my staunchly Catholic syllabus. Evidently, my broad-minded liberal quality was formed in early boyhood for (as my mother was fond of recounting) at the age of six, I informed one of my parents' distinguished friends one evening that my father was Protestant, my mother Catholic, and I Jewish.

There was nothing systematic about my reading. I read without duties, goals, or responsibilities in mind, passing from one book to another, filling my trunk and, later, a bookcase, while also expanding my store of new words, ideas, turns of phrase. My eclectic reading turned me into a mimic writer, someone who was adept at imitating the literary contours of various writers without being able to quite invent his own. Perhaps, however, such mimicry had a virtue: it made me appreciate the value and range of writing, even critical writing, as a highly defined performance, just as with acting, bullfighting, singing, cricket, et cetera. It is possible to find a different voice for a different purpose.

Which returns me to the question of mimicry, an entrenched theme of Anglo-India where the mimicry changed with fashion faster than the inner world did. The English left many place-names in Bombay: Breach Candy (a swimming pool in the actual shape of India reserved for Europeans only), Brabourne Stadium (where, as a truant from school, I took in my first Australia versus India cricket Test Match), Willingdon Club, Warden Road, Kemp's Corner, Queen's

Court, Annie Besant Road, Flora Fountain, Ballard Pier, Cadell Road, Elphinstone College, Prince of Wales Museum. These were names copied from a foreign tongue, and they were relics from an age of parasols, high tea, lawn parties, liveried servants, sculpted topiaries. They were from a tradition in disuse, like old wedding cake or yellowing lace.

There were the queer nicknames, often applied to non-Anglo-Indians: Bunty, Sonny, Queenie, Jumbo, Jiggs, and Piggy (the last metamorphosed into "Piggins" for an obese but sweet-natured lady). There were the school-ties and blazers, a legacy of English prep schools. There were the English *Boys' Own* annuals, English films (classical adaptations, mysteries, romances, costume dramas, and bawdy farces), and English music (orchestras and bands were very much the rage in Bombay, though the trend to Indianization was growing). There were the exotic culinary concoctions, beverages, and desserts: kedgeree, cutlets, sardines on toast, cottage bread, Pimm's Cup, suet pudding, Spotted Dick, trifle: "the food of exiles," as E.M. Forster noted, "[made] by servants who did not understand it." There were the prescribed Cambridge reading lists: Shakespeare, Dickens, and Stevenson (*Travels with a Donkey*) to *Lays of Ancient Rome, Midlothian,* and *Trent's Last Case.* Nothing, of course, by R.K. Narayan, Manohar Malgonkar, Raja Rao, Mulk Raj Anand, Kamala Das, Anita Desai, Ruth Prawer Jhabvala. These were writers I discovered in Canada as a resident alien.

And yet I was not of England. I did not fantasize about living in an aristocratic English past. I knew that as surely as I knew that it was not ridiculous to read of Dickens's wintry London or Wordsworth's daffodils or Shelley's skylark. Nor was it ridiculous to sing "When Irish Eyes Are Smiling," "Danny Boy," or "Auld Lang Syne." We were all colonized, but there were foreign worlds to which we were not denied entry.

I had simply not yet found my place.

My parents were not inveterate readers. My father lacked a formal education. He was taught English by the British in the Mid-East, and when an adult contented himself with journals on automobile engineering, the *Times of India*, and a few Armenian church news-letters. His favourite book was *The Forty Days of Musa Dagh*, Werfel's famous siege narrative set during the Armenian genocide. In this fictionalized version of history, eight hundred families of brutalized Armenian deportees huddle together in a heroic but futile defence against the Ottoman army. I learned (though I don't think my father did) that the number forty was mythic, linked to Biblical symbolism, specifically to an epoch in *Genesis* (where it rains 40 days and 40 nights) and to Moses's 40 years in Egypt and then 40 years in the desert. This iconic book was published in 1933 under a bad sign: the year when Nazism was beginning its wild, demented rise.

My mother, unable to finish high school because of rheumatic fever, did read popular fiction and magazines. She also read children's stories to my two younger sisters and me, activating our imaginations, and encouraging us to perform little playlets. Her older sister Patsy told me that Mother had had several of her school essays held up as models of good writing, though they usually focussed on food. I would never have suspected that was one of her favourite subjects, given that she ate very little at mealtime, preferring savoury Indian snacks and rich desserts to homecooked food. Her favourite pastimes were card games (only small bets) with neighbours or going to the Mahalakshmi Racecourse where her bets were larger, her luck much smaller. My mother was a colonial product who did not rebel against her background. She seemed to have settled for middle-class comfort, resigned to the repeated rituals of Anglo-Indian life—the privileged indolence or ennui, assuaged by what Maud Diver called "promiscuous sociability" in the form of endless rounds of parties. She was not blind to my father's roughness, the near-calamitous state of his temper, but she thought of him as a diamond in the rough, and preferred to acknowledge his good qualities rather than his bad habits. She was not especially curious about his fragmented history or lost culture.

When I entered St. Mary's High School, a Jesuit-run semi-private school that could be attended either as day school or boarding school, I became increasingly aware that my parents' reading would never go to *my* head. Books redeemed the silence between my father and me. I looked to them for the wisdom I believed he lacked, for the language beyond his understanding, for the sheer sensuousness of paper, design, typography, illustration—the very things to which he was indifferent—and, as such, books became my textual father. I could go to them for discourses outside his ken or sympathy. They showed me universes denied to him. I could enter into a mental dialogue with them, and dialogue was one thing truly absent in my relationship with my father. We might as well have been from different planets. I wanted a world that was palpably different from his.

I was exogenous to Armenia, having grown up ignorant of my father's origins and language, but I was also embarrassed at the wastefulness of much Anglo-Indian life. The very word "Anglo-Indian" had changed in significance. An Anglo-Indian used to mean someone of British descent who had settled in India, but the word gradually came to mean someone of mixed ancestry—someone half European and half Asian. There were surely Anglo-Indians of note in the British Raj, but in my Bombay adolescence, I could not find any contemporary Anglo-Indian of special significance. St. Mary's High School on Nesbit Road, Mazagaon, had been originally built for Anglo-Indians and operated under the auspices of The Presidency Education Trust, but in my time there, the students of most exceptional note were Hindus and Parsis. Among St. Mary's famous alumni are Zubin Mehta (conductor), Farrokh Bulsara (later known as Freddie Mercury), Homi Bhabha (critic and scholar), and Dom Moraes (literary prodigy who published his first book at twelve). Much later came Boman Irani, born less than two years before we left India, and now one of the most celebrated comic film actors in Indian film. Boman is the cousin of Indo-Canadian writer Anosh Irani, whose father, Adi, was one of my boyhood chums in Bombay. Adi's older brothers (Kemas and Kaikoo) and older sister (nicknamed "Pinky") were also part of my Bombay boyhood.

Most of the Anglo-Indians I knew seemed to be adrift, either biding their time for some fervently imagined expatriation or resigned to being rejected by India and Britain. Anglo-India was less a concept or visionary place than merely something to be added to or subtracted from. The Anglo-Indians of my acquaintance knew little of their own history and cared even less about it. Intellectually detached from such knowledge, they either despised or romanticized India's contradictions and their own ambivalent attitudes to these. The poor are always with us, they claimed piously, and the poor can teach us so much about humility of spirit and acceptance. But this sanctimony was false, no less than its opposite—contempt. They did not seem to have an idea of the spiritual emptiness in which they lived, much less an ability to define this emptiness. Yet it was all around them. Not that they were unhappy; many were not. The happy or contented ones had found a place—some with security in inferior civil-service jobs, some with positions of petty grandeur. A few Anglo-Indians still played polo, hunted wild boar, and hosted rowdy parties, but they, like their ancestors, failed to make a true bridge between East and West, mistaking hospitality for true intimacy, preferring sport to philosophy. Few of them—only the best educated—knew anything about Indian *Gnosis*. Many of them, pampered by unearned privilege, sought their own bourgeois El Dorado. At best, they were the epigones of Kipling or Scott; at worst, they were bastard progeny of imperial bastards.

I did not glorify Anglo-Indian life; but nor did I seek Indian philosophy. I did not attempt to reduce India to a formula; but nor did I try to understand her enigmas. I did not set myself apart from my Indian peers at school; but nor did I endeavour to become wholly a part of their communities. Despite all too evident deficiencies culturally, morally, politically, Anglo-India was the side I joined with a half-guilty conscience by default of birth. At least Anglo-India had given me a language that was universally recognized, despite the exotic peculiarities of accent, rhythm, and diction. It was only away from Bombay that I became aware that words and phrases such as "*chota* peg," "bush-shirt," "mugging for exams," "Could you give me a lift?" or "box-*wallah*" did not have the sort of resonance to which I was accustomed.

My father spoke English but with a markedly different accent from mine, and with a syntax and diction that I found strange and often excruciating. Where others found his mangled phrases and malapropisms amusing, I was embarrassed to hear him say "oinjment" instead of "ointment." When he declared of somebody "He suffers from magnesia," the gulf between us seemed unbridgeable.

My mother's side, the Alimos, can be charted back to England, and perhaps Spain, Portugal, or Ireland. I have never been able to determine the origin with any certitude. Like any Anglo-Indian side, it is linked to a history of seduction by Europe, though when some of my relatives went "home" to England, they inherited little beyond disillusionment and a weary resignation to the reality of being detached from English history. Dispossessed of imperial grandeur after the end of the Raj and Empire, the English eyed them with misgivings. And the Anglo-Indians, new immigrants, were tempted to forget what they had lost beyond the plagues of snakes, *fakirs*, beggars, dung-encrusted roads, whores with painted faces, green hills terraced with tea, caves with erotic sculpture, high monsoons, the towering silhouettes of palm trees, and the anarchy of wild flowers. England made them want to remember their traces in the solitude of high noon, the raw beauty scavenged by Empire. England forced them to acknowledge that their immigration was an act of alienation, deepened by colonial fantasy. England forced them to experience the fear of having come to the end of their possibilities in a forbidding place.

There was no reflection of this tribe in Indo-Anglian writing, and certainly there was no Anglo-Indian attempt to portray this community to itself during my school years. The Anglo-Indians of my generation were a dying breed, dying not only in terms of number but in cultural significance as well. The best they could hope for in the way of literary identity was in the novels and memoirs of a vanished era. I did not realize this until I was a post-graduate student in the early 1970's at Queen's University in Kingston, Ontario. Recent reading has added to that store of information, and I can share some of what I have learned. G.A. Henty (who died in 1902) commemorated the early version of Anglo-Indians: resourceful men who served the Raj. Henty's immensely popular novels, essentially "tales of derring-do," were meant to capture the imaginations of the young, and his nine Indian novels were more about the Raj, representing the occupying British as humane exemplars of justice and the Indians as "either parasites or rogues, or both." Alice Perrin, daughter of a Bengal cavalry general and wife of an Indian official, published *The Anglo-Indians* in 1912, depicting a lecherous teenage Indian prince bent on sybaritic self-indulgence, and the aspirations of three daughters of a district officer and his *memsahib* wife. The *memsahib* complains that India is "petty, and narrow, and second rate; people are too simple and commonplace out here. There's no life, only existence." And then there was Maud Diver, a soldier's daughter born in India, who was an officer's wife. After she returned to England in 1896, she set about publishing over a dozen romances set in India. *Far to Seek: A Romance of England and India* (1912) deals with Anglo-Indians, and has as its hero the son of an English baronet and a high-born Rajput lady. The novel shapes a moral conclusion that ennobles the Raj, deeming it infinitely preferable to any alternative proposed by nationalist Indians. India was increasingly depicted as a place of the unenlightened.

India has been subjected to extensive literary punishment by foreigners who went to it in quest of spiritual enlightenment only to find poverty, squalor, and disease, while others have discovered transcendental purity and wisdom. But while India, like its Hindu deities, is different things to different writers, what outsiders have seen in her has always been influenced by their own psyches. V.S. Naipaul, for instance, summarizes the subcontinent in motifs of degradation, ruin, and stasis. For him, India is a country that deals only in symbolic action. Consequently, India does not work any magic on him, the metaphysical rebel who feels unhoused everywhere in the world. Decades later, Clark Blaise and his Bengali wife Bharati Mukherjee produced in tandem a literary memoir (*Days and Nights in Calcutta*) after seeking entrance into myths that are still functional, rituals that still signify a reality "forever in creation." Husband and wife engaged in separate but intersecting quests, showing more of India than is generally shown through Western eyes. Yet there was no Anglo-India. Was it on leave of absence in England or simply wiped out?

My own schoolboy reading of Anglo-Indian novels and stories was largely limited to Rudyard Kipling, E.M. Forster, and John Masters, whose books were set in (real or fictive) places distant from Bombay. While it is true that the Anglo-Indians in Kipling are not the same as those in Forster or Masters or Paul Scott, they all share a common fate as victims of Empire, for they are half-castes in a half-world of contempt, self-contempt, recrimination, evasion, and dispossession. Of the four versions of life in Anglo-India, I found Kipling's the hardest to accept because it was filled with vulgar Cockney soldiers and their bawdy barrack ballads, *burra sahibs* and *memsahibs* who flourished in their clubs, and natives who were either patronized or brutalized. Kipling's dialogue was tiresomely mannered, his characters and narrative voice usually representative of the ruling class that eventually left nothing but a shadow of itself in the Indian heat. Forster and Scott (whom I started to read in depth only after we immigrated to Canada) were the most accurate writers on Anglo-India, but their fictional settings were of two different periods, Scott's Pankot postdating Forster's Edwardian Chandrapore by some twenty years. Moreover, Scott was more interested than Forster in charting the dying days of the Raj when the British (in his own words) "came to the end of themselves as they were." Scott saw India as being "even more than England was, the scene of the victory of liberal humanism over dying paternal imperialism." The special fascination that India had for Scott was "the almost tragic atmosphere" he saw as "attaching to it then" as "the mausoleum containing the remains of the last two great senses of public duty" the English had as a people: "the sense of duty that was part and parcel of having an empire, and the sense of duty so many [of the English] felt, that to get rid of it was the liberal human thing to do." Perhaps more than any other English novelist, Scott expressed in social terms the English ethos as a rigid attitude.

By contrast, Forster was easily the most profound and imaginative interpreter of the philosophic tensions between the British and

Indians. His English characters posed as gods in their assurance that Indians liked whatever deities were put in their path. Where Scott worked on an epical plane in *The Raj Quartet*, Forster managed to suggest a massive synthesis within a narrower frame in *A Passage to India*. Forster's novel brilliantly erects a synecdoche: the British Raj is a net cast over the subcontinent, but is itself entrapped by the insoluble mystery of what it seeks to control. When the English hear the enticing invitation, "Come," they are not really promised anything. The call is merely an appeal. And, so, the English come, seeking to take over and subjugate, but they remain invaders in exile. In fact, India catches them in her own massive "muddle." India's apparent formlessness overcomes them, for their imperial arrogance blinds them to the subtle pattern in a civilization "which the West can disturb but will never acquire."

As an adolescent, the novel that appealed to me the most was John Masters's *Bhowani Junction* which is set in 1946, a year prior to Indian independence, when nationalists were testing British moral and political willpower. A technicolour Hollywood version of the novel (starring Stewart Granger and Ava Gardner) drew me like a magnet to the book. A narrative in three voices—two Eurasian (Patrick Taylor's and Victoria Jones's) and one English (Rodney Savage's)— *Bhowani Junction* expresses Anglo-Indian anxieties through a tale of sometimes savage lust and violence. The English despise the Anglo-Indians but need them, if only as visible consequences of Empire. The Anglo-Indians despise the Indians but need them, perhaps as a buffer between themselves and the English. Indian nationalism takes revenge on Anglo-Indians. The widow Sidarni Amrita Kasel, a patriot who has been jailed five times, articulates the Indian vengeance: "We're going to make you realize that you are Indians—inferior Indians, possibly disloyal Indians." Sneered at by the English and Indians, the Anglo-Indians are impelled to sneer at themselves. The emblem is a scorpion trying to kill itself. The picture of the English holds no surprises: these colonials consolidate a class system to ensure imperialistic capitalism, and they are certainly not averse to inflicting any type of indignity as a form of political coercion. In one scene, Savage, the English lieutenant-colonel commanding a battalion of Gurkhas, orders his men to urinate on civil demonstrators lying across railway tracks. But the brutishness is not reserved for Indians alone; the Anglo-Indians, once considered "Domiciled Europeans," are branded "cheechees, half-castes, eight-annas, blacky-whites," and women such as Victoria Jones are considered fair objects for sexual violation. Rape, after all, can be an emblem of contempt and humiliation.

Colonialism breeds "pigmentocracy," as the Anglo-Indians become almost pathologically colour-conscious. Mr. Jones, a senior driver on the Delhi Deccan Railway, and married to a dark-skinned wife who chews betel nuts in secret, encourages his daughter to lie about her background, suggesting that she claim to be partly Spanish in order to account for her swarthy complexion. And in a particularly bitter moment, Victoria recites a racial limerick to herself, in which a young English lady has an affair with a dark-skinned Indian, resulting an "eightsome of twins--/ Two black and two white and four khaki." Unable to be English because she is half-Indian, yet unable to be Indian because she is half-English, Victoria is trapped by a double repudiation. Her people have no moral or political authority.

In Canada, I have often been identified as "Indian," an irony, given the fact that in India, I was considered Anglo-Indian. But none of my family in India seemed to bother very much with investigating the implications of Anglo-Indian history or ways of life. Perhaps this indifference was inherited from the British, lords of colonialism, to whom Indian custom and religion were of no concern as long as they did not interfere with the business of running and exploiting the country, or at least those urban centres that mattered for commerce and rule of law. The English were used to viewing Nature as a beneficent, tender Mother, but in India, Mother changed both sex and disposition, becoming Shiva, Lord of Change and Destroyer of Names and Forms. No matter how hard the invaders tried to subdue Shiva, by bureaucracy or soldiery, they failed. Considering themselves princes and the Indians pariahs, they remained unable to penetrate its interior life and spirit. Most of these English males could be summed up in the image of the colonial with a *chota peg* (a half-size serving of whisky) in one hand, enjoying cigars, English music, billiards, and bridge at the club, while their women concerned themselves with amateur dramatics, garden parties, and *nimbupanis* (lime juice cordials) on the veranda at sunset, while assorted servants scurried about, attending to their whims or needs.

My mother's life as a married woman was very much like that of the English *memsahibs* in the nineteenth century, except that it was not a question of becoming a useful part of the Anglo-Indian community. Married at twenty, my mother did not wish to keep India at arm's length, to look purely inward to the Anglo-Indian community for friendship, amusement, and security. Dressing well, but not uncomfortably, was part of her duty as an Anglo-Indian housewife, and this meant keeping up to some degree with European fashions. There was nothing "native" about her dress, but nor was there anything extravagant. Her most stylish dress was a mauve velvet evening gown, following the contours of her body down to her ankle, and set off by a sash and velvet floweret. This she wore to dinner-dances, after bathing with Pear's soap, powdering herself with English talcum, and dabbing her neck, ears, and elbows with Tosca 4711.

Shopping was done by taxi or horse-drawn carriage (*gharri*), although the daily supply of food was obtained by the full-time cook who undertook an early morning trip to Crawford Market by tramcar. I remember Mother's evening ritual of taking up shopping accounts with the cook. Mutton, beef, and fish, each had its rate in annas rather than rupees. The meat came in large cuts, raw, red, marbled with fat and sinew. Brown, gnarled Bombay duck (lizardfish), high smelling and as chewy as cured leather, lay in heaps. Other fish (usually Pomfret) whole in silver or pink and unscaled. Crabs, however, were received alive in our kitchen. They came in wicker baskets and once the lid was off, they could be seen scrabbling over one another, their pincers feeling the air, trying to find a way out of their enclosure. Any poultry, too (usually a plump hen), was alive, squawking and fluttering its wings, though unable to thrash its legs, which were firmly bound with cord. There would be an occasional partridge or quail, though not from the market; they came courtesy of Alvarez, a Portuguese family friend, who would bring us a brace in a large coop.

I was a witness to the kitchen slaughter of poultry and wild fowl when our cook took his knife (sharpened on a grindstone) to their throats, slitting them with a single firm action, then throwing their thrashing bodies onto the cold stone floor where they bled to death, the beatings of their wings ebbing ever more feebly. Huge pots of boiled water were readied in which to immerse their corpses so that Cook and Maid could then pluck the birds. I still remember the smell of blood, feathers, and raw flesh. Little wonder that I had no appetite for chicken in those days.

Bombay conditioned me to the slaughter of animals. I once saw a pig being killed in the farmyard for a feast-day dinner at a Catholic seminary. A single bullet was used to stun the animal, and as soon as it fell, the slaughterer slit its throat with a knife as other men grabbed its feet. Gouts of dark blood dropped into the dust. Even more vivid was what I witnessed annually after Ramadan, when a goat was ritually killed when my friend Abdel Sattar and his orthodox Muslim family prepared for a feast. A small crowd would gather in a small area beside the side entrance of a large building that was home to a mixture of ethnicities. A portentous hush would settle in the area prior to the *halal* ceremony that included the digging of a small pit in the mud, over which the goat, firm hands restraining its legs, would have its throat slit by a knife in a single quick, deep cut. I would watch with fascinated horror as blood poured into the pit, the animal's sinews and muscles eventually relaxing as life drained away, the day's harsh light intensifying the clarity of animal sacrifice. As the dead animal's dark eyes looked on nothing, there was a sticky smell that clung to my nostrils, while the executioner expertly sliced skin from flesh, his hands emptying the entrails, the stink of fat and raw meat growing sharper. Long flaps of flesh were cut away, ribs exposed, with the sibilance of butchery in my ears. A palpable cornucopia of flesh. A disgusting richness as the voyeurs' circle broke up once the slaughter and butchery were done. No wonder I developed a chronic aversion to goat meat.

Sights, sounds, and smells collected in my reservoir of memory. Topology and geography came to my writer's consciousness late, and they came more as metaphor and symbol than as literal data. It was only when I immersed myself in Canadian literature at university that I began to ponder such things as the lay of the land, the frontier experience, the far north, the true west, the garrison mentality, vertical man/horizontal world, and the gothic wilderness. As a child and teenager, I did not see my native city as a million points of light sprinkled and curved around a hillside and marina. Nor did I contemplate the thousand huts with dung fires burning in narrow, smoky doorways, or the neon glimmer of a multitude of apartments, the tall buildings lit in their pandemonium.

As a Cancerian, water is my element. And there was much of it in Bombay, a schizophrenic bejewelled slum built on a peninsula that was an imperial dowry in a European marriage. Fishermen were in Bombay long before the English. There were, in reality, seven islands: Worli, Mahim, Salsette (once a Portuguese walled city), Matunga, Colaba (formerly noted for European cotton presses and a military cantonment), Mazagaon, and Bombay. Long before the British joined them, turning part of the sea into land, and confusing cartographers who were never sure where sea had been before the land. The goddess Mumbadevi—with variable names, Mumbabai, Mumbai—presided over the sea. Then the Portuguese came and named the place Bom Bahia for its harbour where they sought to shelter their merchant and war ships. Bombay passed into English hands only through marriage, when Catharine of Braganza had to offer it up to Charles II of England as her dowry.

But the sea remained itself. As Alice Oswald has written of sea in general, it is deep, "a dead field fenceless/ a thickness with many folds in it/ promiscuous and mingling/ which in its patience always/ wears away the hard things." But the sea was also something else. It was a world unto itself, large, untameable, yet fascinating. Don Moraes wrote in his memoir *Gone Away*, "The sea is aristocratic in

Bombay, lying under the lighted windows of rich houses, purring to itself and listening to the subdued thunder of cocktail-shakers from within. If the sea were not there, one felt, there would be no parties." I remember the sea misting rocks at Marine Drive, sighing, spitting, or spewing water when drunk with its own power. I remember, too, the parties by the sea, parties in Colaba, where the inevitable male film star was coaxed into making love to himself in an imaginary romantic movie for booze-sodden voyeurs. Or parties on Madh Island where the gentle grotesque, Jiji Goldstein—a professional wrestler (former Greco-Roman Olympian from Romania), married to a diminutive South Indian spitfire—was teased into mock-grappling with the company clown, Noel Reilly, a man whose wife had run off to Europe with a foreign lover, and whose own comic party-piece of mimicked foreign accents gave no consolation to his riven heart.

Parties where Ali, the adulterous Muslim family man, indulged his Christian paramour with displays of ostentatious flattery before returning to his wife in *purdah* in the humble domesticity of a modest tenement. Or parties where the latest executive visitor from Nuffield or Sheffield or Kent or London was showered with sycophancy simply because of his accent.

Parties where bottles of illicit liquor—the product of the grossest fermentation in rubber hot-water-bottles buried in sand—were a surrogate sacramental until the customary raid by C.I.D. officers eager to be perceived as zealous upholders of the Prohibition laws of urine-drinking Morarji Desai. The raids brought panic to the women, avid curiosity to the children, and studied nonchalance to the men who usually managed to flush the incriminating evidence down the toilet and fling the bottles into the refuse heap conveniently located behind the house.

The topology has dissolved in large part from my memory, though I possess a dreaming memory of some of the lay of land:

Malabar Hill suspended in rock and bower, manicured lawns, trellises, sculptured hanging gardens with hedges carefully shaped into animal forms, white villas with riotous bougainvillea, hibiscus, jasmine, and mulberry.

Marine Drive curving like a queen's necklace, and the taupe sands of Chowpatty, flecked with dark coconut shells bereft of their white inner flesh and "milk," abandoned plantain leaves, cigarette wrappers, pebbles unclaimed by the tow of tide, and the remains of fish, spiny, mottled, urned in shell or tattooed by bird beak.

The Gateway of India, Apollo Bundar, overlooking the Arabian Sea, an arch monument of yellow basalt and indissoluble concrete built to commemorate the first British monarch (George V) to visit India, with the water behaving unpredictably, especially in the monsoon season, when waves battered the walls almost ceaselessly.

Having been born near water, I have read water: shallow and deep, limpid, scummy, foamy, amniotic, saline, subversive, tempestuous, placid, psychic. Taken the waters. Tested them. Mixed water and powders. Milk and water. Scotch and water. Stepped into the same river twice, but never the same water. Stirred, like Raphael, the water of memory. Gazed, like Narcissus, at mirror water.

Bombay rose gently above sea level, but the greatest density of life was on low-lying planes, where a sea of people billowed over with the passions of everyday life. The city was so congested that no stray dog, its bones almost poking through paper-thin skin, could ever run the length of a street without bumping into a person. Oaks and banyans, palm trees and fig trees grew in abundance, and fruit and flower preened in their green surroundings, the people entangled among one another in humid exhaustion while ceiling fans and hand *punkahs* whirred and fluttered.

Inside our house, the floor tiles glistened a Morocco red. In the monsoon season, the air was a choking dampness, and the bed linen sucked up this moisture so that we always awoke damp and feeling a little soiled. The hottest months were a perpetual furnace into which we walked like fated creatures. The houses had huge ceiling fans, but these were often futile against the shimmering humidity. A sparrow that accidentally strayed into the circuit of the fan-blades would fall, decapitated. In the hottest months, our bodies broke out in rashes and prickly heat. And as insects collected for their bloodthirsty invasions, our beds were draped with heavy mosquito nets "stranded in the air like the dresses of hanged brides" (in the words of Michael Ondaatje).

Our house was vast. The corners of our living room ceiling soared into a turret, a cathedral ceiling profaned by sparrows that tucked their nests and young into any crevice, unmindful of the broad-armed fans that guillotined many of their brood. Other intruders were sometimes sonar-defective bats that flitted in their prehistoric ugliness, sometimes brushing against our ears, provoking our screams in superstitious fear that a flittermouse would grapple itself to one of our ears, never to be pulled away, unless it also tore off a flap of skin while siphoning off our blood in its death-throes. When servants and adults mounted a concerted attack against the invaders by closing all doors and swinging against the flapping creatures with brooms, we protected our ears and made more than enough noise to harrow the dead.

Nothing could shut out the sun—not the sway-backed palms, the hirsute banyans clumped like aged Orangutans, the intermittent mulberry bushes with sharp thorns, the fig trees raided by song birds discarding pitted fruit skins, or the guava trees smelling of hard green fruit. The birds twittered, whistled, shrieked, and ruffled leaves, vibrating leaner boughs with whirring feathers and choreographed feet. At high noon, everything was a blurred shimmer as the city appeared to turn to sheets of vapour. Dogs panted with exhaustion, beggars shielded their filmy eyes from the unforgiving sun, half-naked bare-footed urchins gathered around shops, whose hoses charitably sprayed short bursts of cold water. Bombay still had horse-drawn carriages in the fifties, and as patrons travelled incognito behind the black window flaps, lean horses laboured uphill and down, slipping on the hot asphalt, wheezing as beasts of burden, with the carriage-drivers flicking long whips at the animals, now foaming at the bit between their teeth. Occasionally a horse would drop to its knees and then feel further lashing on its scarred flanks.

The unforgiving heat exacerbated the stench of dung. "Indians defecate everywhere," wrote V.S. Naipaul in *An Area of Darkness*, pointing to the streets, beaches, hills, and river banks polluted by squatters who were for the longest time deliberately omitted from Indian-language novels or stories, feature films, or documentaries. Canine, feline, bovine, equine, human excrement—all mingled in what Salman Rushdie called "a brotherhood of shit" in *Midnight's Children*. And the excremental vision was ineradicable.

As was the spectacle of beggary. Bombay had a multitude of poor: legless, ragged grotesques wheeling themselves on their versions of skate-boards which they pushed with scrawny hands, blistered and scraped raw with effort; blind children with dark flies gathering around their gummy sockets; lepers with suppurating sores; victims of elephantiasis, disfigured creatures who lumbered along with horribly swollen legs or arms. These indigents besieged everyone, everywhere.

Their spectacle was an expression of Indian stasis. In Bombay, poverty was part of an Indian design of acquiescence to fate, but some of the poor tried turning their deprivation into theatre. There was a fairly young beggar who used to limp into The Retreat to sing for alms. Sensing that English could be useful in this context, he would deliver in a hoarse, off-key voice, "Daisy, daisy, give me your answer doo," or "You are my sun-sine, my only sun-sine." The lyric was always punctuated by resounding slaps to his own bare stomach, as if to dramatize the hollow in its pit. "You are my sun-sine," [slap] "my only sun-sine," [slap] "You make me happee," [slap] "when skies are gray." [slap]

I was compelled to face the grotesque part of mundane life. Some of what I faced sharpened my sense of empathy without reducing my discomfort—as when I came face to face as a boy of no more than five with Estrella, a grey-haired, dishevelled victim of mental retardation. Estrella was part of a Portuguese family who were my parents' friends. Rumour was that she had suffered brain damage when a tree branch fell on her when she was a little girl of no more than three or four. Hugging a cloth doll, Estrella always smiled warmly at visitors, and loved children. But her vocabulary was as frozen as her mental quotient. Whenever she approached me to caress my cheeks, I went slightly rigid with anxiety, not knowing what to expect next, though I suspected she would not cause me any harm. I observed her with a mixture of curiosity and horror.

Later, I learned to force aside such disturbing images and wish for fresh ice-cold lemonade on the veranda or on the beach in the morning or by rock pools near far-off hills. In the hottest months—which were when our schools closed—my mother would take us to a hill-station such as Panchgani or Matheran, leaving my father behind to attend to his work. Over 150 miles from Bombay, Panchgani (whose name means "five hills") was 1,293 metres above sea level and known for its volcanic plateau called Table Land. It was also said to have panthers, a report that darkened my boyhood sense of adventure, though I never saw any of these predators. My sisters and I would accompany my mother as we walked to the top, sometimes using rough-hewn walking sticks to make the hike less arduous. Panchgani was called "the Switzerland of India" because of its natural scenic beauty, high hills, waterfalls, and river. The air was certainly cooler and purer than in Bombay at any time of year, and the colonial cottages and hotels (with liveried servers in dining rooms) were quaintly different from what we were used to in Bombay. Boasting ample strawberry fields, and originally developed as a British Raj resort and sanatorium, Panchgani drew many middle-class families from Bombay and elsewhere. The Raj was long over by the time of my boyhood and adolescence, though Panchgani still had English-style boarding-schools, the most famous one being St. Peter's, founded in 1904, made even more famous for having had rock star Freddie Mercury as one of its outstanding students in the fifties. In my limited experience, not all its tourists were of fine class or manner. I recall an American family of four, where the father (an evangelical minister) and mother told their two young children that they were not to mix with "black Sambos." I suspect that they came from a line of white supremacists and faux-evangelists—the sort that much later defiled the U.S. under Trump. And it didn't take me long to learn in my teenage years why Gandhi claimed to love Christ but not his Christians.

Matheran, a mere 800 metres above sea level, was another favourite vacation spot. Because automobiles were banned, it was accessible only by narrow-gauge railway on small trains that practically crawled up the hill. They were known as Toy Trains, and it was common for many passengers to jump off and then walk beside the slowly moving locomotive as a diversion. Matheran was famous for its *chikki* (brittle made from peanuts, sesame seeds, and jaggery), leather goods (including *chappals* or sandals), and honey. For us, it was memorable for its hand-pulled rickshaws, red dust, and monkeys. Riding in hand-drawn rickshaws was an exotic delight, as if we were transported back to colonial days, when it had been a common, cheap mode of transportation for hire. My sisters (Elma and Audrey) and I loved kicking up sprays of dust to redden our socks and shoes. Matheran had ponies for hire, and monkeys that clambered across rooftops in search of food. These creatures were expert, bold marauders who were wont to snatch sandwiches or candy or any type of food and drink out of the hands of unsuspecting tourists. I recall Elma getting into a tug-of-war with a monkey that was intent on filching her box of cornflakes. Elma lost the battle. She was never of strong constitution—unlike Audrey, three years younger, who behaved very much like a tomboy, scrambling up guava trees, challenging boys, outrunning almost anyone her age.

Other favourite getaway sites were Lonavla with its Sausage Hills (lush with greenery, misty skies, and deliciously sweet, nutty *chikki*) and Khandala in the Western Ghats, where narrow winding roads were dangerous to negotiate at the best of times, but especially when it rained. My Aunt Pat and Uncle Joe De Lima lived in Jubbulpore, their son, Greg, a few years younger than me. Learning from my parents that I needed to put on weight, Aunt Pat fed me thick, fresh cream from buffalo milk, sweetened with jam. Uncle Joe worked for the Gun Carriage Factory, rode a gleaming Triumph motorcycle, and loved hunting wild boar during vacations. Fantasizing that we were hunters ourselves, Greg and I chased a pig that had wandered away from a neighbouring yard. Thrilled with a sense of adventure but nervous about actually making a kill, I fumbled an assault on the squealing animal with a dull spear, only wounding it rather than ending its life. Uncle Joe performed the *coup de grâce*, after scolding us for inflicting unnecessary torture.

Uncle Joe introduced me to Marble Rocks, an area distinguished by a beautiful gorge and soft marble. When I think back to those vacations and getaways, I feel guilty at not having explored much of what they had to offer. I grew up taking too many things for granted, not really seeing the landscape, not really exploring the people. It was only when I began to write seriously, long after we had immigrated to Canada, that I realized how little I had known of places in my boyhood.

What I do remember vividly is that my boyhood was dense with sound. In the first reticence of dawn, roosters crowed the city awake. And in the sunburst of church bell, families clattered to life. Cooks fanned kitchen-fires into a morning crackle, maids slapped cutlery and crockery into place on tables, cars started, buses wheezed, tram-cars clanged or creaked around street corners, and children dressed indolently for school while mothers and *ayahs* urged them on stridently. When it rained, which it did for multitudinous days and nights, the rain went from spattering to flooding, before trembling itself into submission. Mail slots clicked open and envelopes thudded onto stone floors. Vendors began their urgent pitches as maids' coal-glowing irons hissed over cottons and linens. The iceman staggered up flights of stairs, heaving blocks wrapped in sackcloth, and the waterman bore huge bladders of fresh water that went gushing and gurgling into empty metal barrels. Cleaning women scraped and scratched at residues of dirt on wall and floor, and used crude whisks, brooms, and brushes for day-long labours as stray dogs outdoors barked for scraps and at strangers. In the ghettos, women pounded and rolled herbs and spices on slabs of stone, or beat out the soapy water from sodden clothing before rinsing and hanging the pieces to dry in the sun.

At school, bells divided the day into regulated compartments of time and learning, though we always preferred the recess and lunch bells that freed us from the tedium of class and released us into the schoolyard where freewheeling hawks circled, calling to one another before swooping to snatch a sandwich out of an unsuspecting hand. The playground was a din of feet against footballs or cricket bats whacking and cracking hard red balls into the outfield or shouts from the volleyball and basketball courts crowded with leaping and lunging bodies and a blur of legs.

Bombay was a mass of ethnicities—a mosaic of race, religion, colour, and dialect—and its languages, spoken in a variety of pitches, registers, ranges, and shadings, were a rich Babel to those beyond their contours. I spoke little Hindi, less Marathi, no Gujarati, Sanskrit, Urdu, Arabic, or Konkani, so my linguistic decrepitude outside my mother tongue gave me small claim to the accessible Indian world. A person risks real ignorance at times for the sake of unilingual imperialism.

What was it like growing up with elephants pressing in slow motion through streets or with snakes slithering into secret tunnels under porches?

It was never really like that, my Anglo-Indian years. I did ride an elephant once at the Byculla Zoo (formally known as Rani Bagh or Queen's Gardens), but the only snake I ever saw (outside a zoo) was a cobra that danced to its itinerant snake-charmer's flute music or that battled a mongoose to a bloody finish. St. Mary's High School (Cambridge or blue-tie section) had a heterogeneous student body, including shy Indian princes and randy sons of sheikhs who cultivated a repertoire of filthy jokes in which pederasty and bestiality were common themes. I went to school with Iranis who worshipped fire and Zoroaster, and Parsis who, like them, gave their dead to the vultures of the Towers of Silence. Some of our favourite gossip was about driving up Malabar Hill, where an occasional finger or scrap of human flesh was bound to fall onto the windshield. I went to school where Francisco, a Goan boy, stammered for three years in the same grade, talking and smiling so relentlessly to himself that he seemed destined for an asylum. A school where Ashok Sathe, a precocious boy read Ezra Pound's *Cantos* for leisure, and where another, Dom Moraes (five years my senior), was soon to become the youngest winner of the Hawthornden Prize for Literature. I went to school with a Parsi boy whose mother was gunned down by her estranged lover, propelling the boy into a nervous tremor that never left him. There was Pierre, of French ancestry, with curly hair the colour of grain, and with eyes a sky blue, whose grandmother had once run the most exclusive brothel in Bombay. I went to school with Emile, a boy who nervously or lustily played pocket marbles in his short trousers. I went to school with Higgins, a tall, gawky Anglo-Indian, who habitually masturbated in dark cinemas, as he fantasized about seducing the most voluptuous mothers of his peers.

I went to school with others like myself who were not quite in the Indian vein, though not at all certain of their true style. My boyhood was one of mixed codes, and to those not born in India it sometimes sounds like a fabrication, a sequence of invented gestures or lies. Truth is often stranger than fiction.

My first memory is fire. It is from babyhood when I sensed, while lying alone in bed, that there was something red and dangerous at the window. A solitary white candle had accidentally set fire to a white curtain at the window-sill. My baby eyes incandescent, that image stayed with me, as fire became a leitmotif. Indian legend nourished the image: Sita's trial by fire when her ornaments turned to molten lead before turning into flowers with the flames; or Shiva's feet flashing fire. Our Parsi and Irani neighbours prayed facing the sun, and used fire in their daily religious rituals, censers wafting holy smoke at dusk, while Hindus worshipped Agni in their last rite for the dead. Fire was in our home as our cook, a tall, thin black man with a tight body, lit ovens and blew embers; and our maid used a flat iron hissing with live coal as she ironed pleats, hems, collars, and trouser cuffs. In the schoolyard, the sun burned like a merciless oven, sucking the ground dry. And in monsoon season, lightning flashed fire.

Fire had implications of ash. My parents were both chronic smokers. My father's stubby fingers had nicotine stains as he puffed away; my mother was more elegant, as she took care inhaling, exhaling curls of smoke. I don't think she ever thought about ash in any symbolic way. No thoughts of Job repenting in dust and ashes, or of sackcloth Maccabees preparing for battle by fasting, then tearing their clothes sprinkled with ashes. I remember ashen-faced sadhus, grey powdering their naked skin, who buried themselves in sand up to their necks at Juhu Beach. Many years later, when I drew closer to my Armenian side, I read of Armenian women and girls, anointed with oil and set aflame by Turks, being whipped into dancing in a ring of flame.

There were other fascinations in my Bombay boyhood—one especially lurid concerning *hijras* or eunuchs who wandered around Bellasis Road and Kamathipura, though a larger number prowled the sands of Chowpatty Beach. Many had started off as children of prostitutes or as beautiful boys mutilated for sexual gratification. Wearing heavy makeup, and dressed in *saris*, adorned with bangles, necklaces, and earrings, they were treated as deviants. They were prey to particularly perverse homosexuals who liked to inflict pain on them as paid "slaves." However, they did have a positive symbolic role. *Hijras* were hired as dancers at weddings and naming ceremonies, for their blessings would lead, it was believed, to further fertility.

Bombay incarnated contradiction. We lived in an odd Victorian house in a compound of bizarre architectural styles. Our compound, "The Retreat," was a tumult of ethnicities. Set only yards away from the badly potholed main road, it was a dusty cluster of bungalows, villas, two-storey residences with wooden balustrades, wrought-iron veranda railings, and either conical or squat roofs. It was a chaos of bastard styles, a grotesquely comic legacy of British colonialism. Plots of papaya, guava, plantain, and green mango trees made rough territorial boundaries for the houses, and they were freely raided by the compound children, boldly unmindful of the spying eyes behind bamboo blinds. There were also fig trees and a wild mulberry bush for those who dared risking scarred fingers while reaching past thorns for slightly sour berries. Hawks circled and cried in their mid-air copulations, as chattering crows and brown sparrows, serenading tomcats and foolishly strutting poultry thickened the textures of sound.

The houses formed three sides of the oblong compound with a

huge rusting gate, never closed, as the fourth side. At the compound's rear sprawled small huts, derelict garages, congested godowns (warehouses) that housed poorer classes, and a deep well covered and painted white, which became the object of old wives' tales spun to frighten children into staying away from it. The huts had corrugated tin roofs that set up a metallic clatter whenever the rains fell. Dark and smoky within, with several emaciated Hindu occupants coughing away on *bidis* as ground-nut oil cooked on primus stoves, the huts had cool cow-dung spread and dried at the doorways, and on this aromatic carpet were set intricate patterns in coloured chalk powder, many variations of a *mandala*, each configuration a testament to an insistent urge for beauty pushing its way through poverty of means.

The garages had a family of Goans, the parents squabbling, the rampant offspring squalling, all reduced to a decadent nostalgia for a home-place still occupied by the Portuguese. Marwaris and Muslims took to the godowns. Better dressed and with healthier physiques—certainly more glistening skin—than their immediate neighbours, they were the quietest, most private of the three groups, except for wedding days and feast days when they rivalled the Hindus and Goans for festive noise and gaudy accoutrement. So private were they that I did not know for years that the neatly dressed, smilingly polite family man, with camera slung over one shoulder, was, in fact, a brothel-owner and not a professional photographer.

They all lived beside garbage heaps and in a bustling communality, and as they washed their pots and pans, did their meagre laundry on flat stone slabs, and pitched the dirty water an arm's length from their doorways, streams ran dark and muddy at the rear of the compound. They were within "The Retreat" but not really a publicly acknowledged part of it. They were simply the inevitable embarrassment, a fact of life in a city bursting with pluralities. They were a shadow-world, denizens whose will to survive was as strong as their squalor.

When people spoke of "The Retreat" what they meant were the middle-class houses of accountants, store owners, teachers, public administrators, superannuated widows, et cetera. What remain in my memory are thumbnail sketches: Mrs. Davidson, gnarled with age and arthritis, with hands shaped like talons; her daughter Edie, a professional spinster with an older lady friend nicknamed "Buffy" from Simla, who dressed like a man in tweed suits, puffed on cigars, and spoke in a deep voice; Mrs. Saldanha, hobbling around on bunioned, pigeon-toed feet, but full of risible anecdotes, gossip, and Catholic homilies; Khodi Irani (urbane owner of Golden Wafers [potato chips] on Grant Road), a disillusioned, weary alcoholic who died in his thirties; Khorshed, his superb seamstress sister and painter who gave me my first lessons in oils; Dhubi and Tameena, Parsi sisters who lived with their extended family in a long, white villa, and who had a playboy bachelor-brother and a saintly other brother, the St. Francis of The Retreat, who fed twittering sparrows daily; Hannan Ezekiel, brilliant economist, and Nissim, his brother, who was already an eminent Indo-Anglian poet; our next-door neighbours, the Elijahs (with two daughters and a frail son named Samson), who eventually felt out of place in India, and immigrated to England, where the mother Esther, a sweet, kind lady, died too early; and an old couple (whose surname I was too young to remember), the epitome of Bombay colonials.

The husband was a tall, sturdy figure even in old age. Retired from the British India civil service, he remained a thorough Anglophile. Clad in white with a khaki sunhat or *topi*, he would saunter forth, cane in hand, in the noonday sun, like mad dogs and Englishmen in Noel Coward's lyric. Although he and his wife were Parsis and spoke Gujarati at home, the pair read only English newspapers, hoarding the back editions so that all their rooms smelled of old paper. Although she was well past the aid of cosmetics, the wife owned an ornate dresser with three mirrors. More than fifty years after Queen Victoria's death, she assiduously preserved all her Victorian furniture. Every evening at 7 p.m., they would step into the compound, set out two deck chairs, and commence their ritual. He would crank the His Master's Voice gramophone while his wife fanned herself with a hand *punkah*. The couple were obsessed

with John Phillip Sousa and British marches, although their repertoire opened with "Rule Britannia" and concluded with "God Save
The King."

The margins of "The Retreat" held other fascinations. There was
a vigorous, red-haired Pathan who once sliced a Hindu with a knife
during a quarrel. There was a Goan family of seven crowded into a
smoky godown, their eldest daughter, a nubile fifteen-year-old, be-
trothed to a paunchy, aging bachelor but yearning at night for her
secret, teenaged beloved. I witnessed the spectacle when her young
Romeo had to clamber down from the roof, pursued by her irate
father and her two brothers armed with staves and brooms.

"The Retreat" faced St. Anthony's Home, an orphanage for
babies and children abandoned by prostitutes from neighbouring
Kamathipura. The dark, shameless wantons at trellised windows,
who called openly to customers on Falkland Road, a stone's throw
from the orphanage. Many of the whores had started off as children
abducted or bought from families in Nepal, Assam, and Kashmir.
Customers valued hairless genitalia, but if the virgins proved difficult, they were left to the expertise of professional rapists. Sex and
religion had a virtually symbiotic relationship. The babies were bap-
tized as Catholics and reared to be well-mannered youth. Girls, of
course, were tutored to become young brides; the homely ones con-
signed to a fate of further prayer and meditation as potential nuns.

Like some of D.H. Lawrence's characters, I had sex on the brain
as an adolescent. Attendance at St. Mary's, an all-boys' school run
by Jesuits, did not help. Denied female peers, we were left to our
own devices about our hormonal urges, and although I loved to bur-
row in an infinitude of books in my quieter moments, I could not
deny tumescence. There were no easily available sex magazines or
pornographic videos in those days, and parents maintained a discreet silence on all things sexual. Nocturnal emissions were embarrassing because our parents never explained what they were or how
they were caused. Because we all had sisters, aunts, and female
neighbours, we did not regard the opposite sex as creatures of absolute mystery. However, denied the bewildering social truth of their

company, we looked on girls as a conspiracy created against us by
paranoid elders. There were no dances at our Catholic school, and
our socials were the most pristinely homosocial imaginable, given
the overwhelming maleness, though entirely lacking in sex except in
the mind. They were bizarre affairs, chaperoned by teachers and
asexual parents.

St. Mary's had a Jesuit Principal (Father Francis Ribot), and
many Jesuit teachers, some Spanish, some Indian or Anglo-Indian,
and one Armenian. Iraqi-born, bearded Father Serkis (probably a
diminutive of Serkissian) had a robust physique, intense eyes, and a
fiery personality. At cricket, he intimidated bowlers, daring them to
get him out. I never warmed to him even when he visited my father
for drinks and chat. The Jesuits were muffled about sex, though
they explicitly warned us boys against yielding to carnal temptation.
Sin was categorized as venial or mortal, but anything even remotely
sexual was a cardinal sin. To have "impure" thoughts was almost as
bad as actually having sexual gratification. We envied the Protestants
who attended co-ed Christ Church where they could hold hands,
kiss, and negotiate however furtively the first transactions of young
lust. What were their dances like? Where did the boys put their
warm hands? How did they camouflage spontaneous erections? Did
the girls and boys address one another by witty names embedded
with sexual codes? At St. Mary's we had to be content with slandering
teachers ("Big Bum," "Charlotte the Harlot," *et cetera*) or making in-
sulting remarks about the imagined sex lives of one another's parents. Socialization took clumsy forms: we slapped one another on
shoulders and backs, arm-wrestled vigorously, ridiculed shy peers by
vaudevillian mimicry, and exaggerated our own untested sexual
prowess by complicit winks and lies.

As St. Mary's boys, we were lectured relentlessly about self-con-
trol, but in sexual terms, we failed to develop any selves worth con-
trolling. The lives of girls and women were meant to be of no concern to us, of even less significance than the sexual lives of nuns and
priests which, ironically, became springboards for our lewdest fantasies
and gossip. Denied sex, we had to invent it with our imaginations.

We took little comfort in our priests' assurances that there would be something grand ahead for us. Virginity was to be prized, the priests said. Whatever we needed in order to meet the future was to be found in the classroom, gymnasium, or on the playing field. Most of us remained sceptical. Though I loved playing cricket, soccer, ping pong, tried learning to box, and even entertained a ridiculous delusion that I could be a long-distance runner, there was always the private fantasy of forbidden pleasures. Where the boys of Christ Church had dances and socials as carnal outlets, we had to be celibate and amuse ourselves with sports. The boys of Christ Church were given a head start in information about the real world, while most of us at St. Mary's weren't even given dancing lessons, not having anyone except our mothers to dance with. If a seriously carnal girl had come my way, I would not have known how to handle the situation, as was borne out at a family friend's party where a dark-skinned beauty, a year or two older than me, exercised her full repertoire of flirtation. Noticing my interest in the bravura of her sheath-like red dress, she coaxed me into touching the fabric directly at her knee. I blushed, much to the amusement of the adults in the room. The result for me was not even a furtive erection, but stupefying paralysis.

Prior to this embarrassing incident, I did experience two unsettling episodes. One occurred on a train ride back from an international Exposition in New Delhi. At twelve, I was the youngest in a quartet of males from The Retreat (our chaperone being a 20-year-old medical student), but because there was no sleeping space for me in our compartment, I was made to share a bed in a different compartment with a benign-looking bald Hindu male who seemed to welcome my company. Exhausted from the trip and unable to converse with him in Hindi, I merely climbed into the narrow bed, turning away shyly and fell into sleep. I thought I was having an erotic dream that featured a strong hand on my penis, but when I drifted awake, I realized it was no dream. The man smiled at me, nodding as if to say that I should not be unduly concerned as he gently stroked my shaft. However, he did stop, perhaps in fear that I would report him to our chaperone.

The second episode was more sinister. This one occurred during a tramcar ride home, when a handsome adult, probably in his 30s, sat next to me, and tried to engage me in conversation. Once again, my lack of adequate Hindi forestalled conversation, but the stranger smiled, reached into a trouser pocket and brought out what looked like a card with something printed on it. He gestured for me to smell it, but as I leaned in its direction, I inhaled something mysteriously sweet. He motioned me to inhale deeply, moving the card closer to my nose. This immediately aroused my suspicion of something malign. I had known of kidnapped children being forced into sexual slavery, and my face probably registered my fear. The stranger got off at the next stop, gesturing for me to follow him, but sexually innocent as I was, I was not stupidly compliant. He quickly melted into the crowd of pedestrians, leaving me perplexed, unsettled, yet relieved.

Despite these misadventures, sex remained on my mind, as it did for all growing boys. But it was really a matter of ungratified lust. Classes at St. Mary's ran from Monday to Saturday, with a mid-week break on Thursday. Christ Church and Clare Road Convent School had breaks on Saturday, so there seemed to be yet another conspiracy against us by the Jesuits, who forced us into minor self-mortification by their cycles of benedictions, sermons, confessions, and retreats, all very pointedly aimed at getting us to move away from private parts to the saints. Outside of masturbation, the only ejaculations we had were the phrases uttered during church litanies. Spiritually descended from both St. Ignatius Loyola and Torquemada, the Jesuits turned sex into a demonic force. It was sinful to even have thoughts about sex, let alone perform it. They lined us up for weekly confession during Lent, and our confessors demanded an exact accounting of our impure thoughts, words, and deeds. And at the annual retreat, one pink-faced priest in black cassock conducted a highly theatrical presentation on the Last Judgement. A coffin draped in black to the left of the Communion rail, he sat at a long table on the right, scribbling pensively in an imposing black ledger as two neighbouring candles flickered ominously. The penumbral setting heightened the morbidity, and the only thing that precluded terror was our knowledge of this priest's genial eccentricity outside the holy of holies. He often wandered absent-mindedly about the schoolyard in his curry-stained white soutane, with his footwear alternating between sneakers with large holes at the toe or scuffed leather shoes that he would scratch whenever an itch beset him. Consequently, it was impossible to accept him in the role of God decreeing Eternal Damnation. But it made for amusing Theatre.

Our parents maintained a firm silence on all things sexual. They were still suffering from residual Victorianism, which decreed an injunction on sex education. It wasn't simply one kind of love that dared not speak its name. Consequently, young boys received their information from older chums. I saw my first "pornographic" image at twelve. It was an explicit black and white postcard of a Parisian whore and her "john," and I remember the look of amazement on her face as she handled his gigantic erection.

Strange the injunctions against sex in a country where peasant women breastfed their babies openly on buses, trams, and trains, and where *coolies* walked around naked, except for their loin cloths which barely concealed phalluses dangling like slender aubergines. Stranger still the injunctions in a country that was saturated with sexual symbolism and ritual. Indians worshipped the *yoni* and the *lingam*. When passing a sculpture of the Goddess Shri, it was customary for a Hindu to touch her sacred mound, the *yoni*. South Indian temples had a sculpture of two holy men in prayer beneath a giant-sized vulva. Shri Lakshmi, the goddess of abundance, held one hand to a breast (source of milk and nurture) while her other hand pointed to her vulva, the sacred threshold of birth. There were also members of a certain Vishnu sect with emblems of the ripe vulva of a menstrual woman painted on their foreheads.

As countless Westerners must have realized, India (despite its religious and moral orthodoxies) was sensual, for as Paul Theroux puts it in *Elephanta Suite*, "If India seemed puritanical, it was because at the bottom of its puritanism was a repressed sensuality that was hungrier and nakeder [sic] and more voracious than anything" a foreigner knew. The lotus is a sexual emblem in India, its bloom a symbol of women's labia, its bud a symbol of a virgin vagina, and its pistil a representation of the foetus. The entire flower is meant to suggest a womb. Ancient caves (such as Ajanta, Ellora, Khajuraho) had the most amazing erotic carvings with sexual positions that would be the envy of most sex manuals. Nudity was not fig-leafed or veiled. The Hindus believe that every nude woman incarnates *prakrti*, nature, matter, or the primordial substance. She is the prototype of woman. Without her *shakti* or primal energy, the male, human or a god, is dormant or lifeless.

Looking back on my adolescence, I am still confounded by adult reticence about sex. I am especially confounded by my father's silence on the matter of sex education. In any conflict between mind and body, the body would win in my father's case. A lusty man, he could never seem to keep his hands off my mother on the veranda after dinner. Standing a mere five feet four in height, stocky in build, he had pink skin, and his well-muscled arms and legs had power that I admired. He had little body hair and no discernible nicks, bumps, ridges, or depressions in his skin. His fingers and toes were chunky and hard, quite incapable of grace but assuredly suited to quotidian chores. When he washed his oil-stained hands at lunchtime after returning from his business garage, the soap bubbled brown or black, and no matter how briskly he rubbed his fingers and palms together, there was always a residue of grime under his fingernails, a palpable sign of his preoccupation with machines. His feet had a heavy tread, and I could hear his footfall. Sometimes after work, when his socks were off, his feet smelled like Gorgonzola.

When my parents decided jointly to immigrate to Canada in 1961, they knew little of the country, except what was reported by family friends, the two Kulhanian sisters (Kathleen and Lesley) and their long-widowed Indian mother who had first gone to England and then, more wisely, to Canada. My parents decided on Canada by a process of elimination. England, the putative Home for displaced or disgruntled Anglo-Indians, would have been my mother's logical choice, especially as her elder sister, younger brothers, and mother had already settled in such cities as Birmingham, Stoke-on-Trent, and London. Two nephews and a niece of my father were also in England, Aubrey and Stephen in London and Theresa in Middlesex. But my mother recoiled from the reality of English damp and cold. Canada, of course, was even colder, but central heating was not alien to it or deemed an expensive luxury. My mother could not see herself warming up her English bed with hot-water bottles and layers of thick blankets after feeding innumerable shillings to a gas meter. Nor did she fancy English soot or chilly English reserve.

Sent for further training in Sheffield and Nuffield in 1949, my father had a more sentimental view of England. To him it was a country of quaint cottages and inns, easy chatter and choral singing at the local pub, the conscientious cleanliness of gloved vendors, and the proper manners of the English gentleman. Like all other Armenians in Bombay, he insisted on being classified with Europeans. He claimed that his people belonged to the Aryan race, which divided itself into three main branches: the Nordic, the Alpine, and the Mediterranean. As some historians pointed out, Armenians belonged to a family of the Alpine branch, whose original source was Central Europe. The Armenian language belonged to the Germanic group of Indo-European languages. My father believed that all the rights and privileges conferred on the Armenians in India by the East India Company Charter or Agreement of 1688, and since maintained, guaranteed not only the protection of Armenian churches, educational and charitable foundations, or landed properties and commerce, but the important status of British Indian subjects with just claims to be classified with Europeans.

England was my father's first choice because he felt specially protected by the English. Both my parents knew the facts of English racism—the revenge of defeated imperialists who had no more glory. In some ways, my father had a blind spot when it came to Britain. "An Englishman is always true to his word," he maintained, though there was ample evidence to the contrary. He was unaware of the famous *Punch* cartoon of July 20, 1878, depicting Disraeli and the

Lady of Cyprus attempting to hoist a fat Turkish Humpty-Dumpty back on to the wall. Its caption read (with unsteady metre): "Humpty-Dumpty sat on a wall;/ Humpty-Dumpty had a great fall; Dizzy, with Cyprus, and all the Queen's men,/ Hopes to set Humpty-Dumpty up again."

My father recognized some of Britain's insidious use of colonial power in India, but he romanticized her value as a civilized nation. He spoke nostalgically of "the good old days" when there was no Prohibition and liquor could flow copiously at parties, when there was no refugee problem in Bombay, no squatters littering the streets, when pavements and buildings were clean, when clubs could hold swanky soirees when Anglo-India was still the Raj rather than down-at-the-heels. He proudly boasted of his British passport as a guarantee of privileged status. He renounced it only when we immigrated to Canada after my mother decided that Blighty was not Home, after all.

The fact is that no help came from the British when it was most needed by Armenians. Turkish Armenia was to all intents and purposes a British protectorate after the Cyprus Convention, even though the region was never officially given that title. Armenians of the Ottoman Empire foolishly believed that the great powers, led by Britain, would intervene in Ottoman affairs. Britain, supposedly a fountainhead of civilized law, would surely see that the Ottoman system of law was really a denial of law itself. Muslim law was inapplicable to non-Muslims. A Muslim in conflict with another Muslim was guaranteed a fair hearing in civil cases, but a non-Muslim in conflict with a Muslim always lost, because the case was heard before a religious tribunal where non-Muslim testimony was forbidden.

The English did nothing about this. They also did nothing about the fact that Armenians were prohibited from bearing arms—even in self-defence against predatory neighbours. They did nothing about the *devshirme* or boy-collection, whereby officials could seize children from the Christian communities, educate them as Muslims and press them into the Ottoman civil service. They did nothing about the poll tax and property tax, which in practice amounted to unchecked extortion. They did nothing about the obligation to provide free winter quarters *(kishlak)* to nomadic Kurds and their flocks, often for four to six months annually.

The English adopted a stiff upper lip, as usual, but when the evidence mounted about the British government's failure to the Armenians, the Blue Book Report (published in 1916 by Viscount Bryce and Arnold Toynbee) was simply too embarrassing to the British government. Of course, the English had their usual *bête-noire* in the Russians, and they played it for all it was politically worth. In this manner, they could hold fast to the Ottoman connection without really interfering in internal Turkish matters that were intent on exterminating the Armenians.

They had blood on their white hands.

The British in India during the Raj showed that they did not allow too much to deter them from imposing themselves as masters. They introduced railways, roads, canals, schools, universities, hospitals, common law, and gave the country a *lingua franca*, but they also left behind an ugly trail of virulent racism and brutality that ultimately led to their expulsion. To the most intractably racist, Indians were "niggers," "wogs," "black-bellied bastards," while to the inveterately imperialistic, Indians were servile dependents of their masters. The best-intentioned English were given to ironic metaphors where, instead of the colonized appearing as savages or unenlightened unfortunates, Indians were regarded as children in need of a colonial education. Kipling was probably a source for such metaphors. Colonial Headquarters had its own committed views. In tracing the social and political tumult of the Raj, Lawrence James refers to figures such as Winston Churchill (who was chronically nauseated by Gandhi) and Lord Rothermere (an ultra-imperialist) who thought of India as being morally degenerate and in radical need to be ruled under a Divine dispensation.

Why my father did not condemn the British is a matter I fail to understand. Perhaps, denied humanity by the Turks, he mistook English good manners for genuine benevolence, not realizing that these manners had nothing to do with particular interest in him or with Indians in general. English manners in England or in the colonies bear no relation to actual attitudes, for as Germaine Greer has remarked, the Englishman is "uniformly polite to everyone," and, so, his manners "are totally insincere."

Perhaps there was another reason for my father's delusion.

Perhaps humiliation and suffering finally subjugate a victim into misreading grand historical gestures. The British were famous for grand historical gestures, even when these followed centuries of racial intolerance, bigotry, oppression, and repression. The Raj came to an inglorious end, but the English preserved a sense of dignity in panoply, a sense of occasion by dressing up Mountbatten in all his pristine regalia so he could officiate with pomp and ceremony as the sun set on their long rule in India. My father memorialized their leave-taking with nostalgic fondness, quite oblivious to the fact that there was (as Paul Scott came to express in *The Raj Quartet*) something unctuous and evasive about the way the British left. They had been careless in their division of the spoils: India had been badly fractured into rival sects, the princes abandoned to nationalist revenge, the Anglo-Indians left to twice-born contempt. The Quit India Movement had spawned bloody savagery. My grandmother's second husband, an unrepentant Englishman named Ken Face who used to dress in khaki shirt, short trousers, and stockings, had had his skull cracked by thugs in Bombay. And yet, even after all this turmoil and violence, the British had left an undying legacy of racial discrimination. In 1945 it was quite impossible for a British officer to mix with Indian civilians on equal terms; in 1964 (three years after we left India) there were still beach bungalows at Juhu where the English could drink liquor with the tacit understanding that no Indian would be invited to share the privilege. And Breach Candy Swimming Club stubbornly refused to change its "Whites Only" rule.

The British government never wanted to explain its manner of ending the Raj. Perhaps, India had become a burning emblem of their shame; perhaps, India had merely become a bloody bore. And yet, many Anglo-Indians clung to their fantasy of belonging to the culture of England, perhaps fearing that they would lose their attachments to colonial headquarters.

I suspect that for all his liberalism, my father secretly wished that the Raj had continued.

My father had a contentious nature that could be enflamed even by art. He appreciated my godfather's sad Portuguese love songs played on a mandolin, black spirituals and blues music on radio, our Oriental rugs, framed Victorian and Edwardian lithographs reeking of sentimentality, and the tall, blue porcelain vase on which my mother had painted a running horse—but he sneered at the poverty of artists. The thought of anyone starving in a garret for the sake of art provoked his ridicule. The fact that Van Gogh's paintings were now worth millions was a cruel irony of history because everybody knew how Van Gogh had starved in his lifetime. How gnarled his bony face had become, how fiercely stubby his corn-coloured short hair, how sunken his deeply pained eyes, how twisted with grime and effort his fingers. And to have to acquire notoriety by losing an ear to a prostitute—that was the monstrousness of the poor, starving artist. The ultimate horror was Van Gogh's insanity and suicide in a cornfield blighted by crows. When he saw the MGM film version of Irving Stone's *Lust for Life*, starring Kirk Douglas (one of his favourite actors), my father emphasized the agony rather than the ecstasy of the artist. He would point to the pavement artists in Bombay who created beautiful geometric patterns and portraits in coloured chalk, and he would lament their poverty. The lament was streaked with irony, for while he did not doubt that some of these penurious artists had genuine talent, he scoffed that their only fame would come after their deaths. And what good would that be to those who were no more than scattered dust?

I burned with anger at such philistinism. What good was his life? I wondered to myself. What immortality would he ever achieve? His retorts were a declaration of an underground war, a battle of instincts and impulses, to be waged without truce during my adolescence, but he seemed to relish my anger, especially as he knew it could be easily provoked by his mockery. He was not play-acting. He was not being cheerfully aggressive. He intended his insults because, in knowing my respect for artists, he could attack the centre of my intellectual and spiritual refuge and hope for victory by humiliation.

I was to obtain my revenge in my sixteenth year.

My father dearly wanted me to be a doctor. He attached a great deal of importance to that vocation, though his reason was based on the money, prestige, and security that doctors (F.R.C.P. or F.R.C.S.) seemed to enjoy. Whenever I was ill as a child, I was taken to our family doctor, old, gently wise Dr. Balchandra, who always seemed to have an impressively fat medical book on his desk. Dr. Balchandra was a white-skinned Hindu in a *dhoti* and sandals, but he spoke excellent English in a soft bass voice. One of his sons was at medical school in America. Dr. Balchandra had a dispensary on the premises, and I used to watch in fascination as the pharmacist concocted powders and pills, mixtures in bright red or muddy brown and grey. But it was Dr. Balchandra I watched most intently as he slowly thumbed through his medical references or patiently examined me. Because of his age, he had a stoop, but this gave his appearance a benevolent gravity, magnified by his spectacles and slow, careful manner of speech. What especially appealed to me was that he never assumed that his vast experience could do without new technical information. He seemed to be a "readerly" doctor, who would gladly learn as he practised his vocation.

My early and sustained interest in Biology, my perusal of thick medical tomes and the relish with which I sounded abstruse clinical terms ("trephining, karyoplasm, static scoliosis"), conjoined with my viewing of delicate heart surgery (through special arrangement with a young medical student from The Retreat), all seemed to indicate a future for me as a surgeon or specialist. In high school I took Advanced Physics and Chemistry, and enjoyed the special mark that set me and my peers apart from the general ruck of students who elected to stay within the "safe" academic confines of General Science or regular Physics-with-Chemistry. All was well until I ventured deeper into the algebraic complexities of problem solving. I had always detested the formulae, equations, and theorems of mathematics, and as my classes sank into a welter of thermodynamics, valences, refractive indices, and the laws of Boyle, Ohm, and Hooke, my enthusiasm sagged and was eventually completely deflated. I was bright enough to transcend academic difficulties, but I blithely ignored my homework in Advanced Physics and Chemistry, keeping my mind on Shakespeare, Dickens, and Macaulay at school, and Olivier and Brando at the movies.

My ongoing warfare with my father was by now common knowledge among certain neighbours, many of whom sided with me intellectually while urging me to show no filial disrespect. I kept my silence on everything but movies, books, theatre, and fine art, unless my father passed what to me was a remark that simply screamed out for rebuttal. I dreamed of some momentous way with which to punish him for his humiliating slights and indignities. That I was uncommonly good at drawing, painting, writing, elocution, and acting on stage seemed inordinately trivial to him. He didn't care a fig for my collection of books; I certainly abhorred his garage grime and grease. He thought my stage and screen idols patently false; I denounced his coterie of friends for being insincere hangers-on.

I dreamed of getting even with my father. Knowing how dearly he had wanted me to become a physician, I felt a secret pleasure in disappointing him by deliberately failing at Advanced Physics and Chemistry, two compulsory subjects required at the time for university admission to Medicine. When my final Cambridge results arrived, with a cherished Distinction in English Composition, and the inevitable failures in Physics and Chemistry, I blushed. The Distinction in English should have been something to celebrate, for I was one of only four graduates since Dom Moraes five years earlier to achieve that honour. But denied a First in the GCE, I had now defeated myself as well as my father.

Was what I had done really revenge? Was it, rather, a rather wrong-headed attempt to deny my father the pride in a dutiful son?

Was it a scheme to force him to declare his own wounding, his own vulnerability?

And, so, the silence between us grew wider and deeper.

Compelled to face facts (my mother's refusal to settle in damp, green but unpleasant England), he reluctantly abandoned the idea of England as a new home. Australia skimmed over my parents' minds as an option. The climate would be more congenial than England's, and there were long beaches and sparkling warm waters where one could be in one's proper element, despite reconnoitring sharks. But Australia also had vile defects: it fancied itself a supremely masculine culture where women were "Sheilas," and might as well have been drovers' cattle; its class barriers were probably as repulsive as England's; and, even before I ever read Patrick White, Australia did not seem to transcend its dichotomy as a garden-desert, more a desert than garden culturally.

So, Canada was chosen. Or chose us.

We had to apply to the Canadian consulate and give assurances (with references and evidence) that we were solvent, of good character, sound health and citizenship. What was our purpose for seeking landed immigrant status? India held no future for his children, my father maintained. Canada held infinitely more possibilities.

I never felt at one with Bombay. I had always felt a need to look beyond it—for a film, a book, a painting, a life of imagined value. I yearned for a different country, though not necessarily with snow, *portages, coureurs de bois,* and quaint cedar cabins secluded in a bear-dark wood near a lake of loons. Canada came to me in disjointed images and stereotypes. I knew, of course, of the Royal Canadian Mounted Police. Didn't they always get their man? But what did this mean? Canada was a country of resettled felons, like Australia? On the other hand, there were Diefenbaker and Pearson, hardly emblematic of hewers of wood and drawers of water. One had wavy silver hair, the jowls and teeth of a chipmunk, and the eyes of an owl; the other had an absurd polka-dot bowtie, a cowlick, and a lisp. They were both extremely conservative, decent, and safe. Not at all the sort who would send out U-2's or threaten the use of intercontinental ballistic missiles, like the Americans; not the sort who would divide and rule a nation like the British had done. We believed we could entrust ourselves to their governance.

We did not know then about palpable racism in Canada: the existence of slavery till 1834; Sir John A. MacDonald's racism (especially towards Canada's indigenous peoples) or his misogyny; the loathsome abuse of young First Nations males and females at nefarious residential schools; the presence of Ku Klux Klanners in Ontario earlier in the century; or the existence of segregated indigenous, black, and "coloured" communities across Canada. That Canadian history was never taught in Canadian schools till late in the 20th century. Why could it have been? After all, there were legally segregated schools in Ontario till 1965 and in Nova Scotia till 1983. And there were serious restrictions on home ownership and dwelling rentals for people of colour.

We were ignorant of this shameful history, though I doubt whether knowledge of these rancid social, economic, and political facts would have changed our optimism about immigration.

After the obligatory interview with a Canadian *attaché*, during which my mother exaggerated my proficiency in oral French, we manipulated our way out of the muddle of Indian bureaucracy. We discharged our pecuniary duty to the peon who told us that "Pirst, we must have pee" (meaning "fee"), and then, in another venue, we dutifully discharging our real pee into neatly labelled bottles in Dr. Callander's office. Our applications were stamped and classified, we were inoculated, and decreed fit for passage on board H.M.S. *Arcadia*.

Our vessel's name portended utopia, although we knew that the connotation was an act of imagination. My two younger sisters and I were exultant with expectation. My father resigned himself to a social and financial decline in fortunes. My mother was dewy-eyed at a farewell party when friends joined hands in a large ring and sang "Auld Lang Syne." We donated furniture and fine china, gold ornaments, our Grundig record player, and odds-and-ends of our Bombay home to my married cousin, Neville, and were careless about what we tried to dispossess. My passion for collecting was ruthlessly limited to a couple of hundred books, school yearbooks, and assorted papers and clippings having to do with painting, literature, film, and theatre. We were almost obscene in our haste to strip down the volume of our baggage, but I wanted India to fall away like dead skin.

I welcomed displacement, heart and mind open to a long journey across a vast ocean, moving to a new freedom, like a secret thought about a surge of possibilities. As the *Arcadia* ploughed through churning foam, with seagulls above, I looked to the water for erasures. I did not mind the slow rocking when there were large swells, not knowing what came next when the sea stilled to silence.

CHAPTER THREE

SECOND COUNTRY

rriving in Montreal in June 1961, a month before my eighteenth birthday, was the beginning of a new history. My parents had lost a circle of acquaintances and friends, but I was eager for a different life, not concerned about what I had left behind in the act of immigration. Montreal, I was certain, would be a welcome change from Bombay's lazy, noisy, disorganization. Driven slowly by taxi to Notre Dame de Grace, I saw kids playing baseball, not cricket, though I felt a pastoral peace—that didn't last once we settled in an apartment reeking of age, its large rooms disfigured by warped wooden floors. However, it would be a relief not to be bothered by caste. And Canada was not a pigmentocracy, unlike many other Commonwealth countries.

I never experienced raw racism personally, though I did encounter a certain indefinable condescension at times because my spoken English had a foreign lilt before I was able to flatten that without also becoming boringly toneless. "Where did you learn to speak such excellent English?" I was asked frequently, as if my verbal facility was akin to the talent of a dancing dog.

I had never thought of asking my mother Lorna (a Scots name, coined by novelist R.D. Blackmore for his novel *Lorna Doone*) why she had selected my baptismal name Keith (another Scots name). I later guessed the significance of my middle name Stephen, because that had been my father's middle name, as well as the Christian name of his own father, whom he had lost while he was a little boy in Dikranagerd. I did not know my paternal grandparents because they had perished in 1915, and there were no photographs of either of them. In fact, my father had but the slightest memory of his own father disappearing when he was "recruited" by the Turkish army. It was only in my adult years that I realized how many uncertainties surrounded my father. I have no confirmation of the year of his birth. His Indian and Canadian passports give 1909 as the birth-year, but my parents' marriage certificate records 1911 as his year of birth. The earliest surviving Canadian passport I have of his declares Dikranagert Sum, Armenia as his place of birth, except that there is no city by that name. There is a Dikranagerd, and a Dikranagerd Sur, but perhaps, the passport error was simply a case of misspelling, especially as Canadian immigrant officials were not familiar with Armenian names. There is no surviving document that shows when my father arrived in India. Nor do I know much about his early life in Bombay, or the year when he met my mother.

My mother's side also has biographical gaps. I have not been able to pin down the etymological source of her maiden name, Alimo, which sounds vaguely Spanish, less vaguely Portuguese, though there is a name Alaimo traced back to medieval Sicily. The Alimo family name was found in the USA in 1920, with ten families by that surname living in Connecticut, but I have never discovered either the primary etymological source or the meaning of the name. As for the Alimos in Bombay, I never saw my maternal grandfather Ewart Reginald Alimo, except in family photographs, and my only memory of him was through family anecdotes. I do remember my maternal grandmother Nellie Margaret Haller because she was a beloved part of my life in Bombay and even visited us in Canada for my sister Audrey's wedding in 1972. My grandmother's second hus-band, Ken Face (who had had his skull bashed during a Partition riot), licked his fingers before turning the pages of a newspaper, and spent many hours glued to BBC radio, listening to County and Test Match cricket. He was disliked by all my grandmother's children, some recalling that he had dared to flirt with Nana while she was still married to Ewart Alimo. Ken may not have been overtly racist, but he was given to making snide remarks about Indians. His long stay in India stamped him as Anglo-Indian, but he never felt at home in the subcontinent. It was inevitable that he would leave India for good, taking my grandmother with him. Though Nana had two surviving married sons (Edmund and Reginald, Valentine, the oldest, having died on his first wedding anniversary), a married daughter Patsy, and numerous nephews and nieces in England, Blighty was never Home to her, but that was where she died. England would always be a place where the uprooted Alimos would feel a sense of loss or a radical estrangement. I share their estrangement to some degree, but in an ironic way. I have cousins in Birmingham (through my Uncle Reg's marriage) whom I have never met and whose names I do not remember. And in India the closest relative was my married cousin Neville who settled with his wife Joyce and children in Goa, and whom I never saw again after 1961. In a nutshell, one side (the Armenian) was mostly a blank; the other side (Anglo-Indian) was partially known, most of the family tree lost. In a genealogical sense, I was an incomplete person, and unfinished in a radical sense.

Being half Armenian and half Anglo-Indian, I had always felt a part of someone else's story. It was a hard thing to try and live as solely one or the other: I did not speak, read, or write Armenian; I felt more Anglo than Indian, but always with a sense of continual subtraction. After the deaths of my sister Elma and my parents, I wrote *Pain*, my post-modernist memoir that mixed various literary forms, and decades later, I wrote *Against Forgetting*, an autobiographical narrative poetry sequence in the service of remembering, recovering, and remaking pieces of me and other lost selves of humanity. In Montreal, wedged between English and French, the language and the people, I was trying to adapt to my status as a New Canadian, though first I had to deal with being a new immigrant. In other words, my accent, my style of clothing, my habits set me apart from Canadians my own age. I did not, of course, realize that my Anglo-Indian accent was exotic until I heard myself a few years later on an audio recording. My pronunciation, however, was considered English, which baffled many Canadians who were often woefully ignorant of India's imperial connection. English had been spoken in the subcontinent long before it had been in Canada because the East India Company had sought trade in silk, cotton, indigo dye, tea, and opium from as far back as 1608, when agents landed at the port of Surat. Originally called the *Bombay Times and Journal of Commerce*, the *Times of India*, an English-language daily newspaper, was founded in 1838 to serve British residents of western India.

Immigration is always an act that demands new ways of looking at reality. In India the obvious was overwhelming, but Montreal was far from obvious for me. My parents rented an upper duplex on Monkland Avenue, Notre Dame de Grace, and as we had arrived in summer, there was a pastoral peace quite different from the pastoralism of *maidans* in Bombay, where as a boy I had played soccer, field hockey, and cricket. There were fewer people on the streets—hardly the thronging bodies on buses, tramcars, and trains in my home city. And all the streets were clean, almost gleaming under sunlight. India had been an assault on my senses in general and on smell in particular. Its geography had been vast and generally undeveloped in terms of settlements, highways, boulevards. Its buildings, such as The Retreat, were old-fashioned or a bit ridiculous in architecture. I felt compelled to challenge stereotypes and clichés: I never lived in a hut; my mother never wore a sari (although my two sisters did at a costume party with neighbourhood girls their ages); not every street or zone was poor and dirty; I never consulted astrologers; I never spoke "Hindu" (the Canadian misnomer for that country's national language) at home; I never questioned how it was that my mother's side of the family spoke only English; and neither our civic government nor our provincial government was run by village headmen. My Bombay, my India was not Gandhi's or Nehru's. Although I did attend a school where one of my classmates was a prince or prince's son, I never personally experienced the Raj.

Dispelling common misconceptions of where I had come from increased the problem of adaptation, let alone assimilation. Part of me wished to remain separate. I did not necessarily wish to speak about my family or origins, unless required. I did not want to sound tonally flat in speech, as flat (as prolific Bruce Meyer puts it) "as someone announcing that the next train to somewhere is delayed." I was never a conformist, so I did not wish to be a follower or "group-ie" anywhere. I did not wish to be anonymous, though I guarded my private, inner life, or whatever I had as such. This push-and-pull tendency wrinkled my life significantly. My father looked and sounded like an immigrant, with his workman's cap and heavily ac-cented, mangled English, so I felt uneasy about inviting new friends into the home. My curiosity and my language were far wider than his, although he was not a man for whom his own life was the only story. He cared about us, though he felt humiliated having to return to manual labour as an automobile mechanic after having been the equivalent of Vice-President of a car factory. And there were no ser-vants in Montreal to reinforce his status or ease the domestic life of my mother. There was no clan for him to claim as his own in Montreal—not till he discovered and befriended a few members of the Armenian community, but even then he felt out of place.

My mother, too, felt out of place. Compelled by a radical change in economic fortune by our immigration, she returned to the work-force at forty. When I saw her struggling against the cold, snow, and ice, and multiple bus routes to get to her place of work each workday morning, I felt sorry for her and frustrated. I was annoyed when I gave up a seat to an older person who barely thanked me, only to see that no Canadian was prepared to do the same for my mother. Was it because she looked like a helpless foreigner? There was nothing even superficially Indian about her—not her dress, not her manner of speaking, not even her complexion which was lighter than mine.

To be a colonial or neo-colonial was to be restricted by history, as well as to be the subject of a special hate. Or a submerged bias, at any rate. Canada was not Australia, America, or Britain, with their separate histories of virulent prejudices, but there were pockets of racism, and it was not uncommon for certain groups of immigrants to hear such derogatory terms as "Paki," "nigger," "wop," *et cetera*.

Racism also infiltrated the school system. I know of an otherwise genial, expat, moustachioed Scots Principal (who favoured wearing a polka-dot bowtie) at a suburban Elementary School in Peel region who declared at a staff meeting that he would find it very hard to accept any school being named Mahatma Gandhi Public School. He did not say whether he might feel the same way about a school named after William Wallace or Rob Roy.

Although I was hardly a victim of Canadian racism, I did experience radical cultural difference. There was a difference in the way emotion was shown in public. The Indian (and Armenian) ways are candidly open, sometimes raw, sometimes extreme. But in Canada, feelings tend to be pent up so as not to seem insincere or intrusive. This contrast is crystallized in situations of grief or loss. Canadian funeral parlours are spotlessly clean, fragrant with the smell of fresh lilies and floral bouquets, and the dead wear makeup and are dressed well in their coffins. In Bombay, mourning was rarely private, and it was generally loud, verging on spectacular in a literal sense.

Bombay was also far more communal. Parties were held weekly, and friends ate, drank, played card games complemented by gossip, or chatted (often at the top of their voices). I shrank from rowdiness, but there was no mistaking the vitality of social gatherings or get-togethers. As a young teenager I was invited to a Muslim wedding banquet, where I shared in a big meal arranged on a large *thali* (metal plate), from which guests ate with their hands—scooping the food only with the right hand, not the left. One of the greatest pleasures was enjoying rich *Dhansak* (a mixture of Persian and Gujarati cuisine that combined lamb, vegetables, and lentils in a rich sauce) at a Parsi *Navjote* ceremony—equivalent to a Jewish bar-mitzvah or Christian confirmation. I was never much of a meat-eater when young, but the aroma of *Dhansak* and the flavour of the gravy were enough to satisfy me, as we ate off long, clean plantain leaves to live music by Nelly and her twelve-piece dance Band. Nelly (really Nellie Batliwalla) was immensely popular at the time, and her repertoire was heavy with pop tunes or easy-listening music for those who preferred not to dance. However, Bombay also had its sinister side.

Certain alleys and streets were fraught with crime, and one would risk life and limb wandering in them at night. Montreal streets, however, were generally safe at the time. There was no rushing disorder, no thick crowds, and if there were ghettos, they were kept away from foreign visitors who would probably have reacted negatively at the sight of them.

Montreal has a history, of course, but this shows less obviously than Indian history in Bombay. In Montreal, one has to search for it in a small number of historic churches, markets, statues, buildings; in Bombay, one was surrounded by it, street by street, zone by zone. History seeped into daily life, inviting meditation about desire, suffering, and the body each of us lives in. There was a palpable sense of a mythical past, in which terrible battles had been fought, grand battles on plains, fates decided by the gods with many avatars. French-Canadian Montreal remembers the Plains of Abraham, when General James Wolfe defeated French troops under the command of the Marquis of Montcalm, resulting in the loss of Quebec to the British in 1760, but forts (as in many other parts of Canada) are mostly empty relics, their short history gussied up for costumed parades or rituals. It is very possible (as J.L. Granatstein contended in the March 2021 edition of the *Literary Review of Canada*) that "Canadians don't like to think about war," citing the fact (as outlined in Tim Cook's *The Fight for History*) that "Canada largely forgot about the Second World War for fifty years," until the mid-1990s when the country was "finally moved by the CBC's coverage of D-Day and V-E Day anniversaries—coverage that showed what our soldiers had done and how they were remembered by those they liberated." Historical sites in India have auras; historical sites in Canada have auras that are less distinctive and forceful.

Commissioned to do a short travel piece for *Montreal Calendar Magazine* in 1981, I took my wife Caryl and young son Michael to Fort Henry National Historic Site in Kingston, Ontario. The location was picturesque, the site on Point Henry, an elevated point near the mouth of the Cataraqui River where it flows into the St. Lawrence River at the east end of Lake Ontario. The fort, named after Henry

Hamilton, former Lieutenant-Governor of Quebec, had been con-
structed during the War of 1812 to prevent a possible American attack and to monitor maritime traffic on the river and lake. Its historical genesis varnished by memorabilia, the newly-renovated fort
had become a popular tourist attraction. It boasted spick and span
uniformed military guards, and offered historical re-enactments of
drills and battle tactics. But these rituals were empty. "When did the
attack happen?" I inquired of a military guide. He blushed: "It never
did." No actual battle had occurred, so everything—the Garrison
Parade, the Victorian schoolroom, the Muster Parade, the gleaming
black cannons—were gilded mementoes of something absent at the
centre. The Sunset Ceremony, conducted every Wednesday in July
and August, with a full program of drill, music and artillery, was a
glamorous illusion. In Bombay, real battles (not *possible* ones) were
part of folk legend, and the country as a whole had its ancient historical epics in Sanskrit, and though these texts had an emphatic
religious intent, many parts had a basis in historical fact. Indian
history did not need defining. Canadian history did.

But there was another crucial difference between Canada and
India. Apart from some romantic and false glorification of the
Western builders of the nation, to the detriment of the ever-ma-
ligned and traduced indigenous population and the Chinese who
actually built the great Canadian railroad, Canadian history did not
overplay its heroic side, not even when it came to the soldiers who
had fought valiantly during two world wars. (Canada keeps apologizing for historical injustices: the physical and sexual abuse of First
Nations children in residential schools, and the vicious internment
of Japanese-Canadians and Italian-Canadians during the Second
World War. The depth of sincerity may be in question, but the rituals are politely exercised.) Indian history, on the other hand, was
forever glorifying the past, without vital self-criticism. It was as if
Indian historians were assured that the past required no serious re-
examination because the country would go on, sanctified by Indian
spirituality. India adored itself. And this adoration is part of the
Indian stasis, as when Indians look back at Gandhi and see, not his

struggles against intrinsic anomalies, only his myth, finding what they wish to find in him. It is rather like the way the English do with Winston Churchill, a distinguished, theatrically heroic, racist and, therefore, much lesser man.

An important aspect of existence is learning how to attend to quotidian life and its banalities, and not expecting everything to be dramatic, melodramatic, or extravagant with sensation. I was a reader and observant voyeur, so I eased myself into knowledge, learning to pay more attention than I previously had to my environment, taking less for granted, realizing that I was *in medias res*, as it were, not at the beginning of things, but in the middle of a journey to know myself and my immediate world. My past in Bombay, divesting myself of Indian concerns about language and custom, I was eager to be Canadian in my own way. But what was that way? And how could I achieve it?

Montreal had four distinct seasons, unlike Bombay, where heat prevailed over cold most of the year, and where the worst season was the wettest one: Monsoon. That was when streets were flooded, cars put out of service when their engines drowned, and where raincoats and gumboots became the season's pragmatic fashion. I did not miss the heavy rain, but my parents did not take well to snow and ice. My mother, a small, dainty lady, feared slipping on ice and cracking a bone, so she always walked with a bag of sand, so she could scatter a handful before her. Being young and thrilled at the sight of falling snow and glistening ice, I felt more Canadian when I learned how to keep my balance on tight-fitting skates I found abandoned in a school locker-room, as I held on to a young helper's hand and cut wobbly circles around a rink. It did not take long for the romance of ice-skating to fade away. Nose-bleeds and frostbitten earlobes hastened my antipathy to winter. Feeling very much as if in the unpitying custody of winter, I quickly decided snow was not my element.

I missed cricket, so I joined a team aptly named the Wanderers because every member was, in fact, an immigrant—from the Caribbean, Pakistan, India, Australia, England. But outdoor cricket, pastoral cricket, was limited to the summer months, and the game was alien to most Canadians, except those who had been sent to private schools set up and still run by English administrators or Canadians trained in an English system. My family and I no longer had a home of privilege, and though our apartment on Beaconsfield Avenue, N.D.G. was roomy, the floors were warped and scuffed. In winter, with tightly-shut double windows, we felt cooped or caged, with no circulation of fresh air. So, when my father made curry or an elaborate biryani that took hours to prepare, the apartment reeked of garlic, onion, and strong spices. I worried about the smells of Indian food clinging to my clothing.

My parents had given me a choice to make quickly. Because their savings (following currency conversion) had been reduced drastically, they could not afford to send me to university, unless I could find work immediately after securing a degree. Teaching seemed the most practical option because once I obtained a Teaching Diploma and the B.Ed. degree, I could find a job and pay back my parents. I had been drawn to the profession because of some memorable teachers in Bombay who were models of dedication and commitment. I applied for admission to St. Joseph Teachers College, where I encountered yet another example of condescension during my interview with a nun who, because I was a newly landed immigrant, doubted my ability to keep up with other students in terms of language of instruction. Sister Mary Desmond, pink complexioned, slight of stature, was sceptical of my Cambridge Distinction in English. She was not persuaded by the fact that I had been only one of four St. Mary graduates after legendary Dom Moraes to have earned a Distinction in English in the Cambridge exams, and she assumed that English was my second language, unaware, of course, that my reading habits were voracious. She sent me to Dr. Thomas Francoeur, whose opinion mattered. He was a gentle, quietly-spoken man of immense professional achievement, whose warmth was palpable, though I almost crashed in our brief chat. He asked if I liked to read, to which I replied, "Oh, yes!" "Well, could you tell me what you have read recently?" I was a reader by habit, but I froze, unable to remember a single title of the three or four books I was reading at the time. Noticing my brain freeze, he put me at ease, suggesting that, perhaps, it was just a case of nerves, for my conversation was otherwise fluent. He approved me for the "A" stream, that is, the four-year course leading to both an A Diploma, as well as the B.Ed. degree (granted by the University of Montreal). And it wasn't long before I justified his confidence in my English or finished as the top student in his Theology course, as well as in all my courses in English Literature.

St. Joseph's on Durocher Street was a modest institution that had the appearance of a school-building—sober, if not altogether grim—a small cafeteria, and a staff especially oriented towards training pedagogues the conventional way. Founded in 1955 by His Eminence George Emmett Cardinal Carter as a separate government-operated college for the preparation of male and female teachers, it was called a Normal School, as many teaching colleges were, because the name was derived from the French concept of an *école normale* to provide a model school with model classrooms to teach model methods of pedagogy. Headed at the time by Father John Hilton (a handsome, avid golfer), the college offered two streams of training: a two-year course for a "B" Diploma, and a four-year stretch for the "A" Diploma and B. Ed. I was granted admission to the second year B.Ed. courses because I had arrived with a year's academic credits from St. Xavier's College, Bombay.

The first summer of my first year at the college passed with part-time work of manual labour which was totally beyond my interest or aptitude. A working-class Jewish family, down the street from me, hired me to tutor their son in high school English for the grand fee of $2 an hour, and I remember their apartment reeking of fried fish. In due course, I was hired by a Prep School in N.D.G. to tutor its students at not much more. However, my three years at the college were among the best years of my young life. I managed the French course (André Provencher being a ruddy faced, genial instructor); suffered through a bland History course by Robert Lavery (who went on to become Associate Director General of the Montreal

Catholic School Commission and other administrative positions elsewhere); absorbed William Lawlor's lessons in Theology; enjoyed the wit of Trigonometry and Pedagogy courses by dandruff-flaked Norman Henchey (who also went on to much bigger things at McGill University); actually flourished in Math under the dynamic instruction of Dominic Modafferi; endured an Introduction to Philosophy course that never seemed to go past its own Prolegomena (though Socrates Rapagna was a patient, well-intentioned instructor); grit my teeth through a rigidly dogmatic course in Epistemology and Metaphysic by rigidly dogmatic Sister Mary of the Nativity (nicknamed "the Native" by irreverently cynical students); was amazed by the fluency of instruction in Educational Psychology by Edward McCracken until discovering that virtually every lecture was memorized verbatim from a textbook; and passed other courses (some entertaining, others mediocre, a few barely tolerable). Apart from Dr. Francoeur (who was greatly influenced by Pierre Teilhard de Chardin's Vitalist concept of the Omega Point), the one professor who motivated me to be my best was Thomas Francoeur's brother-in-law, J. Martin O'Hara, a former Rhodes Scholar, a humanist in the best sense, with an empire of cultural lusts. A slim giraffe of a man with long loping strides, he could have been any aspiring teacher's model for patience, cultural curiosity, and democratic discussion. His two biggest interests, among many, were Literature and Art, that also happened to be two of my biggest interests, and his lectures radiated allusions to both genres that stirred my curiosity and widened my knowledge.

He also encouraged (as did Prof. Brendan Fahey, Prof. Robert Burns, and Mr. Mederic Primeau) my indulgence in Theatre, appreciating my efforts in producing, directing, and acting in one-act plays, and scenes from Ibsen and Shakespeare. An enthusiastic group of peers constituted the nucleus of my theatre group: Roman Wodzicki (for makeup), John Zawada (actor and director of some shows), Nancy Banville, Michelle Brisebois, and Susan Campbell (all three for acting). Martin O'Hara was probably the most instrumental one in securing me a special award for Theatre. The trophy was a smaller version of the Oscar, an amusing nod to my acting and genuine fondness for film. Martin also organized art exhibitions and sales for the Thomas More Institute, where he offered evening courses in literature, art, and bilingual theatre. Seeing me sketching quietly in the college library, he peeked over my shoulder, and said: "Would you like to meet the artist you are copying?" That was how I met Louis Muhlstock, who had been celebrated for his paintings about the Great Depression, landscapes and urban scenes around Montreal. Charmed by my pencil homage to him, Muhlstock gifted me a signed lithograph of a goat lying on barn straw, and later sold me a pastel drawing of a female nude at a price that was probably half of its normal going rate. Martin also brought me into contact with Stanley Cosgrove, painter, draughtsman, and muralist, who (as the National Gallery of Canada put it) over a long career "maintained a consistent artistic path, creating serene figurative representations that explored three principal subjects: forests, women and still life. In his paintings, he placed a strong emphasis on formal relationships through an economy of means, with simplified forms and a limited palette." After I wrote a column on him for a glossy Montreal magazine, Cosgrove showed his appreciation by gifting me two books (one in English, the other in French translation) about his art and signing an exhibition poster.

One of the imperishable memories from my undergraduate years at St. Joe's was of November 22, 1963. I happened to be ordering lunch in the cafeteria when news broke of President Kennedy's assassination in Dallas. Time stopped as everyone froze with shock and horror. That evening all the television coverage numbed me with melancholy. JFK had been a hero of mine: a young, bright, vibrant champion of humanist ideals, the most inspiring American President I had seen and heard. In his short term in office, he had transformed not only America but much of the world. His witty eloquence was only one amazing factor in his genius. He was for human rights at home and abroad, and though he came from an extremely wealthy family, he and his family were not narcissists or filthy super-elites. They supported numerous charities, and some of them literally gave their lives for their most cherished beliefs in true democracy.

My sense of difference as a new immigrant was brought to the fore when one of my classmates, Miles B. (of East European ancestry), steeped in mass media headlines of China's military invasion in 1962 of disputed territory along a 2000-mile Himalayan border, asked me if I was eager to return to India and support her in this Sino-Indian conflict. I had already known that his general knowledge of international affairs, especially Indian, was abysmally low, but his question startled me because I had never expressed any sense of political chauvinism or jingoism, let alone any sense of militaristic bravado. Moreover, I have always believed that patriotism is often the last refuge of scoundrels. What made him think to ask the question, and if his curiosity was genuine, why wasn't he eager to rush to his own ancestral European country and fight proudly for whatever ethnic or cultural or religious cause his people defended?

Was Miles suggesting that there was so much more I could be doing back in Bombay rather than in Montreal? I was an undergraduate, not yet anyone of any significance in any science or art. Of what practical use would I have been to anyone in India, my birthplace that I was never given to romanticizing? Was he simply suggesting that somehow my real place was not Canada but India? Even if I did harbour a secret need to return—which I didn't—it wouldn't have been Home in the same way it was in my childhood. But it did make me wonder if the longer I lived in my new country, the more I would need to ponder whom I was becoming. My parents were past that anxiety or curiosity, though I knew that my father frequently lamented what he had lost by leaving India. As for my Anglo-Indian uncles and aunt in England, I suspect that many of them had regrets over what they, too, had lost by immigrating. But any interpretation of who we were as immigrants depended on who the interpreter was.

It was but a passing moment, but it has stayed with me because it adds weight to what many new immigrants continue to feel in

Canada: you do not really belong here if you weren't actually born here. There's always a shadow that falls across your new adaptation or assimilation.

Miles went on to be elected Head of the Student Council.

After graduating from St. Joe's *magna cum laude*, winning the Lieutenant-Governor's Medal and being selected as Valedictorian at a ceremony on October 16, 1964 at the Plateau Auditorium, I began evening courses for my B.A. at Thomas More Institute for Adult Education (also founded by G. Emmett Carter) while teaching Elementary School during the day. I relished taking other courses by Martin O'Hara, who later (with the approval of Charlotte Tansey, another key figure at the Institute) managed to bring me on board as Discussion Leader (in tandem with Basil Holland) for a course in Bilingual Theatre.

In celebration of my B.A., my colleagues (led by Mildred "Bunnie" Phelan) at St. Monica's Elementary School gifted me a full-length LP recording of the National Theatre of Great Britain's production of *Othello,* directed by John Dexter and starring Sir Laurence Olivier. Years later, after two unsuccessful marriages and long settled in Ontario, I was invited to be a Guest of Honour at a Thomas More Convocation, where I was formally interviewed by Martin O'Hara about my writing career. By this time, however, Martin was showing signs of age. He still drove a Volkswagen (now unsteadily), walked more slowly, showed creases on his face. But his mind stayed alert on all matters of books, art, and theatre. He treated me and my partner to a delightful lunch, where he shared memories of me as an enterprising undergraduate with a passion for theatre. He enjoyed relating how I worried about the costume I was to wear as John Worthing in Wilde's perfect comedy. "Sister Mary Desmond came to me and said, 'You won't believe what's bothering Keith. He's fussing about whether the ironed crease in his trousers looks right.'" Martin was delighted to receive every new book I produced, wrote letters of reference on my behalf to universities, and remained ever true to his humanist self. He was a man who knew in his bones that Dante is differently valuable than Derrida, and his life and career showed how the art of teaching is the art of discovery. He was living validation of Yeats's dictum that education is not the filling of a pail but the lighting of a fire.

Martin O'Hara taught me the art of discovery. He was a great teacher. He set my mind on fire.

CHAPTER FOUR

ALMA MATER, ACTING, AND GETTING DEEPER INTO SHAKESPEARE

F ilm came first, and then Theatre and Poetry as my artistic obsessions. When I was 3, my mother took me to *Nyoka the Jungle Girl* at a local cinema, and I subsequently became an avid movie-goer, sometimes spending the better part of the day at the Alexandra, a short walk from our compound, where for the low price of six annas, I could see a cartoon, a short documentary, and a Hollywood feature film. Indeed, as a very young boy, I practically lived at the Alexandra, watching double features. My mother had to dispatch our cook to fetch me home where I had to content myself by inventing my own mental movies, spinning out of the ones I especially enjoyed on the silver screen: westerns with Roy Rogers and Dale Evans, Tarzan movies with Lex Barker or Johnny Weissmuller (who had the best physique and swimming ability of any Tarzan); and B-movies from Warner Brothers, MGM, or Paramount. There was another genre that I greatly enjoyed: comedy, especially as performed by Buster Keaton, Charlie Chaplin, Harold Lloyd, Laurel and Hardy, Abbott and Costello, the Three Stooges, and Martin and Lewis. I was such a big fan of Hollywood movies that when I was still a pre-schooler, I drew a stamp on an empty envelope and announced in block letters: Hollywood Here I Come. The local postman had a good laugh before quietly returning the envelope to my mother, who shared it with the De Souzas and Soares downstairs who claimed to be related to film star Merle Oberon.

They weren't exaggerating. Nicknamed "Queenie" in honour of Queen Mary who had visited India in 1911, along with King George V, Oberon had deliberately concealed the truth of her parentage, creating an elaborate fiction that she was born in Tasmania to a British mechanical engineer and a Eurasian mother (from Ceylon) with Maori ancestry. She was able to get away with this by claiming that her birth records had been destroyed in a fire. The truth was she had been born in Bombay to a young girl who had had a relationship with an Anglo-Irish foreman of a tea plantation. Her biological mother, Constance, eventually married Alexander Soares and had four other children: Edna, Douglas, Harry, and Stanislaus (Stan), who grew up believing Merle to be their aunt, when in fact she was their half-sister. Later, when she was a famous movie star in London, she pretended that her mother was her maid. In black-and-white films, such as *The Scarlet Pimpernel* (with Leslie Howard), *The Private Life of Henry VIII* (with Charles Laughton), and *Wuthering Heights* (with Laurence Olivier), close-ups revealed the skin-whitening pancake makeup on her dark face. Oberon never had children of her own, and the prevailing suspicion was that she was afraid that they might turn out to have dark skin. I have only a dim memory of her step-father, Alexander, while he was living with sisters Priscilla (Doc) and Kitty, along with Mrs. D'Souza and daughter Dorothy. Edna and Douglas moved to the UK at an early age, so I did not know them. Stanislaus was the only child to keep his father's surname of Soares, and I do remember him as Stanley or Stanny, a tall, skinny man with a friendly disposition.

I have stronger memories of Priscilla and Kitty, the former a retired medical practitioner with a small library of medical books that fascinated me with their strange illustrations and language; and Kitty, a soft-spoken seamstress, who entertained me with stories of *shikars*, *machans*, and man-eating tigers as she carefully worked her sewing needle and thread. She promised to make me a Tarzan loincloth, such as the one worn by Johnny Weissmuller. To assist her, I drew a human figure, replete with body parts, and added a caution: "You know, Aunt Kitty, those two dots at the top of the body are not buttons."

Kipling's India of British dash and daring had dominated cinema screens in Anglo-India, as in Hollywood versions of the Raj, with battles in mountain passes, vividly suggested by Gatling guns, cannon mounted on elephants, and spectacular charges by Bengal lancers, though most of the British cavalrymen were played by American actors, serving under fiercely-moustached English actor Cecil Aubrey Smith, epitome of the *sahib*. Marked by extraordinary historical distortions, films such as *Gunga Din, Lives of the Bengal Lancers, Clive of India*, and *The Charge of the Light Brigade* celebrated heroic self-sacrifice for the sake of Empire. Indian films were of no concern to me or my parents. My parents went only to English-language films, and never at the Alexandra cinema that used lurid advertisements of upcoming films (some "adults only") that eventually outraged very conservative Indians. These "puritans" demanded that school-bus drivers switch routes so that their impressionable children might not be exposed to "dirty" posters. No surprise that in 2013, the Alexandra turned into a mosque and Islamic institute. But in my boyhood, that cinema was where Western celluloid dreams unspooled.

Indian films seemed to wallow in arbitrary song and dance, cheap melodrama, exaggerated folklore or legend, historical epics beyond my ken—and all in Hindi, Bengali, or Urdu, languages that were not of any interest to me. Although my own world was dominated by Hollywood film magazines, such as *Photoplay, Silver Screen, Movie Classic*, and *Modern Screen*, I did know the names of some of the most popular film magazines and successful Indian film stars: *Filmindia, Filmfare, Picturpost, Screen, Film World*, with pieces on Nargis, Meena Kumari, Geeta Bali, Suraiya, Dilip Kumar, Raj Kapoor, Dev Anand, Ashok Kumar, Johnny Walker (though I wonder if his surname was linked in any way to the scotch whiskey my father drank), and Sabu (someone I knew from Hollywood movies, such as *Elephant Boy, Jungle Book, Thief of Baghdad*, and *The Man-Eater of Kumaon*). My parents knew Anglo-Indian dancer and actress, Cuckoo, whose full name was Cuckoo Moray, and later there was another Indian film actor who crossed our paths at a dinner party, entertaining guests with an example of his cinematic acting.

Mother's puppet plays were my entry into the dream world of theatre, as were itinerant marionette shows, Punch and Judy, and peep-hole entertainments. Indian puppetry had a long tradition, and the cheapest, most popular form was glove puppetry derived from Bengal, aimed at the lowest social rung. Contrary to the salacious nature of European or North American peep shows, there was nothing pornographic, and, indeed, one of the most fascinating experiences for us youngsters were kaleidoscopes that dazzled with their shifting colours and shapes. Bombay also had radio broadcasts of drama, comedy, and music, so my ear was trained to pick up textures of sound while my mind opened onto imaginative landscapes of story. My first role in a school production was a literal pain in the neck. It would have been when I was around six or seven and was cast as a cherub in a religious tableau honouring the Blessed Virgin Mary. As with other little boys cast as cherubs, I was required to place my head in a hole cut out of the tableau décor and look up at Virgin Mary. However, my cut-out was quite far down the painted décor, and the strain was too much for my little neck. But I did not give up, doing all I could to look devotedly angelic. In Grade 5 I was cast as a female gypsy dancer at all-boys St. Mary's. Costumed in a flared skirt with ribbons, wielding a tambourine, I applied light red lipstick for makeup, and insisted on borrowing a pair of my mother's knickers so that I would feel authentically feminine.

Perhaps there was a method to my boyhood "madness."

My boyhood was part of an oral and aural culture that was to prove of some benefit to me as a writer. I grew up in a predominantly radio and film culture. Few people in India at the time owned television sets, which helped us to concentrate more sharply on sounds and develop long attention spans, along with a modicum of mimicry. Having been exposed so early to film and radio drama, it was only natural that I would become producer, director, and actor in live performance. I organized scenes to be performed for neighbours at The Retreat. I created handmade tickets, and my sister Elma collected the admission price. On some occasions, she would even dare to perform, though her performances were almost invariably in the same Queen of Hearts getup that my mother had sewn for a costume party. Being inordinately shy and stricken with a stutter, Elma had absolutely no performing talent, but Audrey, my youngest sister, five years my junior, would serve as supporting player on occasion, such as the *corpse* of Julius Caesar as I delivered Marc Antony's famous funeral eulogy, at the end of which, lacking a curtain or appropriate lighting to demarcate the end of the scene, I had to call for her to get off the floor and exit, much to the comic delight of the neighbours. Bigger comedy occurred when the Baby Jesus in a Christmas special indulged himself with crisp potato chips in the most improbable Bethlehem ever imagined. Or when another of my chums, a boy with an unfortunate stutter, was all but dragooned into playing one of Richard III's soldiers at Bosworth Field. As I (in the lead role, of course) cried out vehemently: "A horse, a horse, a kingdom for a horse!" he retorted: "Come, my horse, I'll help you to a lord," raising uproarious laughter from the audience, much to his blushing embarrassment.

At 12, I felt I was born to read, recite, and perform Shakespeare. I loved attempting all the roles in the "Pyramus and Thisbe" play-within-a-play of *A Midsummer Night's Dream*. My sense of exhibitionism was not to be curbed. As a teenager, I dressed in drag to perform comic monologues, but my best impersonation was of an Indian speaking pidgin English or Babu English in a heavy accent. "My wife and I have lots of problems making both our ends meet." These party pieces endeared me to many guests at my parents' dinner parties, where booze flowed freely and where food was a veritable repast. Why was I drawn to acting? Was it the false glamour of the profession? Was it a dream of fame and money? Was acting simply an escape from what I felt to be monotonous Anglo-Indian life? Or was it a case of egotistic exhibitionism: a "Look at me, look at me, look at me" syndrome? As all truthful actors know, ego is an essential factor for their vocation. Dirk Bogarde expresses this succinctly in *Snakes and Ladders*, the second volume of his autobiographical tetralogy: "Well, ego, for better or for worse, is very much involved in this business of being an actor, because we are creatures who are obliged to use our own beings as our instrument, and we tend to have to keep reassuring ourselves—and looking for reassurance—as to how good that instrument is. It tends to make us very boring as people unless we are on constant guard against a total self-preoccupation." Whatever was the root of my mimetic or histrionic talent, I delighted in participating in virtually every play at St. Mary's School for Boys (Cambridge section), whether it was comedy or drama, an adaptation of Dickens or Shakespeare.

My earliest experience of professional Shakespearean theatre was at St. Mary's. It was a performance by Geoffrey Kendal's travelling troupe, Shakespeareana Company, later memorialized in the 1965 Merchant-Ivory black-and-white film *Shakespeare Wallah* that provides a vivid sense of the nature and travails of touring players. Kendal's troupe "pounded the highways and byways of India, taking versions of Shakespeare to schools, convents, village squares, maharajas' palaces; anywhere that would cover their costs, from the North-west Frontier Province in what became Pakistan down to Travancore in the south." All I remember of their version of *The Merchant of Venice* in an auditorium at St. Mary's were some wan drapery, tacky painted sets, florid acting by Kendal who (I think) played Shylock, and the mocking raspberries some cynical students sounded during the Jessica-Lorenzo moonlight duet. One of the British cast members dared to bray back at the hecklers, raising even more laughter in the student audience. I do not remember if Kendal's daughters, Jennifer and Felicity, acted in that production. They probably did, but at that time we teenage students did not know the cultural significance and implications of Kendal's itinerant troupe, though I was fascinated by the English performers and their actor-manager.

At St. Xavier's College, I did not have an opportunity to play any Shakespeare. In fact, my sole acting opportunity was in *Weatherwise*, a very dated two-scene comedy by Noel Coward, about the turmoil caused by a mentally deranged aristocratic dowager who imagines she is a dog. I was cast as Dr. Twickenham, a psychoanalyst who is summoned to observe and treat Lady Warple who, following a séance, growls and rushes about on all fours at every mention of the weather. He recommends that at a signal from him all the family should pretend to be dogs. His trick seems to work well, until seeing her knitting calmly, the doctor deems her cured, but then makes a casual reference to the weather, provoking Lady Warple to leap for his throat and worry him to death. I relished playing the ridiculous role, but because some of the cast (perhaps feeling like fish out of water in a 1923 British comedy) began to skip rehearsals, the production was cancelled by the director, Alyque Padamsee, an alumnus of the college and a fellow much older than any of us in the cast. He would later gain international fame as a screen actor in Richard Attenborough's Oscar-winning *Gandhi,* in which he played Muhammed Ali Jinnah, the founder of Pakistan.

Shakespeare reinvigorated me later at St. Joseph Teachers College in Montreal—where Sister Mary Desmond progressed from sceptic to my eager supporter as I was a regular literary contributor to the college newspaper, and adapted, directed, and acted in scenes and plays by Albee, Ibsen, Wilde, and Shakespeare. It did not take long for me to earn the nickname "Shakespeare" (bestowed on me by colleague, Leo Venditti) and be called "Will Shakespeare's favourite collaborator" by Professor Brendan Fahey, a man with a real appetite for theatre. Blissfully free (because of my young age and inexperience) of political correctness or of any militancy about cultural appropriation, I knew instinctively that Shakespeare was an artist of the highest degree, who had the absolute right to create or appropriate whatever character of whatever colour, race, or religion he wished in whatever country of a map or mind, because the ultimate journey of any real artist is the journey into the human heart and soul. His plays "bestride the world," with characters in them (as Andrew Dickson points out) hailing "from Tunisia, the Levant, Algeria, India; his dramatic imagination roams restlessly across France, Denmark, Austria, Turkey, Greece, covering a veritable gazetteer of far-flung destinations." It was only in later years that I became aware of his moral and ethical ambiguities when it came to studies of power and virulent passions as in *Othello, The Merchant of Venice,* and *The Taming of the Shrew,* though even now I am not convinced that he was a racist, anti-Semite, or a male chauvinist. Though an unparalleled genius, Shakespeare reflected some of the biases and ethical limits of his time. It seems unforgivably silly for a contemporary critic to view Shakespeare wholly through post-Holocaust, post-feminist and other 20th and 21st century Woke lenses, just as it is absurd to measure the morality of the Old Testament or the New by modern tenets. People, especially artists, change with the changing world, and artists should be judged primarily by aesthetic criteria, and not by the precepts of a cancel culture. Otherwise, we end up with Thomas Bowdler and Guillermo Sanchez's numerous equivalents in every century.

Shakespeare's religion and politics did not matter as much to me as his other facets. He was a man of the theatre, which is to say that many of his arch villains, rogues, and morally compromised characters are the most fascinating characters in his plays: Iago, Petruchio, Shylock, Edmund, Richard III to name but five, and to which could be arguably added Macbeth, Othello, even Henry V. He wrote with such artistic freedom, authority, and poetic verve that his characters were thrilling. Although I did not know the full connotations or resonances of his language, I felt the rhetorical force of Shakespeare's verse, and when I did get the opportunity to see Laurence Olivier on screen—first as Richard III, then as Henry V, and only later as Hamlet, I knew that an essential part of my core was changed forever.

Olivier's Crookback was dazzlingly spectacular, grotesquely comic, daringly seductive, thrillingly horrific. As Henry V, his trumpet voice (in a different pitch and timbre) rose to glorious heights of eloquent bravado at Agincourt and Harfleur. In my senior year in high school, I saw his Hamlet, a portrait of wounded melancholy and choler, a glamorous blonde-haired prince of "shreds and patches" with a resolve challenged by self-doubt or misgiving or disgust yet carried to a climax of unmatched excitement in the duel with Laertes and the subsequent spectacular assassination of Claudius. There was simply no screen actor who approached Olivier's heroic proportions, and it was clearly his voice that was singularly unparalleled. I appreciated this extraordinary genius years before I read Tynan on Olivier's voice:

> It is so important as an incentive to tragic writing that we must dwell upon it; most of all when it hits the hoarser rallying note and becomes a roaring-valiant fanfare; when one's vision is of an unpent charge of black stallions, bearing a legion on their arched and warlike backs. One monstrous shot of his in *Henry V* made it momentarily impossible to be cynical about patriotism: 'Cry God for Harry, England, and Saint Geo-o-o-orge!' In gentler moods the power remains, and it is depressing to be forced to the conclusion that there is no dramatist alive who could write a line worthy of the noble ferocity, the almost muscular fury of this actor's best cadences.

Olivier died in 1989, yet I can still hear his virtuoso voice in my head. As I studied all his film performances, I realized how a great actor's technique could make the climaxes higher, the tense lulls deeper in the big roles. His protean technique enlarged a role imaginatively, revealing facets of character that other actors could never match. Those critics who suffer from Woke rapture would undoubtedly disagree, pointing to his use of stereotypes of Blackness (nappy hair, animal stride, racial pride, sexual vitality) in *Othello* as gross parody or even rank racial cliché, but what they miss completely is Olivier's brave defiance of racialist obsessions. He was not mocking or parodying anyone or anything: he was celebrating the character's *immense self-pride* by flaunting those very physical qualities that marked him as the Other in an imperial, colonial society. And he was moving precisely because of the poetry of his physical movement and his interpretive imagination. Much was made by his sternest critics about his being an actor of externals, a brilliantly cold technician, but Kenneth Tynan had the best rebuttal to this imputation. In his essay "The Death of Kings" (in *He That Plays the King*), Tynan argues:

I know of only two actors who can play both the heroes of mind and the (to me) much more important heroes of body: Olivier and Valk. It is, after all, the physical things which go to make good theatre; noises and body movements are theatrically far more significant than the qualities and essences they cloak. The actor is the tangible foreground of the tragedy; he is primarily a plastic bundle of techniques, not a feeling or a mind. He should build his part from the outside inwards, at whatever cost of private exaltation; his is the business of artificially conjuring up emotion in an audience, not in himself. (Though he exudes sweat, he may be quite cold-blooded.)

Because Olivier was larger than life, he was grossly parodied by inferior actors but never matched in genius. Even as his body went into massive decline in his later years, his muscles shrunken, his voice losing its silver trumpet tone, Olivier remained an actor's actor, especially in roles that required heroic scale and temper, whether romantic or self-destructive. A diary entry by me for November 11, 1987 reads:

At 10.30 p.m. on Channel 19, Laurence Olivier read Shakespeare, Larkin, Auden, Waller, Milton, Hardy, Graves, Barrett-Browning, C.S. Lewis, Thomas, et al. Frail as a crooked stick, his hands gnarled and grotesquely misshapen, his cheeks rosy in their high relief of a rather emaciated face, he showed the spirit, wit, and virtuosity of an aging, great actor. Milton has never sounded as melodious or romantic, C.S. Lewis as moving, or Shakespeare as tender. Sometimes the breath was a little wispy, but the phrasing was impeccable, the rhythm firmly defined, and the colouring of words quite wondrous—although Olivier confessed, after a virtuoso reading of Auden's 'Lullaby': 'I didn't understand a fucking thing of that.' He did Prospero's farewell with acute feeling, yet when asked by Patrick Garland, the interviewer, if he was ever tempted to do The Tempest, he was unhesitating in his response. He found the play too sonorous and humourless, and as for Prospero: 'There isn't a fucking smile in him!'

At St. Joseph Teachers College (1961–64), I directed and acted in scenes from Shakespeare, Oscar Wilde, and Ibsen, did a solo reading from Charles Dickens, and performed the main role in Albee's *The Zoo Story*. In the full-length *Valiant Woman*, written by Sister Mary Desmond about a female European saint, I had a short scene in which I played a rather eccentric elementary school teacher, modelled on Mr. Joseph Fern, a tall, bulky Math teacher of mine at St. Mary's High in Bombay. He was a mild-mannered man who tried to camouflage his gentleness by a mien of dignified solemnity, but his bobbing movement down the classroom aisles was the stuff of comedy. I added my own character details: absent-mindedness, obliviousness to his own eccentricity, and a lack of classroom control. I was supposed to teach my young pupils (around 10 years of age) the proper pronunciation of "flourish," while they raised risible anarchy by throwing chalk at my black robe, making silly faces, and totally ignoring my lesson. I was so comically convincing that my professors commented with relish: "Keith, you have just failed your teaching practicum."

On another occasion, I played John Worthing in Wilde's *The Importance of Being Earnest* at the Gesù Theatre. The college production rented professional costumes from Malabar on Parc Avenue, but the budget was not high enough to afford anything more than sets that could only hint minimally at Victorian ambience. The Gesù on Bleury Street was a perfectly marvellous theatre, with excellent acoustics and sight-lines. It was a mismatch because we clearly lacked the proper technique and decorum to bring off Wilde's high comedy in such a reputable theatre, though Sydney Johnson (drama critic of *The Montreal Star*) remarked that my performance as John Worthing had the right appearance and vocal tone for Wilde's wit.

(In my student years, my voice was my best physical asset, and probably accounts in some measure for my tendency to write poems as a spoken art.) I fared better in Marchette Chute's *Scenes from Shakespeare*, also staged at the Gesù, in which I played Henry V in two scenes: the king's Harfleur oration ("Once more unto the breach, dear friends, once more"); and Henry's wooing of Princess Katherine. Strong memories of Olivier in my mind, I felt that my voice (tending towards the tenor range) suited the stirring poetry for the battle speech to the troops, though I was, perhaps, a little too self-conscious in the wooing scene. Drama was always my strong suit in acting. I played a poignant Oswald Alving in scenes from Ibsen's *Ghost* (adjudicated by Henry Hovenkamp, who had acted at Stratford), though my Oswald was decidedly neurotic in a Geraldine Page manner, because I had just been bowled over by her performance as Alexandra del Lago in the film version of *Sweet Bird of Youth*. And when I played Jerry in my own staging of *The Zoo Story*, I won wonderful plaudits both as director and actor. I was only 19 at the time, but the play and central role touched a nerve. I identified with Jerry, the disturbed, acutely lonely young man—not because I was psychologically disturbed (at least not to my knowledge!), but because his complaints about the world and God ran parallel with mine. I relished the play's rude humour, spontaneously hysterical eloquence, and its keen intuition of despair. My performance was intensely passionate, and I won applause from actress Ann Wickham, who suggested I should audition at La Poudrière, the professional theatre located in a powder magazine built in 1822 on St. Helen's Island, and run by Jeanine Beaubien. However, charged with youthful romantic idealism about playing leading roles in Shakespeare and other classics, I frowned at the prospect of doing boulevard comedy or Whitehall farces by Ray Cooney, John Chapman, and Tony Hilton. Alas, Hamlet was not to be. I appeared in a bad community theatre production of Chapman's *The Brides of March*, in which I played an Arab sheik's emissary named Haroun El Bahn.

Theatre rivalled Literature in my student life. After a performance of *Cages*, I chatted with its two stars (Mercedes McCambridge and Michael Lombard) separately at the opening-night reception. My conversation with Lombard was dominated by a discussion of the relative merits of Anne Bancroft in *The Miracle Worker* and Geraldine Page in *Sweet Bird of Youth*, with my preferring Page to Bancroft. When I asked Lombard what advice he would give to any young person about to get into an acting career, his answer was a swift: "Don't!" McCambridge was chattier, warmer, and sensitive to my ardour for theatre and film. Attractively tanned, with a strong facial profile and wavy hair, she was the least affected actress I had met to date. Only 5'2" in height, she had wonderful power and authority on stage and screen, as in her Oscar-winning supporting role in *All the King's Men*, and later, her Oscar-nominated gritty, butch portrayal of Luz in *Giant*, opposite Rock Hudson, Elizabeth Taylor, and James Dean. She was utterly candid about her own history of alcoholism, her Hollywood films, and her great love for Adlai Stevenson, whom she believed (as most humanist liberals did) should have been President of the United States. I was all ears as she recalled the late James Dean, one of my early screen idols. And she listened to whatever green, naïve opinions I had as if they were worth her attention. When I asked shyly if she would consider visiting the college to address the Drama Club, she agreed willingly, though, alas, nothing came of the offer because the college lacked funds to extend her proper remuneration.

At least I hadn't been tongue-tied in her presence, which was not to prove the case when I finally met Laurence Olivier backstage at Place des Arts in Expo year. Determined to meet him, no matter what, I was lucky that there was no attendant at the stage-door after the performance of Strindberg's fierce black comedy, *The Dance of Death*. I had written a "fan" letter to Olivier months before he was scheduled to arrive in Montreal, expressing my admiration for his genius in the most poetic way I could muster and asking to meet him. He replied in a typewritten letter from the Old Vic, March 16, 1967:

Dear Mr. Garebian,

Thank you very much for your letter. I am delighted that
you have enjoyed my work and extremely grateful to you for
your kindness in writing to express such generous thoughts
about it. It is kind of you to ask to see me but I am afraid I
already have a tremendously heavy programme of
engagements during my short visit to Montreal which makes
it impossible for me to think of arranging any personal
meetings. I am so sorry; but I would, of course, be happy to
autograph photographs or programmes for you if you would
care to leave them at the stage door.

All good wishes and again so many thanks for your
kindness and interest.

Yours sincerely,

Followed by the great one's actual signature!

This polite rejection was easy to swallow. His signature alone meant
he had actually bothered to read what a callow youth from Canada
(by way of India) had gushed forth in a small geyser of purple prose.

I walked quietly to the dressing rooms where I caught sight of
Geraldine McEwen changing out of her costume as Alice, before I
stopped outside the door of Robert Lang (the Kurt) who proceeded
to chat with me, probably sensing my huge enthusiasm for the production. He didn't seem to be put out in any way when it became
eminently clear that my idol was Olivier, and he remained unfail-
ingly polite and open to a long chat. But my nerves were on edge as
Lang pointed me in the direction of Sir Laurence's dressing room. I
knocked gently, and a serious-looking man (probably Olivier's dresser) politely but silently accepted my request to have Sir Laurence
autograph my house program. I was halfway home. All I needed was
to wait till Sir Laurence emerged. I waited for what seemed an

eternity till I caught sight of Joan Plowright, in white cap, white jacket, white mini-skirt, and white boots walking past me. It was the Swinging Sixties, after all, though Montreal swung less than London did. Plowright had evidently just flown in from London, and eventually the dressing room door opened, and out strode my idol of idols—in tweed jacket and cap. Despite a recent history of ailments, Sir Laurence looked physically strong. He doffed his cap to a little boy held in his mother's arms, smiled charmingly, and made very brief small talk with them. My turn came next. "What should I do at first?" I silently wondered. "Bow? Please, God, don't make me lose my head and genuflect." I had planned what I wanted to say, formulating and reformulating something eloquent and sincere. I didn't want to sound ridiculously purple, nauseatingly flattering. But when I opened my mouth, nothing seemed to come out except a rather hoarse whisper: "Oh, Sir Laurence, I am one of your biggest fans!" or some such vapid twaddle. He smiled benignly at me, but I wondered if his politeness really masked a pity for yours truly. And that was the one and only time I have ever been at a loss for golden words in the presence of someone I adore.

I briefly crashed a reception for cast and invited guests in one of the foyers, where I tried to make conversation with Jean Gascon (who didn't know me from Adam), asking him what he thought of Olivier. "Oh, Larry, he's on the way out!" he replied, referring to recent reports of Olivier's thrombosis and cancer. I couldn't quite ascertain if his tone reflected sympathy. He then remarked huskily: "You know I played Edgar at Stratford." I did know, but he seemed to be slyly insinuating that his performance had been, at least, a match for Olivier's.

Unless they attend theatre school, most stage performers start with community theatre. In fact, the relatively short history of professional Canadian theatre begins with little regional and community theatres—amateur groups in Montreal, Ottawa, and Toronto leading the way. Some of the very best professional English-speaking actors in Montreal (Len Watt, Walter Massey, Victor Knight, Norma

Springford, Ann Wickham) had their start as part of such community theatres, and one of the leading producers in that city also formed a company that mixed amateur and professional actors. That was English-born and bred Mary Morter, the founder of Instant Theatre in 1965, a lunch-time group that included actors who were well known to local television and radio audiences. I was among the performers in one of her amateur groups—more of an *ad hoc* group, aptly named The Unknown Players of Westmount. But Morter recruited professionals George Carron and Don Scanlon for a one-act piece, *Coffee House*, directed by Scanlon. Carron, who had a significant reputation for comic acting on television (*Comedy Café* and *Comedy Crackers*, for instance), played the leading male role, for which he was not really suited. Even less suited to any role was the actress in the female leading role—a young lady whose acting was as thin as her physique. Her diction and acting were as flat as Norfolk or the prairies, depending on what geography is more familiar to you. But she was young and attractive enough to Carron who, partly out of genuine concern that she was letting down the production, invited her to rehearse with him in the privacy of his condo.

His coaching did not help.

Not that this unfortunate production had anything to do with his death from cardiac arrest at the age of 40 in 1970, but it certainly did not improve the health of anyone connected to the show.

My experience in community or ad hoc theatre included playing the stuttering, outwardly timid but sinister Professor in Ionesco's *The Lesson*, the male lead in the first English language version of Henri Ghéon's *Passion Play*, and two roles (Second Tempter and First Knight) in T.S. Eliot's *Murder in the Cathedral*, about the assassination of Thomas Becket. I loved playing the very odd Professor, but that was the only role in which I was never word-perfect because of the convolutions and "nonsense" words in the text, and the production itself was badly directed by a man who (harbouring a virtually caricatural perspective of the absurdist play), forced me to wear a wool cap that was totally out of character for the Professor. I did manage to add my own sexual body language in the "seduction" section, adding an orgasmic shudder at the climax of a "sexual" assault on the unsuspecting student. The director (whose name I have long forgotten) moved on to the CBC, where he rose without a trace.

The venues for the Ghéon and Eliot productions fortified the religious connection, for *Passion Play* was performed outdoors at St. Joseph's Oratory in an English version in 1967, whereas *Murder in the Cathedral* was staged in St. Patrick's Basilica in 1978. Both venues were tourist attractions, as well as holy sites. Dominating the skyline facing north of Mount Royal, the Oratory is said to be taller than St. Paul's Cathedral in London, Notre Dame Cathedral in Paris, and St. Patrick's Cathedral in New York. The massive size and grandeur could be overwhelming, but there was another extraordinary feature at the Oratory: the heart of Brother André (who died in 1937 at the age of 91), locked in a vault as an object of veneration. I and my almost equally young fellow-players were Catholic, but we indulged ourselves in profane banter. I (at 24) and my younger fellow-players (such as Veronica Hollinger, Alana Forrester, Elaine Creighton, Viviane Côté, and Mary Robert drawn from Marianopolis College, Westmount, and the youngest member Paul Della Pena) would indulge ourselves in profane banter before growing suddenly solemn in time and in tune for our enactment of what were representations of the Stations of the Cross. We had to resort to more acting when, after the performance, we were complimented by more than one audience member for our extraordinary conviction of feeling. The Oratory had huge stone and cement statues depicting scenes from Christ's passion and crucifixion, and as darkness fell over its large garden, given extra lustre by moonlight, nature complemented artifice. One night, claps of thunder and flashes of lightning lent an unexpected dramatic effect to the moment of Christ being nailed to the Cross. All the cast felt a special *frisson* that night, a sort of *duende*, even though we did not know what *duende* meant.

At the end of our first summer season, I was made assistant director, while continuing in the role of male lead. I was also selected (I don't remember how or by whom) to receive a special monetary award as best actor. However, I never saw the money. I guess it was "donated" by the rector or, possibly, taken by him as a sacramental. The only palpable relic or evidence of my performance is in an official Oratory calendar—a full-colour shot of me making a very dramatic gesture at one of the Stations of the Cross.

Alas, where the *setting* added to the quality of our presentation of the Ghéon, the elaborate Gothic Revival architecture of St. Patrick's worked against our version of the Eliot. Our Genesian Players production, directed by tall, tanned, silver-haired Rudy Stoeckel, was impressively costumed, well rehearsed, and seemed destined for acclaim. However, none of us knew that our struggle with bad acoustics would require the energetic labour of a Hercules, but without a satisfactory result. I was chagrined to learn that my fellow thespians and I were audible only as a dreadful rumble. There went Eliot's glorious text. There went our acting pride. Nevertheless, what this production emphasized for me was the value of concentration. In scenes with lengthy monologues, it was very important for each actor to really listen to what was being delivered as text. Such listening has to be convincing, not mimed, and I was delighted to be complimented by one of my young fellow-tempters for showing focus and how to be truly present in a scene when required to remain eloquently silent during one of the long monologues by another actor. I seemed to know instinctively about how much energy was required for such intense concentration, and how such energy helped to express conviction or verisimilitude. I had learned a lesson from careful observation of some great film and stage actors.

With each new role, I was discovering something new about acting. Steinbeck's *Of Mice and Men*, staged by the Teachers Drama Guild, had two exceptionally good actors playing the unlikely buddies: Joseph White as George (a small, wiry, quick-witted man) and William Shore as Lennie (the large, lumbering mentally challenged migrant worker who does not know his own awesome strength and the tragic price he will pay for it). I was cast as Curley, the nasty son of the ranch boss. Rumoured to have been a champion boxer, Curley is aggressively confrontational and neurotic—choosing to compensate for his small physique by picking fights with much larger ranch-hands. Now, apart from having played the usual game of Cowboys and Indians as a boy in Bombay, and having been a fan of classic Westerns, there was nothing much I had in common with Steinbeck's ranch hands. I was much shorter and smaller in physique than the Lennie of big, burly Bill Shore (a real-life Vice-Principal). Therefore, there was a natural visual *frisson* in my having to threaten the much larger Lennie, and the fact that in one scene I was to cry out in pain when one of my hands was crushed by Lennie brought special delight to students who dared not challenge me in the classroom. Stage villains are much more fun and far easier to play effectively than saints.

This production, ably directed by Michael Lieberman, was a huge success in the eyes of all who saw it, including some bigshots from the CBC. But what was especially significant for me was a startlingly new insight into the deception or "fakery" of stage acting. Tall, handsomely bearded William Brier playing Slim, the "prince" of the ranch—the only character in the story who is at peace with himself—was anything but a natural-born actor. In fact, both in rehearsal and performance, he had difficulty remembering not only his lines but which scene followed another. At one performance, while I was sitting quietly in a corner offstage, getting into character, "Slim" approached me, anxiety creasing his face. "Which scene is coming up, Keith?" he asked, throwing me totally out of character. However, on stage, he was able to fool just about everyone in the audience. He looked sure of himself, quietly poised and in control—everything the actor wasn't in reality. And it brought to mind the old theatre joke: The soul of acting is honesty, and the sooner you can fake it, the better.

These amateur credits (very modest in number) expressed my development as a creature of the theatre. Their practical lessons stood me in good stead years later when I became a professional theatre reviewer and scholar. They certainly helped me sense the moods of audiences, as well as discriminate between good acting and bad, effective directing and inefficient, competent reviewing and incompetent. They also taught me about focus in directing and acting, and how to find the "spine" of a role, as well as the overall shape of a play. They made me take Theatre seriously and not treat it as a lark or a way out of serious subjects at university and beyond. In other words, they made me increasingly aware of Theatre as a craft, made indescribably incandescent by the art of actors of special genius. My own list of such actors is discriminatingly short because I draw fine distinctions between talent and genius—distinctions I apply to all creativity.

While teaching English and running a Drama Club at Marymount Comprehensive High School in Montreal, I directed an English-language version of Anouilh's *Antigone* in 1970, with myself as Creon, and fellow teacher Paul Board (tall and bearded) as Chorus (the role I had really wanted). Two students alternated the title role, and their contrasts in physique, voice, movement, and dramatic scale were an early lesson in ranges of interpretation. One, firm in physique, handled the language well, stressing the heroine's stubborn pride vividly; however, the second, taller, but with a smaller voice, used her supple body more effectively, allowing her innate passion to power through the language. My student cast included Susan Peacock as Ismene. Susan was the daughter of David Peacock, then the General Director of the National Theatre School, and a most generous man who had earlier graciously accepted my invitation to address, without remuneration, my fellow teachers at a workshop on Drama. (I did not know then that one of Susan's younger sisters was Lucy Peacock, who has become one of the outstanding leading ladies at our Stratford Festival, and someone who would figure prominently many decades later in my book *Colours to the Chameleon: Canadian Actors on Shakespeare*.)

Anouilh's original French version had recast Sophocles with intense political and philosophical meaning with touches of metatheatre to remind audiences that they were watching a play. My production eschewed his politics of 1944 when Paris was occupied by the Nazis while an underground Resistance was at work. I sensed that such specific period politics would mean little to student audiences, and despite violating the neoclassical unity of time by having black lighting in one dramatic sequence, my production succeeded because I elected to focus on a conflict of generations in the play. By having an adult as Creon and a teenager as Antigone, it was easy to dramatize a clash of ages, temperaments, and volitions. The production was widely praised, drawing visitors from the CBC, as well as Jacob Siskind of *The Montreal Gazette*, not exactly a fuzzy, warm-hearted critic. I was grateful for his review that claimed we had succeeded where many professionals had failed.

But I did not receive much encouragement from the Department Head of English who suggested that I was possibly treating my extracurricular activity as a passage to Broadway! His remark put me in mind of Sheila Fischman's earlier suggestion that perhaps I was aiming too high over the heads of Montreal newspaper readers.

A pattern seemed to be forming. I was always deemed out of place or missing my real path by aiming too high.

Fortunately, there were students who appreciated me for daring to shake up the custom of staid productions, as with my staging of Albee's *The Zoo Story* and *The American Dream*. These one-act plays were certainly not to the taste of a Catholic school, and though they were not banned (as they would be today in Texas, Florida, Arkansas, or any number of the more culturally and intellectually backward American states), they generated *frissons* of outrage among certain nuns, chronic moral spinsters, and the irredeemably religiose, while concomitantly raising the delight of more creative and liberal-minded students. Teresa Paucha, who had played vapid Mrs. Barker in *American Dream* and was a first-rate essayist in my top English class, articulated this in a 2022 memoir for *Marymount Moments*, culminating in the question: "How did Keith Garebian manage to get away with introducing our young, truth-seeking, rebellious ironic hearts so such darkly rowdy avant-garde material in an academic context where 'Drama Club' had for many years meant only Miss Doyle's impeccably proper staging of Shakespeare plays?"

Tessa was diplomatic. Miss Doyle, for whom Shakespeare was her Bible but whose theatre aesthetic was closer to Earle Grey's than Peter Brook's, loved designing costumes. Alas, her colourful costumes often sat like museum pieces on students who had no business being in them any more than they had any business playing Shake-speare without adequate direction or an understanding of blank verse—theirs being quite blank.

Montreal is where my passion for theatre flourished. As an under-graduate, I attended several National Theatre School productions, and saw Joseph Ziegler, Nancy Palk, Marilyn Lightstone, Seana McKenna, and Colm Feore, for instance, before they became big names in their profession. I also saw Martha Henry, Donnelly Rhodes, and Heath Lamberts on television while they were students, and was particu-larly impressed with Lamberts's comic improvisation where he and Rhodes were supposedly trapped without water in a desert. With not even a cactus plant to provide a trickle of much-needed water, Lamberts cunningly resorted to slitting a vein in his buddy's wrist and drinking the blood. Here was comic genius in an early display.

Montreal was where I did my M.A. thesis on *Hamlet* at Sir George Williams University (before it became known as Concordia, merging with Loyola College in the west end), a strange place at the time, and not just because it was a concrete campus downtown at 1400 De Maisonneuve Boulevard West. A large portion of the English faculty was American and acted like imperious neo-coloni-als. They always seemed to be advancing their own ambitions rather than their graduate students' interests, and there was one man in particular who took delight in failing as many graduate students as he could in the M.A. French Translation exam.

Sir George's English faculty had its share of eccentrics and mis-fits. Rytsa Helen Tobias was a short, plump, good-natured lady who liked a fag (the nicotine version) now and then. Her lectures were tests of concentration and focus because she had an unfortunate tendency to hem and struggle for words in the course of explaining a text, so her students were often more intent on observing her man-nerisms rather than concentrating on the content of her lectures. But she was benign, as was Roslyn Belkin (not one of my professors) who insisted on reading all literature as allegories or analogies of Scripture. Less benign, because of alcoholism, was Betty MacLean, a bony, middle-aged authority on Victorian literature, although it was difficult to verify her literary authority, given her tendency to fall into a stupor during seminars. It was reported with somewhat malicious glee that the faculty head was able to invite her to lunch, ply her with booze, get her drunk, and coax her into signing a letter announcing her retirement, much to the relief of colleagues who were embarrassed by the frequency of her stupors.

Fortunately, there were professors of real substance and integrity. Soft-spoken Neil Compton was Head when I had applied to the graduate division. A humanist scholar, he was wheelchair bound, but his inquiring mind was a mile wide, and he delighted in the academic achievements of students—as did Sidney Lamb, who also served as CBC film critic. Both men were close friends of each other, and both, alas, died in 1972, within ten days of each other. Compton spoke quietly and modestly, but his scholarship was widely acknowledged. Lamb was more direct but just as sincerely interested in his students. I liked both of them, and both of them liked me. Two other outstanding academics were guest professors: F.E.L. Priestley (authority on the Victorians) and Matthew Hodgart (who offered a summer course on James Joyce). Another impressive faculty figure was Henry Beissel, from whom I took a course in Chaucer and his contemporaries. His long, flowing dark locks and beard made him seem bohemian, as well as bardic. Beissel was an extrovert, widely travelled, deeply well-read, and with broad areas of curiosity. He edited a journal called *Edge*, wrote poetry and plays, and welcomed discussion. He read Chaucer aloud in a manner that sounded convincingly Middle English and with colourful flair. Years later, when I began my freelance career as literary and theatre critic, he and I became good friends.

My M.A. thesis got off to a bad start. I had wanted to write about Olivier's Othello (which I had seen multiple times in a badly recorded film version of John Dexter's National Theatre production), but academe decreed that such a topic was not within the bounds of a literary thesis. David McKeen, then the Head of the English department (who revelled in minute research in the most arcane Shakespearean subjects), felt that my topic belonged to film studies. A handsome, bright scholar, McKeen preened himself on his expertise, but his findings were really footnote annotations rather than full-length scholarly essays. He could establish, for example, that the Rhenish wine consumed by Claudius at the banquet had a cooling rather than heating effect on a drinker's system, and he delighted in pointing this out to me in order to rebut my claim that wine in *Hamlet* could be taken as an expression of something hot in the prince's temperament. "You'll never be a Wilson Knight!" he charged with a supercilious flourish. I could have pointed out that neither would he. Moreover, much as I admired some of Wilson Knight's essays, being a second Wilson Knight was the farthest thing from my mind.

I naively switched topics for my graduate degree, opting for an academic exploration of Hamlet as a case-study in depth-psychology. My supervisor, Leonard Mendelsohn, an orthodox Jew who always wore a *yarmulke*, proved to be critically orthodox only as far as punctuation was concerned. I doubt that he did much more than scan the bloated thesis, which was very correctly rejected by examiners, much to my bitter resentment for having been so poorly supervised in the first place and for being compelled to spend more time than I wanted on the M.A. I was given a new supervisor, Michael Brian, at whose suggestion I explored the subjects of Extravagance, Mediocrity, and Fire in *Hamlet* in order to show that the prince was not simply a victim of melancholy but of black bile or *choler adust*. My thesis viewed the play as "a complicated ritual of purge where the prince is stirred not only to avenge his [murdered] father, but also to vindicate his wounded name." I argued that the play's dramatic tension is generated by two contrary styles of life, Extravagance and Mediocrity, and that these styles are really forms of disposition and distemper on one hand (expressed by fire imagery) and modes of balance and good temper on the other.

Brian was the first of my professors at Sir George who actually read every word, line, and paragraph I wrote, clearing out the wool, the fog, the empty purple passages, challenging every generalization or loose assumption. I began to understand the New Criticism, the formalist movement in literary theory that demanded close reading to discover how a literary work (especially poetry) functioned as a self-contained, self-referential text. Brian was a superb lecturer, as I discovered in a huge class (packed with students) where he discussed a scene from *Hamlet*. In language that was *au courant* with current slang and idioms, he was able to highlight verbal connotations, focus on imagery, and produce coherent insights without resorting to narcotic academic jargon. His lecture was like theatre: he spoke directly to his audience, treating them like collaborators, and spun anecdotes related in some way to the text, luring his students to soak up information enthusiastically. His passion was infectious. I doubt any student left his lecture with brain in neutral. And, as I discovered in the course of my thesis, he could be sharply critical without devastating you. He took a genuine interest in your progress, probably because he subscribed to Samuel Beckett's dictum: "Try again. Fail again. Fail better." When he thought you had come up with something brilliant, he would point to it with excited admiration, which, of course, was balm to the ego. He was a man with high standards, but kind at heart. In private life, he was a considerate husband (to a wife, a Mathematics professor at the same university, who never seemed to be in good health) and father of three playful daughters. On a visit to his home, I noticed how tolerant he was in allowing his young daughters to scrawl in crayon all over a wall as if they were creating a mural. At university, it was a different matter: no arbitrary or spontaneous literary scrawling, no irrational or hasty guesswork. At his prompting, I did an enormous amount of research into such things as Renaissance psychology and philosophy, in addition to covering medical treatises by Galen, Levinus Lemnius, and others.

My selection of *Hamlet* was a daft decision because I was venturing into territory already staked at Sir George by Shakespearean scholars such as David McKeen and Edward Pechter. I was very anxious, because I feared that my research was leading me away from the text as *poetic* tragedy into areas of arcane scholarship. Nevertheless, I consulted every major Shakespearean critic in

English up to 1970, and when Henry Beissel saw my bibliography, he joked that that alone should have automatically earned my degree. At my oral defence, I kept a discreet and judicious silence as various professors argued their competing views of the play. Their heated and often irrelevant *ad hominem* exchanges done, they finally got around to passing my thesis, but not before one or two of them took credit for *my* scrupulous research. One of the consequences of this experience was my inveterate post-graduate hostility to desiccated academic theory that fattens on what it feeds—mainly huge clumps of jargon and mounds of pompous intellectual claims.

When news of my successful thesis defence reached Mike Brian in England, where he was spending a sabbatical, he sent me a brief, hastily type-written letter: "Congratulations on getting the thesis accepted—of course they had to accept it. Quality will out. I was just a little worried about the politics of it all but it sorted itself out nicely. Well, I think part of the trouble is that if you're teaching the same subject as the thesis is dealing with you tend to be a bit dog-in-the mangerish [sic] about it. By carping you seem to enhance your own standards—but it is a very cheap way of going about things isn't it? Professors are not noted for their emotional maturity you know." That I knew well, indeed!

However, as a literary and theatre scholar, I could not afford to shut out all academic writing, so I practised critical discretion, selecting those writers who didn't lose themselves in labyrinthine thickets of hifalutin post-modernism. As I moved deeper into theatre studies, I devoured books on theatre by James Agate, J.C. Trewin, Alan Dent, Felix Barker, Eric Bentley, Peter Brook, Jonathan Miller, Ronald Eyre, Michael Benthall, Walter Kerr, Jan Kott, Kenneth Tynan, Robert Brustein, Charles Marowitz, John Lahr, Simon Callow, Antony Sher, Stephen Greenblatt, James Shapiro, *et al.* And I learned how vivid, penetrating, and enlightening these writers were in their distinctive styles. It wasn't a matter of agreeing with all their views on actors, directors, or texts. In fact, I often disagreed with them, but they all excited my lust for theatre, even when individual actors, directors, or playwrights disappointed me. Most of these writers had had some practical experience in varying degrees with professional theatre. It was not surprising that those who had been inside the profession often had the best insights into processes of acting and directing.

It was in Montreal that I first sampled the acting of Maxim Mazumdar and Richard Monette: the first, a flamboyant prodigy who lacked artistic discipline; the second, a sensitive, stylish young actor who showed he could play Albee as easily as he could an unemployed jester as nobody's fool. Montreal also brought me into contact with Michael Springate and David Rimmer, ambitious directors and playwrights, who launched their own independent theatres. Springate was the founding director of several experimental theatre companies, and became the Artistic Director of Playwright's Workshop Montreal. Of mixed heritage (English on his mother's side, Canadian on his father's), he was committed to new works, combining them with plays by Mishima, Beckett, Shakespeare, Stoppard, and Buchner. David Rimmer operated on a smaller scale in the English suburbs of the West Island, specifically focused on audiences in Dollard des Ormeaux and Pointe Claire. His miniscule operating budget contrasted with his bold, raw expressionistic style of directing. His little group had Tony Nardi as a lead actor before Nardi discovered greater fame at Soulpepper and in Canadian films.

Montreal offered me, on the French-Canadian side, Denise Pelletier, Jean Gascon, Jean-Louis Roux, Albert Millaire, Marthe Mercure, Monique Mercure, Jean Archambault, Yvette Brind'Amour, Guy Hoffman, Kim Yaroshevskaya, *et al*, and some exciting productions of Molière, Brecht, de Musset, and Tremblay, performed with verve, elan, or panache. Montreal also had the Saidye Bronfman Theatre and the Centaur Theatre, where I was able to practise my theatre criticism as a fledgling reviewer, interviewer, and feature writer for such journals and sources as *Scene Changes* (edited by Jeniva Berger), *Performing Arts in Canada*, and the *Canadian Theatre Review* (before it devolved into almost stultifying academic dullness). The Saidye could have brought me wider prestige as a freelancer had its world-premiere of Arnold Wesker's *The Merchant* ever opened. Preparing to do a production history, I interviewed Wesker, discovering his fundamental distaste for Shakespeare's "comedy" that he branded anti-Semitic and riddled with clichés about the arch Jewish usurer and his pound of flesh. I quickly realized that, in berating Shakespeare's play, he was promoting his own as superior. Though infused with genuine conviction as a socialist, and celebrated in his twenties for writing plays such as *Roots* and *The Kitchen*, Wesker was no wild-eyed, raving extremist. He disliked being labelled one of the Angry Young Men in English theatre, though the label put him in the company of such notables as John Osborne, Keith Waterhouse, and Harold Pinter. When I asked about his motive for writing *The Merchant*, his eyes lit up as he condemned Shakespeare's Shylock for being "a professional Jew" unreasonably and perversely clinging to his bond. Wesker's Shylock was a passionate father, a devoted friend of Antonio, and a sympathetic character. His bond was not designed to be cruel but to mock Venetian law of its time for forbidding all contact with Jews except through contracts. An exciting perspective intended as a passionate counter to Shakespeare's, but loud protests from official representatives of the Jewish community and many of Saidye's season subscribers forced the cancellation of the production before it really ever got started. This was but the first in a succession of mishaps for Wesker's *Merchant*. When the play managed to obtain financial backing in the U.S. in 1996, its lead actor, the formidable Zero Mostel, died suddenly during early rehearsals in Philadelphia, prior to the play's debuting in Washington and New York.

The life of a freelance theatre critic is often precarious, especially when theatres expect critics to play sides and tamp down criticism. During Maurice Podbrey's tenure as Artistic Director of the Centaur, he and/or his chief publicist and Head of Media Relations took exception to an article I published in *Performing Arts in Canada*, in which I asked the provocative question: Why is English theatre in Quebec becoming politically irrelevant? I have never put political considerations ahead of aesthetic ones, but politics are most germane to considerations of culture and humanism. In Quebec,

French-Canadian playwrights were always emphatically political, with Michel Tremblay, Robert Gurik, and Marcel Dubé leading the way, whereas the only English-speaking Quebec playwright at the time to address sociological and political themes appeared to be David Fennario, Alas, his slices of life were far from artistically sophisticated, but the Centaur, under Podbrey, seemed to be thriving at the box office because of him, Anne Chislett, and Linda Griffiths who, despite some entertaining qualities, hardly matched any of their French-Canadian contemporaries, much less American, British, Australian, or South African playwrights of that period. To give Podbrey his due, he did stage plays by Athol Fugard (whom I got to interview for *Scene Changes*), but excellent as some of these were, they did not address social or political concerns of Quebec or Canada. However, the Centaur expected fawning tribute, and so, without formal forewarning, I was summarily removed from its media list, which was an action that did not damage my life in the least. It simply emancipated me from having to endure another *Balconville*, *The Tomorrow Box*, or *Maggie and Pierre*, plays that were nowhere on my Must-See-Again List. Apparently, my critical word had more weight than I had suspected. Roughly a year later, I was mysteriously and quietly restored to the Centaur's media list. At least, the Centaur's decision to cut me off comps was *politically* motivated— unlike the case of the present regimes at the Shaw and Stratford, where box-office is the prime concern, and where freelancers are treated like beggars at the Barmecide's feast. I loathe bureaucrats, administrators, and publicists who fancy themselves Grand Panjamdrums, when, in fact, their contributions to art are abysmally minimal, if not negligible.

The situation in Toronto was worse, as I discovered after moving to Ontario in 1982. The large established theatres (Mirvish Productions and the short-lived Dancap Productions) did offer real treats from time to time, as did some of the independent theatres, but my heart usually sank when a new Canadian musical was announced with much hype in the press because, with a few notable exceptions, the new musicals generally looked and sounded as if they properly belonged in a cemetery after being embalmed in formaldehyde. While Canadian kids were fortunate to have stage adaptations of *Anne of Green Gables* or *Jacob Two-Two*, Canadian adults had to submit to tuneless, witless, dreary material that was chronically depressing or cornily unsophisticated, with music that no one could remember, and with choreography only a cut above what was being practised in a suburban school for tap-dancing. I exempt *The Return of Martin Guerre* and *The Drowsy Chaperone* (the Broadway version, not the original Toronto one).

On the "legitimate" theatre side (whatever "legitimate" means), there were oddities that linger in memory like bad odours:

> ~a play mixing puppets and human actors, where the puppets often looked and acted like time-travelling escapees from *Sesame Street*;
> ~plodding multi-racial dramas;
> ~serious plays with serious themes that seemed like forms of therapy for their playwrights;
> ~an epical Oriental concoction by a thoracic, vascular surgeon, who definitely should never be allowed to give up his day job;
> ~a play by the son of a famous Montreal architect that had no plot, merely an academic situation that devolved into a battle between intellectual pit-bulls, making the piece a débat rather than a play, and fittingly titled *Private Jokes, Public Places*.

And that was all in just a single theatre season! But later seasons (say, 2018 and 2019) were hardly better with the following:

> ~a modern version of *Hamlet* (properly titled ~~Hamlet~~ with a cancellation sign) that mixed rock 'n' roll, radio play, concert recital, and stage play, without finding a way to merge these into a satisfying whole, and where the eponymous hero was

played like an angry musician performing on what could be
called "Denmark's Got Talent";

~a long one-act drama about Marshall McLuhan, who once
suggested that our country is just an hallucination, and at
the end of which I felt that the play itself was a sort of
hallucination;

~yet another modern version (a very muddy one) of *Hamlet*
in which Gertrude and Claudius fucked on a mud heap;
Ophelia collapsed into a mud pile, soiling herself in despair;
Claudius exposed his tortured conscience while observing
himself in a mirror before kneeling on the same mud-pile he
had used for intercourse with Gertrude; Hamlet was given a
handful of mud in lieu of Yorick's skull; a performance of
Horatio entirely in dumb show; and a First Gravedigger who
seemed to want to sing and dance his way into our hearts.

My admiration for Shakespeare and topflight classical theatre has
often made me *persona non grata* to Canadian theatre professionals.
Many of this breed seem to doodle at their crafts, and many are political commissars who promote cheap reverence that makes artistic
discrimination difficult, if not impossible. Mercantilist and colonial
attitudes (firmly established in the nineteenth-century) contributed
to the cultural deprivation for many of our playwrights who were
not given the advantages of an indigenous theatre tradition. The
shallowness of a cultural past accounts in some measure for major
deficiencies in their craft. And facile ultra-nationalism produces
nothing more than mediocrity. Rather than condemning or slight-
ing the invaluable contributions of "Brits" (such as Tyrone Guthrie,
Michael Langham, Robin Phillips, and Christopher Newton, for
instance) to the development of Canadian theatre, Canadians should
be celebrating and building upon them. But pet slogans carry the
day for the culturally stunted. When I was a member of the Toronto
Drama Bench, I put forward the name of Robin Phillips for the
group's annual award for Outstanding Contribution to Canadian

Theatre, prompting a quite remarkable silence, and a sense of a few jaws dropping to the floor. Herbert Whittaker, who had been the first elected Chairman of the group, remarked, "I notice a chill descending" in a tone that was not far from cool itself. Don Rubin, for whom Phillips was a confirmed *bête noire*, could not countenance such a nomination, and managed to get enough support to eliminate Phillips from further consideration. Of course, a much lesser artist (but an "authentic" Canadian) was voted in for the award.

I learned that no matter how much I praised Canadian actors, actresses, designers, and select directors or playwrights, I would never be considered anyone other than an elitist with a penchant for that damned foreigner Shakespeare and (slightly less damned) classical theatre. The thing is that I don't believe elitism is necessarily a bad thing, *vide* V.S. Naipaul, Vladimir Nabokov, *et al.*

CHAPTER FIVE

THRIVING AT QUEEN'S, LANGUISHING AFTER

With the invaluable assistance and company of my expatriate American friend Leon Martin, who owned a manual-transmission van at the time, I drove to Kingston, the limestone city, with a load of books, clothing, a bed, mattress, pillows with sheets, a small television set, and a few basic supplies for kitchen and bath. I had rented a bachelor's apartment at 544 College Street (a short drive from Queen's University), whose superintendent was an older married lady of impeccable manners and understanding. The apartment had a stretch of windows that I managed to cover with a motley collection of cheap curtains. A bachelor's hasty home decoration, colourful in a haphazard way, or accidentally fauve. After loading my books in the cupboards above the oven and kitchen-sink, I was ready to begin a new life, apart from family, close friends, and my teacher fiancée Caryl, who was to become my wife in the middle of my studies.

Queen's University in Kingston was an academic world in which I thrived. Its official Coat of Arms, based on that of Edinburgh University, bears these emblems: a pine tree for Canada; a thistle for Scotland; a rose for England; and a shamrock for Ireland. As if this were not enough to establish a colonial connection, the red border is decorated with eight gold crowns symbolizing Queen Victoria and the university's royal charter. Below the shield is a Latin inscription, *Sapientia et Doctrina Stabilitas*, which means "Wisdom and Learning shall be the stability of thy times." And the colonial link is further underlined by the rousing university cheer, "*Cha Geill!*" (a Gaelic war cry) which means "No Surrender!" The fact that I could not pronounce the Gaelic war cry was hardly of any importance to me. Nor was the Coat of Arms, though the Latin motto bore significance.

Queen's faculty for Graduate Studies in English boasted celebrated authorities on Spenser (A.C. Hamilton), Hopkins and Yeats (Norman H. MacKenzie), Coleridge (George Whalley), Fredric Philip Grove (Doug Spettigue), and Canadian and Commonwealth Literature (John Pengwerne Matthews). My admissions interview in 1971 was with Professor MacKenzie, a short, very slightly built, balding, bespectacled scholar of gentle disposition, whose voice was so soft that his lips seemed to be moving on silence, rather like a white mouse nibbling gently on cheese. Perhaps it was his sly way of compelling a listener to lean forward and focus more intensely. It was rumoured that his emaciated physique was a consequence of his having been a prisoner-of-war. He was courteous but very much to the point, advising me not to pursue Shakespeare or the Elizabethans as my area of specialization, but urging me to specialize in Commonwealth Literature, a new and fast-growing field of studies that would surely result in new teaching opportunities. He sent me to Professor John Matthews, an expatriate Aussie, and a most cordial scholar, whose book *Tradition in Exile* was well-known to scholars of 19th century Canadian and Australian poetry. Welcoming me with great enthusiasm, he recognized the urgency of my situation (I was on a year's sabbatical from my teaching position in Montreal), and assured me that I would not need to waste time with the usual term essays. I could begin my research immediately into R.K. Narayan and V.S. Naipaul, whose names I knew, though not their literary works as yet.

Wavy-haired Matthews was a pipe-smoking, friendly sort, who had the best interests of his students at heart. He and his wife hosted a small group of doctoral candidates to a wine-and-cheese function annually at their home, where the cellar boasted homemade wines with fine labels branded with the Matthews name. His two courses on Canadian and Commonwealth Literature, rife with diagrams about the interrelationships of man, landscape, and cultural history, were not as relaxing. I wrote essays and participated in seminar discussions, while reading a book a day for the first year, simply to narrow the immense gaps in my knowledge of Commonwealth Literature.

Many of the books did not require to be read in depth, but many did—especially novels by Raja Rao, Wilson Harris, Patrick White, Janet Frame, George Lamming, Hugh Hood, Robertson Davies, Wole Soyinka, and Malcolm Lowry. I made extensive notes, while also preparing for Comprehensive exams scheduled in the second year of studies. And then there was the issue of a dissertation, not to mention the academic courses I had to take in conjunction with audited courses: W.C. Ferguson's Bibliography and Research, J.S. Baxter's Renaissance Drama, and George Whalley's Coleridge and the Victorians. I loved Matthews's courses, tolerated George Clark's idiosyncratic lectures on Anglo-Saxon poetry (entertaining on the sociological, historical, and cultural sides, but generally lacking deep textual analysis of *Beowulf*), and enjoyed disagreeing at times with Baxter about Shakespeare.

I sat in twice on Whalley's undergraduate course on the Victorians, where there was a palpable chill in the room as the students seemed bound to silence, even when Whalley urged them to share their opinions on a poem or prose passage. His scholarly reputation had simply magnified their terror, and as far as Ph.D. candidates were concerned, almost all of us quaked with anxiety about having to deal with Whalley's questions on the Moderns for the Ph.D. Comprehensives. This paper produced the highest failure rate in the Comps, and Whalley did not allay our fear when he softly assured us that nobody would be able to complete the three essays in the three-hour exam time. But not to worry: we could concentrate fully on one essay, do a rough draft for a second, and then merely outline the main points for the third. Which is what I did, though I made at least three false starts on the first essay. At the orals, he questioned my interpretation of one of Hamlet's lines concerning "conscience," and I wisely conceded his point, while waxing eloquent enough in answers to other examiners.

The dissertation was easier to write, though I lost Matthews as my supervisor midway through my research. He went on sabbatical following a generous SSHRC (of over half a million dollars) for editing and annotating a huge cache of Benjamin Disraeli letters he had discovered in England. R.T. Robertson (from New Zealand, and an authority on comparative studies in national literatures) replaced him, and though my dissertation ("The Spirit of Place in R.K. Narayan and V.S. Naipaul") was not rigorously scholarly—certainly not in the vein of my M.A. thesis on *Hamlet*—it covered a lot of literary ground, its over-arching theme an extension of D.H. Lawrence's ideas about the spirit or genius of place—a subject germane to my ethnic background. The dissertation's principal conclusion was that the "spirit of place" has more than one form and effect: "when localized (as with Narayan) it yields a literature of acceptance containing benign answers and commentaries about a human condition it believes is consolidated; when delocalized (as with Naipaul) in a sequence of landscapes that affords no permanent Home, it makes art a literature of protest or rebellion with a psychic centre (affected by nihilism) from where the writer questions the meaning of history." Viewing it now in a rear-view mirror of history, I realize I may have Naipaulian residue in my core sensibility and psyche.

There was one major regret: I never got to make use of a wonderful handwritten letter from V.S. Naipaul in response to questions I had raised in a letter sent to him on January 14, 1972:

Dear Mr. Naipaul,

I have just read *In A Free State* and have enjoyed it immensely. Perhaps, this is not quite the sort of reaction I should have to a book about neo-colonialism, fear, and disillusionment. However, my enjoyment derives from your literary skill, the pith and virtuosity in your narrative power, and your confident way with irony. There is no doubt in my mind that this book ranks alongside *A House For Mr. Biswas* as the two peaks in your literary career.

Here, however, is where I have a question. Obviously, as you yourself have indicated, *In A Free State* makes a final statement about human placelessness and lostness. Where then do you expect to turn next? Am I wrong in thinking that you have nothing else to say about the colonial dilemma and that I see your next phase along the lines of a *settled* neo-colonial in England?

Please do not misinterpret my remarks. I am not suggesting that you will *ape* any tradition. However, I wonder what viable alternative there is to neo-colonial despair. Obviously, London is now more than just a commercial or metropolitan centre for you. You have lived in England for over a decade and surely your artistic sensibility is now closer to England than to any other part of the Commonwealth. Indeed, there is no Eden but a man finds a place to erect his own abode. Am I wrong in thinking that you have made at least some peace with yourself in the matter of a national building?

I wonder what you think about critical reaction to your latest book. I exclude, of course, the inane critics such as Auberon Waugh who sacrifices accuracy for slogans. Angus Calder suggests that you have an anti-climactic vision and I would be interested to know your reaction to this remark. I hope you do not feel that I have imposed myself upon you, but I am most interested in your career and its problems. I trust that you will not find my questions too insignificant to merit a reply.

His handwritten response in black ink (dated September 19, 1972) arrived from 105 Great Russell Street, London too late for me to incorporate as an appendix in my doctoral dissertation. However, I shared it with Robertson, and now re-reading it decades later, and years after Naipaul's demise, I cherish it:

Dear Mr. Garebian,

I wonder whether you remember the letter you wrote me on Jan 14. It wasn't sent on to me, and I have just found it on my return to England after nearly nine months abroad (in Trinidad, Argentina + New Zealand). Your letter was intelligent, generous + extremely pertinent. Where does one go from here? Well, one goes nowhere. What has happened is that I am no longer a pioneer; the world has changed around me. Countries like India—although you may not agree—are becoming metropolitan in their own right, with their own glamour, their own beginnings at self-analysis; and it is no longer necessary for someone with my instincts to make the journey I made. Not a pleasant journey. But it is over now: the world rights itself. Just when England is insupportable, other countries become exciting. Neo-colonialism is not really a problem to people like myself any longer. If you read—it is a book of articles I am publishing in about a month—my first writing about India, you will see how much the world has changed. Not a good answer, I feel, to your profound question. But a proper answer would be a book itself—and I perhaps may write it.

Thank you for a lovely letter.

Yours,
VSNaipaul

I was grateful for the time it took him to write it, and for the fact that he treated my questions with dignified courtesy and genuine interest. Much to my relief, he did not find them puerile or pointless or, even worse, the graceless spadework of a desiccated academic. I published parts of my dissertation in the *Journal of Commonwealth Literature, Ariel, International Fiction Review*, and *The Literary Half-Yearly*. Akin to dipping a little toe into a huge pool of Commonwealth water, even though the term "Commonwealth Literature" was a delusion. Had I read Derek Walcott's essay "What the Twilight Says" at the time, I would have seen that only English Literature was hallowed ground to the English. As every tribe "hoards its culture as fiercely as its prejudices," Commonwealth writing was "filial and tributary."

And just how sincere are the white Commonwealth nations with regard to their non-white partners? I pondered this at a Conference for Commonwealth Literature at the Loyola Campus in Montreal, where Aborigine writer Kath Walker (small in stature, with an apple face) was seated away from the Head Table. Was it because of her notorious feistiness or her unpredictable candour? Whatever the reason, I thought it exceedingly strange that this Aborigine poet, political activist, a Member of the British Empire, should be slighted. I invited her to sit with me. During one of the essay presentations, I noticed her drawing with coloured markers. I looked over her shoulder and was struck by a very colourful representation of the Aboriginal cosmos, rendered in pointillist detail. I expressed my admiration and in little more than a blink of an eye was presented with the drawing which she graciously autographed. I had only a superficial knowledge of Australian history and that nation's racist policies against its indigenous population, and my innate empathy for the dispossessed was heightened by listening to her account of her grandmother raped at twelve by a white man. Reading her face and the glint in her eyes was to be in the presence of living pain. Yet there was a strange moment in our conversation when I told her of my own mixed ethnic background. She remarked that in her tribal culture, I would be met with disapproval for being rather like a tree with an extra root that needed to be torn out lest it damage the health of the tree. Was this reverse racism, I wondered, but quickly realized that trees are sacred for her people, and perhaps my own mixed ethnicity was a tangential point for her because of a long history of white racist violation where Aborigines were often raped and where the mixed-race offspring inherited further cultural, psychological, and emotional violation. Where she wrote movingly of the real threat of Aborigine disappearance, I had already seen the waning of Anglo-India and the radical shrinking of Armenia.

Years later, I read of her sangfroid in 1974 when the British Airways flight she had taken was hijacked by terrorists for the Palestinian cause. During three days in tense captivity, she kept her cool, using a blunt pencil and an airline sickbag to compose two poems. This bravery was matched by her moral integrity when in 1987 she returned her MBE in protest against celebrations to mark the 200th anniversary of British colonization of Australia—or from the Aborigine point of view "200 years of sheer unadulterated humiliation." She changed her name to Oodgeroo Noonucal, an Aboriginal name with deep, poignant significance, Oodgeroo meaning "paperbark tree" (whose bark is used for drawing), and Noonucal being the name of her people, owners of Minjerribah, an island in south-eastern Queensland, where she was born and where her people had lived for over 20,000 years.

Kath was my "shadow sister," a phrase invented for her by the great Australian poet Judith Wright. Small in physical size, she was a giant in cultural significance.

Family

Wedding Portrait of my parents (1942).

Aged 2, Juhu Beach, 1945. My father, his face turned away, is behind me, while my mother, pregnant with her first daughter, stands behind him. My father's best-man, John Condor is bent over behind my father. Others in the pic were family friends who moved to Australia.

Aunt Rose, my father's
older sister, looks deeply
sad in this pic for losing
her newborn infant. n.d.

My godfather Charles
Ronald Williams (Billy)
sits front row centre. n.d.

With my sisters in
Panchgani, India
(circa 1954).

Elma, my ill-fated sister
(1945-1981).

Acting

Striking a dramatic pose in an English-language version of Henri
Gheon's Passion Play, St. Joseph's Oratory, Montreal (1967).

As Creon with a student Antigone in an English-language version
of Jean Anouilh's Antigone, Marymount Comprehensive School,
Montreal (1970).

Friends

With Armenian students at the Hamazkayin launch of Pain:
Journeys Around My Parents, Toronto (2000).

Acceptance Speech for the William Saroyan Medal,
Yerevan, Armenia (July 2013).

William Hutt posing on the front steps of his Victorian home, Stratford.

Nonnie Griffin's peals of laughter at one of my parties in Mississauga.

With poet-editor Elana Wolff at the launch of my haiku book (2013). Elana's 2021 interview with me was the greatest I have ever done.

With Allan Briesmaster at the launch of Frida: Paint Me as a Volcano, Victory Café, Toronto (2004).

With my son and Atom Egoyan at a commemorative celebration of the Ararat film, at Roy Thomson Hall, Toronto (2015).

Letters From The Famous

LAURENCE OLIVIER.
Old Vic Theatre,
London S.E. 1.

16th March 1967.

Dear Mr. Garebian,

        Thank you very much for your
letter.   I am delighted that you have
enjoyed my work and extremely grateful
to you for your kindness in writing to
express such generous thoughts about it.

        It is kind of you to ask to
see me but I am afraid I already have a
tremendously heavy programme of
engagements during my short visit to
Montreal which makes it impossible for
me to think of arranging any personal
meetings.   I am so sorry; but I would,
of course, be happy to autograph
photographs or programmes for you if you
would care to leave them at the stage
door.

        All good wishes and again so
many thanks for your kindness and interest.

                Yours sincerely,

Mr. Keith Garebian.

From Sir Laurence Olivier (1967).

V.S. NAIPAUL
André Deutsch Ltd
105 Great Russell
Street
London WC1
September 19 1972

Dear Mr Josselson,

I wonder whether you remember the letter you wrote me on Jan 14. It wasn't sent on to me, and I have just found it on my return to England after nearly nine months abroad (in Trinidad, Argentina + New Zealand). Your letter was intelligent, generous + extremely pertinent. Where does one go from here? Well, one goes nowhere. What has happened is that I am no longer a pioneer; the world has changed around me. Countries like India — although you may not agree — are becoming metropolitan in their own right, with their own flavours, their own beginnings at self-analysis; and it is no longer necessary for someone with my instinct to make the journey I made. Not a pleasant journey. But it is over now: the world rights itself. Just when England is insupportable, other countries become

From V.S. Naipaul (long before his knighthood) (1972): Page 1.

exciting. Neo-colonialism is not really a problem to people like myself any longer. If you read — it is in a book of articles I am publishing in about a month — my first writing about India, you will see how much the world has changed. Not a good answer, I feel, to your profound question. But a proper answer would be a book in itself — and I perhaps may write it.

Thank you for a long letter.

Yours,

V S Naipaul

From V.S. Naipaul: Page 2.

Keith Garebian
16 Mansfield Place
Dollard des Ormeaux
Quebec H9G 2B4 P.Q.

200 Glen Rd.
Toronto, Ont.

From Irving Layton (1977).

c/ MOONGALBA,
P.O. DUNWICH
STRADBROKE ISLAND, 4163
TEL. 075-499169 QLD

18th April, 1983.

Dear Keith,

Thank you for your very good thought provoking poem about me. Excellent.

I am as busy as ever. I leave for Wayalla, South Australia next week for a fortnights hard labour at the schools there.

How is Canada these days. We are about to go into winter here so I guess Canada is about to go into their ~~cold cold winter~~. summer.

Our winter here, lasts for about three weeks of really cold weather, otherwise we just get a cold nip in the air. I do like living in the sub-tropics for that reason.

As you probably realise we have a change in Government in Australia and we, the Aborigines live in great expectiins of a better deal. The socialists have so promised anyway.

"Shadow Sister" is still being shown on television as people here keep asking for a re-play of the show.

I do not get enough time to myself to do any creative work. Am attempting my sixth book but not being able to really get into it. Perhaps after June I shall get some time. I have also being asked to go to Japan as the television there did a programme on so called famous Australians, I am supposed to be one of them. Famous, I mean.

Hope they ask me to go there during the summer. I can't stand cold weather.

It was nice to get your letter. Hope all goes well with you and give my regards to all my friends there.

Love,

Kath Walker.

From the feisty Aussie Aborigine poet Kath Walker (1983).

P.O. Box 2700
Station D
Ottawa K1P 5W7

Jan 8. 86.

Dear Keith,

I'm editing a book of essays for ECW — a book entitled The Bumper Book. It's made up of about 15 essays by divers hands all taking their CanLit hobby horses out for a canter. For example, Woodcock has written on the concept of "cultural industries", John Mills on nationalism, George Bowering on being audited, Fraser Sutherland on Atwood and Survival, Larry Matthews on the CanLit canon — and so on.

The idea is to be provocative and, if possible, funny. Thinking of all your trenchant stuff on the theatre, I wondered if I could interest you in writing an essay about Canadian Theatre — what's wrong with it, why we don't have more, whatever. Or whatever you'd like to write about concerning theatre in Canada.

From John Metcalf (1986).

4242 Hampton Ave., Montréal, Québec, H4A 2K9
Sunday, November 4th, 1990.

Mr. Keith Garebian,
2001 Bonnymede Drive, Unit 150,
Mississauga, Ontario,
L5J 4H8

Dear Keith: I'm writing to thank you very gratefully for the long,
careful and very favourable review-article in the October Books in
Canada and for your continued support and understanding of the serial
novel and my other projects. I could not have persisted as long as I
have with this work without the careful reading and vocal approval
of you and a small number of other readers like John Metcalf, Tim
Struthers, Michael O. Nowlan, Laurence Matthews, Pat Morley, and a
few more. At present there are reviewers who seem to take pleasure in
asserting quite falsely that I have no readers and that interest in
The New Age is rapidly dwindling. It is true that I don't sell as many
copies as I did in the beginning, but at that time books sold for
$6.95 in hard cover, and now they are $24.95, with the GST about to
be added on top of that. The dollar volume achieved by a given book
of mine in its first season is slightly down from earlier days. In a
given September to December period, with prompt distribution and at least
some promotion, a book of mine will draw about $15,000 in gross sales.
If the book costs $25.00 I will sell about six hundred copies in the
first fall season, after that follow-up and back list sales will usually
get the book up around 1,000 copies reasonably quickly. Then it goes
into permanent back list, rarely out of print. Every serious writer in
Canada will tell you the same thing except for half a dozen who are
featured in any given publishing season. The number of potential readers
of a serious work of Canadian literature has somewhat dwindled 1960-1990,
but so it has all over the world, with competition from video and audio
cassettes, home TV, and many other sources. I've managed to persuade
publishers to do twenty-five of my books to date with two more contracted
for and scheduled for production in 1991. This is not a dwindling
activity.

Your review article was the first publication I know of to go forward
from the beginning of The New Age to look closely at the books in
sequence and show how they build towards the point I've reached in
Property and Value. This seems a natural thing to do, but it does take
both time and space, and I am very pleased that Books in Canada allowed
the review; apart from anything else it informs booksellers and readers
across Canada that my book has in fact come out and is now available in
stores. Of course this is invaluable and necessary promotion. I can't
hit the road and visit the seventy or eighty bookstores in Canada--that's
really all there are--who might stock Property and Value. The most
effective means of reaching them are Quill and Quire, Books in Canada,
and the radio show Morningside. I've got a series of five brief broadcasts
across a week coming up on Morningside, and the publishers tell me this
is the best promotion you can get in Canada.

You might have seen Joel Yanofsky's review in the Toronto Star. It
will not surprise you to hear me say that it was in almost every respect
inaccurate about matters of fact. But a double-column review in the Star
with a picture and a useable quote is very useful even if the review is
a sharp criticism, as this was. It's immensely valuable space just as an
announcement of publication. Better if favourable but very useful anyway.
I don't know if the Globe will do a review. I hope so; it would be great
if it turned out a favourable one. The Gazette review was done by a former
student of mine and was carping and petty, which surprised me. So thanks
for your kind and encouraging treatment, old buddy, and hang in there.

From Hugh Hood (1990).

William Hutt

Dear Keith:

As you know, over these many years, I have waived and waived and waived until my arms are sore! But for you I will waive once more. However, in return, I would be pleased to see a full page solo shot of me well identified as Ramsden. Do you think you can manage that?

Hope so — mean time best of good fortune with the book

AND

my most affectionate thanks for your birthday remembrance

Ever
Bill

May 3/91
Stratford

From William Hutt (1991).

Shaw Festival

August 17th, 1993

Mr. Keith Garebian
3375 Pony Trail Drive, #1006
Mississauga, ON
L4X 1V8

Dear Keith:

Please forgive my inordinate delay in writing to you. This year has been so hectic - rehearse one play, rehearse a second, rehearse and - God, forbid - act in a third. Now I can see my desk - just! Thank you for all the work and most especially for the signed copy.

The book looks splendid and the manager of our Shaw Shop tells me she has trouble keeping it in stock - I hope sales are good elsewhere, too - for your sake, as well as ours.

Sincerely,

Christopher Newton
Artistic Director

Truly excellent. Thanks

C.

From Christopher Newton, Artistic Director,
the Shaw Festival, Niagara-on-the-Lake (1993).

August 26 1993

Dear Keith:

I am humbled by and in awe of the beauty of your gracious letter. I will ever hold it dear to me and my experience with this show.

You have given my work some invaluable light. I thank-you for giving of your talents, your generous observations, and positive ideas of what this fragile world of artistry is about; of what we must continually strive for and believe in. I am so grateful to be a part, some small part of that world, from time to time.

I wish you all goodness.

I hope to express my sincere gratitude to you in person, some day soon.

With warm regards

Respectfully   Brent C.

From actor Brent Carver (1993).

Harold Prince · 10 ROCKEFELLER PLAZA · SUITE 1104
NEW YORK, N. Y. 10020

Telephone
(212) 399-0960
Facsimile
(212) 974-8426

February 26, 2010

Keith Garebian
1515 Lakeshore Road East
Apt. 1704
Mississauga, ON
L5E 3E3

Dear Keith Garebian,

That you want to dedicate your book to me is an honor, and I don't suppose I should require reading it to accept.

As for your many questions, I'm going to shortchange you on that, because it seems CABARET has a life of its own. It's genesis was in my office, with Kander and Ebb and Joe Masteroff. And our version clearly led the way to all the subsequent interpretations.

There's no question in my mind but that we fudged a little on the love story, but remember, it was 1966, and throwing the Joel Grey character (really, the lead) at an audience, complete with the unparalleled depression in Germany, which directly led to Adolph Hitler and the National Socialists, was an awful lot to expect of an audience, so we deliberately eschewed Cliff's homosexuality and allowed a more conventional view of Sally and Cliff's love story.

As the years passed, Bob Fosse was able to take more advantage of social change, and that again happened when Sam Mendes mounted his production, so I'm unable to answer your specific questions, except to say I do not think there is any need to add any more to Sally's character, or Cliff's role, other than those changes that occurred in the film.

I do think both the film and the Mendes production did not quite dramatize the metaphor that was central to my production, which is at the beginning of the musical, Joey Grey was no more than a pathetic emcee with lousy taste, desperate to entertain, and clueless. I had met such a man in Germany when I was in uniform in 1951, and he was the inspiration for that character. I felt that the emcee presented in the film, and the subsequent productions did not undergo the same changes. He was evil in the beginning and evil at the end, and I would quarrel with that.

The most important of all your questions is will there be future interpretations of CABARET? You bet there will be. It invites that kind of invention, but I take great pride in knowing that our version was the first. Thank you for writing.

Sincerely

Hal Prince

Hal Prince

From Hal Prince of Broadway (2010).

CHAPTER SIX

LITERARY FRIENDSHIPS

I reviewed Henry Beissel's poetry collection, *The Salt I Taste*, positively in the *Montreal Star*, but the first of Henry's letters in my archives was about a different review. I had criticized a bad Véhicule poetry collection (*Montreal English Poetry of the Seventies*), much to the dismay of many of those poets but to the considerable approval of better poets elsewhere. Henry reacted with "considerable glee," remarking in his lengthy letter of March 14, 1978:

> It's about time someone took the hacks to task. There has
> been altogether too much self-congratulation and backslapping
> on the Canadian literary scene, especially here in Montreal.
> The arrival of busy-body pseudo-poets [...] has aggravated
> an appalling state of affairs. Any kind of verbal mush passes
> for 'poetry' these days. Anyone spilling his puerile fancies
> and pre-occupations across a page in any jumble of scraps of
> words passes for a 'poet' these days. Any bubble and squeak
> from the bowels of a neurotic or hysteric, so long as it's laid
> out to resemble verse, parades as a 'poem' today. I realize that
> illiterate 'literature' has flourished in the past, but never as
> luxuriantly as in our own time. And never has it received the
> critical acclaim it enjoys today. Never before have its
> perpetrators been held up to an ignorant public as the 'literary
> luminaries' of the nation, shipped back and forth for display

and emulation, given the highest titles and awards. In such a situation criticism such as yours, impartial, concrete, sensitive and intelligent, is more than just a fresh breeze. It's a beacon in a starless night. I daresay if there had been more of your kind of critical reviews over the past 20 years we wouldn't be wallowing in the cultural cesspool that engulfs us now.

Such heady praise was just what a budding reviewer needed. But Beissel was not merely flattering me; he had genuine issues with the Canadian literary scene in general and with Montreal's coterie of back-slapping comrades in particular: "I am not bitter. I am disgusted, angry, sad, because for 20 years I have had to live my intellectual and creative life in a world of cultural con-men and charlatans. Writing for me is both a way of life and a craft which demands of me everything I have to give." Ten years later, Henry would claim: "I am convinced there are not 200 people between Victoria and St. John's who actually read serious literature. The audience for quilting is about ten times as large. The rest is beer and baseball."

Born in Cologne, Germany, Henry had a rich cultural background, although his home life was in turmoil and his country in political *Sturm und Drang*. He was born out of wedlock to a musician father and a mercurial mother given to bouts of anger "mysteriously morphed to pity," as he and a younger brother struggled to survive the war where brown-shirted, goose-stepping barbarians enflamed his own "fevers of the human heart and mind," and his city ravaged by bombing. He was shocked by the depraved savagery of the genocide, and yearned to leave for foreign shores. When he escaped his homeland, he sparkled as an academic and writer at universities in Alberta, Trinidad, and Montreal. By the time he arrived in Canada in 1951, he already had a reputation as poet, translator, essayist, playwright, and editor. Our paths first crossed at Sir George Williams University, where he, with dark flowing locks and a flourish of gestures, coloured every lecture on Chaucer by a full-out reading in Middle English (replete with a repertoire of highly energetic vocal modulations). His elocution was a veritable performance.

After I had begun my freelance career in mid 1975 and become his friend, I attended the celebration when he wed Arlette Francière, a brilliant translator from France. The party was held in Sharon Schwartz's home on Arlington Avenue, Westmount, on a fine April day in 1981, and attendees included Gary Geddes, Per Brask (who was Artistic Director of the Saidye Bronfman Centre), Michael Brian (my M.A. thesis supervisor), American expatriate Ronnie Brown, Louis Dudek and his wife Aileen Collins, and Frank Scott and his artist-wife Marian. Tall, lean, and thin-haired, Scott had the manner and mien of a mandarin authority; his wife was shy and quiet. She seemed quite content to let Frank do the talking. Louis Dudek, tall, lean, and balding, liked discussion on a wide range of topics, but particularly of local writers. A passionate admirer and defender of Ezra Pound, he had an excellent reputation as a professor at McGill and as a poet who helped define Modernism. He had waged intellectual battles against such Canadian literary heavy-weights as Northrop Frye and Marshall McLuhan, and was very supportive of small publishers and new poets. I had admired his collections *Europe*, *En Mexico*, and *Atlantis*, and listened patiently as he denigrated Irving Layton, apparently never able to let their famous literary and political feud begun in 1958 pass into history without further comment. "Oh, Louis, must you go there again?" Aileen asked, tired of his rehearsing an old grudge.

When Henry and Arlette settled in Alexandria, Ontario, about 60 miles each way from Ottawa and Montreal, I visited their home named Ayorama, where Henry had a comfortable studio across a path from the house. The bucolic ambience, complemented by the couple's vegetable garden, seemed a perfect site for Henry's writing and, eventually, Arlette's strong, expressionist painting. It was easy to see links between this rural life and some of Henry's poems. The solitude afforded by Ayorama was a richer catalyst to creativity than the solitude of his boyhood and youth, and Henry's literary productivity was astonishing. It was heartbreaking to the couple when the infamous ice-storm of 1998 destroyed forests and much of the natural vegetation around Ayorama, as well as many areas of eastern

Ontario and southern Quebec. Worse was to come, as Henry expressed in a letter to family and friends (Yule 2006): "On the night of January 17, Ayorama burnt down. What that has meant for us, most of you are aware of. I built Ayorama with my own hands, and Arlette and I lived there for thirty years in our own forest, raised Clara there, sharing the challenges, the joys and woes of a not always benevolent, but always healing Nature. Suddenly our home, our retreat, the habitat of our creativity was gone, the victim of an arsonist." But in 2006 they moved to a house in Ottawa spacious enough to serve both their respective arts. Henry's study had its own "creative disorder," but he and Arlette winterized a hot-tub room, converting it into a studio, windows on three sides, where she could produce new paintings.

Henry shared my interest in theatre, and appreciated my own passionate concern about matters in Montreal, where the Centaur was being run by South African Maurice Podbrey, a man known for espousing what he often did not actually practise. In 1971, Henry clashed with Podbrey in a dramatic exchange of Letters to the Editor at the *Montreal Star*. Henry rebuked the Centaur and the Saidye Bronfman Centre for having "yet to show that they belong to Montreal rather than to Johannesburg or New York." This drew a response from Podbrey which essentially claimed that flag-waving was easier than finding satisfactory Canadian plays—a point he was able to prove by his selection of second and third-rate Canadian plays in subsequent seasons.

As a playwright, Henry was most praised for the puppet-play *Inuk and the Sun* (which had a first-rate staging at Stratford), *Goya* (given an excellent Expressionistic production by Alexander Hausvater), and *Under Coyote's Eye* (which I have read but never seen performed). He shared my criticism of contemporary Canadian theatre's being "a cultural circus for non-discriminating patrons," as he lamented that "in an environment that puts laurel wreaths on the heads of prematurely superannuated mediocrities like Carol Bolt and David Fennario."

As a poet, Henry has enjoyed even larger praise for works such as *Cantos North*, *Seasons of Blood*, and, more recently, *Fugitive Horizons*, *Sightlines*, and *Footprints of Dark Energy*, one collection following another with convincing evidence that Beissel is a poet of successive summits. Though he has a natural empathy for the unjustly oppressed, victims of political tyrants, and indigenous tribes in the Americas, he recoils from any suggestion that he is a romantic—as I discovered after I had questioned what I considered his romanticism in *Cantos North*. He made his case in a letter to me (March 18, 1985):

> Sure, the poem acknowledges an appearance of harmony in nature, but it is a harmony enforced over millions of years by laws that are brutal to both individuals and species and that must be obeyed by both at pain of death. The 'native' Indian had learnt that lesson and had therefore become integrated into the landscape. But that didn't make him a 'noble savage.' The poem refers to him as 'no nobler than upstream/ salmon or a hawk on the wing.' The Indian, it says, 'had long left the paths of innocence.' In other words, he had become part of nature, sharing its harmonies but also its constant fears and cruelties. All this is anti-romantic. This land (archtypically [sic] the northland is for me the land dominated by death) which some have come to in their search for Eden is 'an inferno/of ice' where we must 'bury our dreams in stone caches' as 'we bleed from birth/to death.' Perhaps all this isn't clear enough in the poem. Perhaps the archetypal level is too closely fused with the personal, with the celebration of this country and its pioneers. On its most immediate level CANTOS NORTH is an account of my 30-year old love affair with Canada. That theme was intended as the counterpoint to the meditations on the fragility of life. Well, maybe some day we should have a long talk about it, although I don't really want to become the exegetist of my own poetry.

It read almost like a university lecture, but the intent was clarification rather than an attack on labels, and Henry loved discussion. Even when, on one occasion at Ayorama, he stuck doggedly to his claim that he was an agnostic atheist (or was it an atheistic agnostic?), much to ironic laughter by me and Arlette, who scoffed at his casuistry.

Henry's poetry has always struck me as being more in a European than North American vein because of its dynamic investigations of histories, cultures, and contemporary issues. As an exile, he knew what it meant to be uprooted and caught between radically different cultures. Perhaps this had a lot to do with shaping his own cosmopolitanism. Henry had taught university in the Caribbean, presented his poetry in the company of Derek Walcott, and there wasn't a sliver of racial bias in anything he ever did as a professor or writer. His letters and postcards are filled with details of exciting travel experiences in Peru, Guatemala, France, China, Germany, England, Mexico, Iraq. Some letters report on interesting theatre productions he had seen, or cite numerous guest readings and lectures, or include clippings of nationwide teaching opportunities (for which he was ever-ready to write letters of reference on my behalf). Others celebrate Arlette's evolving painting style, report on writing projects he was undertaking or bemoan the rancid state of politics in academia. An overarching theme is his chronic antipathy to cultural mediocrity, as in this message to me in 1982: "I care about a genuine culture: a people confronting the complexities of an ever-changing reality and trying to create order and meaning where there appear to be none. I care because mediocrity diminishes and degrades us all. If life is not a continuous search and exploration of the mind and through it of the many conflicting dimensions we call reality, what is it? Joe Clark in leather shorts taking a flying fuck at a doughnut?"

That he has not been appointed to the Order of Canada is a reflection of a cultural disorder. I join Gary Geddes in calling the whole sorry business the Disorder of Canada.

While attempting to ice-skate rather unsteadily at the Lower Canada College rink in N.D.G. where I was living, I met Hugh Hood. He didn't know who I was, but graciously offered helpful advice on elementary skating technique. Off the ice, I could hardly equate the casually dressed man in baggy trousers and running shoes with the rather famous writer and English professor. But I soon learned that his casualness of dress and manner (he loved eating Campbell's soups out of their cans) was the opposite of his intellectual sophistication. Perhaps I should modify this statement because, in fact, when he wrote a story or started a conversation, there was a relaxed informality in the way he allowed ideas to play in his head and on the page. Our friendship began on ice, but warmed up in time, though I was not a big fan of his novels at the outset when I started my freelance career as literary critic. The first book review I ever published was a short one in the *Montreal Gazette* of *Horse D'Oeuvres* by a group known as the Four Horsemen. I was paid the princely sum of $30 for the privilege of having my surname misspelled by the copy editor. I was paid just a little more for a much longer review of the first novel in Hood's New Age series. My review was negative, finding *The Swing in the Garden*'s narrative too placid, and the book too much in love with documentary details. Whatever he privately thought of that review, Hood had the good grace to befriend me, inviting me to his home, where his wife Noreen Mallory, a painter who had once worked in the props section at Stratford, also became a friend. Shy and a bit uneasy at a dinner hosted by the couple, I allowed a roast potato I was slicing to skip right out of my plate to the floor. Hood cracked: "Well, that's quite a jumping potato!" to put me at ease, and Noreen's delicious meal became even more enjoyable.

That dinner puts me in mind of another dinner where Hugh's pet green parrot played an unexpected role. Jack David recalls that when he and Robert Lecker were Hugh's dinner guests, Hugh's pet green parrot suddenly flew to the table, where it proceeded to act like an invited guest. The same parrot had made me clammy with sweat when it flew from its open cage to Hugh's shoulder on one of my visits. Hugh had not known of my boyhood trauma in Bombay when my godfather had tossed a fowl at me in order to stifle my complaint about being left in the car by my parents while they shopped at Crawford Market. The creature's feet were bound by string, but its wings flapped hysterically, and its squawks made me shiver in fright. Hugh's parrot was a much quieter, relatively well-behaved bird, but its free movement in the room unnerved me.

Hugh was teaching at the University of Montreal, and was nominated for a Governor General's Award for *Swing*, compelling me to mentally review my own review of the novel, fortified by Hugh's discourses on the nature of his analogical and allegorical methods. Hugh plotted all his novels in minute detail, and sometimes this worked against them because they lacked spontaneous surprises of characterization and story-telling. "That's a honey of a sentence!" or "That's a honey of a book!" he was wont to say as a prelude to a brilliant discourse on his literary sophistications. Never one to hide his light under a bushel, Hugh could make grand claims for his own writing, ranking himself in the company of Dante, Balzac, Anthony Powell, and Proust. He was absolutely sincere about what he was hoping to achieve. To this day, no literary critic has successfully named his style, and although I don't think that any single novel in his New Age Series measures up to the greatest Canadian or American or British novels, the 12-part series uses emblems and exempla in an enviable sweep of regional history, culture, politics, sociology, and manners. Hugh was better at short fiction and the essay (as in *None Genuine Without This Signature*, *Dark Glasses*, and *Trusting the Tale*), although his best single work is probably *Around the Mountain: Scenes from Montreal Life*, a unified cycle comprising scenes, sketches, incidents, and full-fledged stories. As John Metcalf observed, Hugh created a place for meditation in the service of fiction, although Metcalf (a superb close reader) and I eventually clashed in our respective readings of some of that fiction.

John and I both recognized Hugh's encyclopedic mind. A sample informal chat with Hugh was usually a test of one's concentration and parameters of knowledge. A typical conversation could encompass such things as cartoons, baseball, Bing Crosby's crooning style, Dante, Wordsworth, ice-hockey, Canadian Tire, Anthony Powell, Catholic theology, numerology, a comparison of Woody Allen with Ingmar Bergman, the *Carry-On* films, and P.G. Wodehouse. I am exaggerating, but only a little. John Metcalf provides this satiric vignette: "My wife and I were once driving with Hugh to Toronto to read at Harbourfront. As we pulled out of the drive, my wife asked Hugh why he had not put on his seat belt. Taking in a comprehensive survey through the ages of the doctrines of Free Will, Salvation, Law, and the nature of the Social Contract, the answer lasted until we were approaching Oshawa."

The first letter from Hugh that survives in my archives is from November 22, 1982, in which he praises a review-article by me on the damnable rubbish published on Canadian theatre, taking note of my "windmill arms, flailing all and sundry with forcible blows" and continuing:

> Of course what you say is so damned right—that we will not get a theatre by multiplication of scholarly apparatus or by training thousands of young actors and technicians for whom no genuine and dignified employment can be provided. We will only get a theatre when we get two or three or four WRITERS like Soyinka or Fugard or Beckett or Derek Walcott. We have to find a few creative artists— not interpretive artists but originative [sic] artists like writers and composers—who can work at the frontiers of invention. I don't know how or why this happens. The 'funding' available for the theatre of Yeats and Synge and Lady Gregory—the great Irish theatre from 1900 to 1940, say, was trivial and minimal by our standards.
>
> A few unpaid elocutionists with no formal training as actors speaking the lines of these strange plays quite unlike any others in the English language theatre of the day. The cost in money spent was absurdly tiny. Funny, isn't it? We have such a finance and business oriented, moralistic and puritanical community that most people here think of art in terms of 'funding.' Think of the great magazines churned out on somebody's dittograph magazine in a back room.

Hugh appreciated my reviews and articles, though I felt somewhat embarrassed to be included in what he termed "the Hood-Rooke-Metcalf-Lecker-Garebian-Tata mafia," because while I delighted in scaring philistines "shitless" and keeping them "on the run," I shrank from being part of any mafia. When Twayne published my book on his work till 1983, he sent me a letter of gratitude, complimenting me on packing immense information into a format that usually produced books "of thinness and an eked-out argument." He genuinely wanted me to succeed in my own dual and sometimes duelling vocations as teacher and writer. Knowing that I felt like a fish out of water in the school system, he wrote numerous letters of reference on my behalf for university teaching jobs, even trying to convince me that I should apply for the position of Department Head of the English Department at the University of Montreal. He failed to convince me because I was too insecure about my proficiency in French, but I deeply appreciated his faith in me. In one such letter (sent to the Chairman, Department of English, York University), he explained why he would place me in "the very front rank of contemporary critics of Canadian literature and drama." He claimed my writing on Canadian authors was "highly esteemed by other writers like John Metcalf, a notoriously difficult man to please, where literary standards have been invoked," and then went on to summarize my style in a Latin epigram, "*suaviter in modo; fortiter in re*," translated as "gentle in manner; resolute in deed." Which author could ask for more?

John Metcalf also became a literary friend. He did not offer the literary equivalent of Scotch or Lorazepam—something to numb his readers, to take them out of themselves. He did not think that fiction should translate us to another world; rather, it should drive us "deeper into this one." As a polemicist and critic, he was caviar. I loved his acid wit and his courageous take-downs of some of the biggest overrated names in Canadian literature. He, in turn, liked my own acerbic wit, especially when I turned my attention to the woeful mediocrity of Canadian playwrights or a shockingly shoddy biography of

Irving Layton. I was delighted when he (a true connoisseur of the word) saw no need to alter a word, much less a comma before publishing each of these pieces in his Bumper books (*The Bumper Book* and *Carry On Bumping*). I also liked his barbed wit in black ink on yellow paper when it was aimed at my writing, as when he generously edited an early, bulky version of my first biography of William Hutt. I knew full well that all wit has an element of rude candour. When I mailed him a blank cheque and asked him to enter his fee, the amount he charged was astonishingly low. He, too, thought I was in the wrong teaching system, and often offered to help me find work. But there wasn't much work to get. Part-time college and university teaching received shamefully little money, and freelance book reviewing was worse. In all the years I wrote for *The Toronto Star* and the *Globe and Mail*, I cannot remember a single increase in the basic fee for a book review. Irony was that I made a lot more money as a consequence of a highly successful class-action lawsuit against these dailies and others for their digital use of reviews without fair compensation.

John had his own economic and professional struggles, but he never missed an opportunity to send up absurdity, as in this brief message to me in January 1988: "I'm working for 6 months as a 'writer-in-res' in Nepean public library—a far flung (and carelessly flung) suburb of Ottawa (1 ½ hrs. on smelly bus) where people come in to grill me on where to take their video/manuscripts on dinosaurs or how to obtain a copy of the Coroner's Act. This is true. It is quite awful. But the Visa situation had become possibly life-threatening."

John sometimes had too much faith in me. I disappointed him when he commissioned me to write an essay on Alice Munro's "Walkers Brothers Cowboy," because I failed to take proper measure of the story's texture and technique. He suggested that I look very closely at the opening paragraph, at the opening sentences and perspective and images, and it was only after I had read his own essay on the same story that I realized what he had meant for me to do. His essay is a classic of close reading, an example of what Cyril Connolly (his model for critical taste) meant when he asserted that "an expert should be able to tell a carpet by one skein of it; a vintage by rinsing a glassful round his mouth."

Informal conversation with John was always delightful, as he deftly spun satiric anecdotes about academics and writers known to both of us. He often spoke the way he wrote, with perfectly-timed understated wit. At every word a reputation died—not out of sheer malice, but because his devastating deflations were utterly on point. I detested much of what he detested. He was a Brit and he could sneer as no one else could, but his purpose was not self-promotion. Rather, it was a deliberate attack on the mediocrity or awful provinciality of much Canadian writing. He was antagonistic to prevailing literary standards, only because he wanted Canadian literature to be better. He detested academic jargon and its heavy breathing practitioners, and he satirized them devastatingly by representing them wallowing in the muck of words and phrases such as "heteroglossia," "deconstruction of binaries," and the "monological egocentricity of conventional lyric discourse." Metcalf's high standards gave him cause to take aim at a variety of targets: Morley Callaghan, Robin Matthews, W.P. Kinsella, John Moss, Patricia Morley, and even the novels of Margaret Atwood. He most admired Alice Munro, Clark Blaise, and Norman Levine. He believed that form and content should be indivisible because "the way something is being said *is* what is being said." Alice Munro, whom he championed even before she had published her first book, has said of him, "Praise from him, you feel, is real gold ... He will be kind and loyal and affectionate, but he won't tell you he likes your writing if he doesn't. I have the feeling that he is one person who can tell where the soft spots are, where the words are pasted over the cracks, can tell what's fake, what's shoddy, what's an evasion, maybe even mark the place where a loss of faith hit you."

I knew he had his blind spots—especially about confessional poetry—but which critic doesn't?

Many years later, in reviewing *An Aesthetic Underground* for *Books in Canada*, I wrote:

If hanging, drawing, and quartering were a punishment available to the most fervent Canadian nationalists, John Metcalf would probably be first on the executioner's list. Whether it is the assorted buffooneries of the school system and departments of education or the Canada Council and the major publishing houses, whether it is yesteryear's overrated literary lions or today's pop stars of CanLit, whether it is slavering celebrity journalists or pompous academic hacks, Metcalf makes all flinch. I have known rational men of respectable education to turn apoplectic with rage at the mere mention of his name, and I suspect that many of his critics equate the deadly strength of his venom with the nefarious effects of SARS or mad-cow disease.

Metcalf did turn his barrels on me, though I did not know this until years later, long after I had shoved aside academia and battles of the books. When I read his long-winded Foreword in *Light Shining Out of Darkness: And Other Stories* (Biblioasis, 2018), I was surprised that anti-academic Metcalf now imitated the fervid polemicists he had so often decried. Eschewing Hood's own explicit remarks on secular analogy, allegory, and emblem, he lumped my interpretations of "Flying a Red Kite" and "Fallings from Us, Vanishings" in a category he branded "bizarre, if not flatly comic." But what was particularly bizarre was his deliberate act of reading *against* Hood's express emblematic intent. He even seemed to have forgotten some of his own remarks about Hood's intentions to reinvent allegory and "invent new shapes for his stories, shapes unlike what had become the traditional shapes of 'modernism'." John pointed out that the "'new shapes' turned out to be very old shapes, refurbished shapes where 'realism' was almost beside the point." I had spelled out Hugh's literary quality: "From the beginning, then, Hood's sensibility was emblematic, and it tempered a classical sense of order and form with a romantic sense of mystery and wonder."

John quoted Hugh on the "Flying a Red Kite" story, *while*

disbelieving him, refusing Hood's representation of "the flying red thing" (the red kite) as "a reference to the Pentecostal tongues of fire which descended on the Apostles," and which "pulled the story into a very expressive formal design." John commented: "Only a clairvoyant could have seen 'the flying red thing' as Pentecostal tongues of fire and I'm not sure what tongues of fire pulling the story 'into a very expressive formal design' *means*. Bill Keith wryly commented that kites go up and Pentecostal tongues descend." Well, Keith was partly right—but only partly, because these tongues have a special connotation, quite apart from the physics of ascent and descent. Hugh Hood meant to point to a new way or articulating or expressing the spirit, which is precisely the point of the Pentecostal tongues of fire. But John was simply having none of it: "Only Hugh could have imagined a kite as Pentecostal tongues. Similarly, I still remember his sheer *astonishment* that I had not *immediately* grasped that the three grocers in 'The Fruit Man, the Meat Man, and the Manager' represented the persons of the Holy Trinity." Sometimes irony can rebound. John should have known that, when dealing with Hugh's short stories, the merger of symbolism and naturalism is a dynamic feature. I am an agnostic (having renounced my Catholicism many decades ago, long before I published anything on Hood), and John, I am guessing, is possibly irreligious, but our religious scepticism should have little or no bearing on our respective interpretations of Hugh Hood. While I'll stand by my interpretation, I will not allow this literary quarrel with John to alter my opinion of him as an excellent short story writer and an extremely careful, witty editor who has done far more for the cause of Canadian Literature than most of our university professors combined.

Almost twenty years after our last conversation by phone or epistolary exchange, I suddenly had the urge to call him on September 19, 2020, though unaware of the circumstances of his life and career at this point. He was five years my senior and had done marvellous work for Porcupine's Quill and Biblioasis, winning awards for his expert editing, culminating in his investiture as Member of the Order of Canada in 2005. But would he even remember me? He did. It was almost as if the long gap in our communication closed immediately, our mutual delight in repartee bubbling over the phone, the lacuna of time melting away or not mattering.

"What is the new book you have been working on, John?"

"*Temerity and Gall,*" he said, chuckling wickedly, exploiting the phrase cranky ultra-nationalist Robin Matthews had hurled at him, a damnable Brit, for daring to criticize Canadian writers.

I look forward to receiving future letters in black ink on yellow paper from him because "John doesn't do email," as his wife Myrna declared.

CHAPTER SEVEN

THEATRICAL FRIENDSHIPS

Technically adept at lying on stage, actors lie offstage with ease, and I react with special loathing to feigned friendship. Perhaps, too, they have learned to distrust critics, fearing that some inner vulnerability might be exposed nakedly and cruelly. Acclaimed English actor Michael Gambon once remarked of his colleagues, "Actors are show-offs, big-headed bastards, egomaniacs." I could not generally disagree.

Leaving aside Joan Heney (with whom I had an amorous relationship decades ago, and who remains a great friend), I count only two actors and one actress—William Hutt, Heath Lamberts, and Nonnie Griffin—as my most significant friends. Although each had a monumental ego, each had an inner vulnerability hidden beneath a façade of some sort of audacity, unorthodoxy, or rebelliousness. I was privileged to be a trusted confidant when they needed to unburden themselves of certain anxieties. I produced three books on Hutt, a lengthy, substantial interview with Lamberts, and wrote articles on Nonnie Griffin before performing excerpts from Shakespeare, Wilde, and Neil Simon opposite her at art soirees.

I have said all I really need to say about Hutt as an artist in *William Hutt: Soldier Actor*. Not as naturally gifted as Christopher Plummer, not as versatile or internationally renowned, Hutt was our true Northern Star. His personality was called everything from "pompous, arrogant, and strangely contradictory," to "warm, generous, witty, and caring." He had a strong ceremonious self-importance, and an ego that had all the colours of a peacock. Whatever his flaws as a person, his towering talent was matched by undisputed generosity, a point that *Soldier Actor* makes eminently clear. I now offer select diary entries about Hutt as examples, many dating back to the year my first biography of Hutt (*William Hutt: A Theatre Portrait*) was published by Mosaic Press. I have selected sequences that reveal several of Hutt's anomalies. Manners make the man, and oh, what manners, what a man! The excerpts also reveal the complex, difficult journey a biographer has to make with a "live" subject. (An annotation: Matt in the entries is none other than Matt Mackey, Hutt's loyal, loving companion, caregiver, confidant.)

> March 5, 1988: A bright drive down to Stratford. Was greeted at 4 Waterloo North by Liz—Matt's girlfriend—who looked healthy and happy. Bill came downstairs, beaming at me warmly. He looked fit—a bit paunchy—and led me to the dining-room table ... Bill was the soul of amiability, and we had a long, fruitful session on my manuscript. Although he forewarned me that certain things would be painful to me, there was nothing I could call unpleasant or difficult about his demands for alterations or cuts—many were things I had wanted to do myself. I was a little apprehensive about his remarks regarding the Matt section ("This is the only thing I want said about Matt in the entire book!"), but he delivered a tender testimonial to his companion that is touching in its frank love.
>
> We worked for five hours—excluding the odd minute or so for telephone calls or trips to the 'loo.'

> March 6: Another long, fruitful session with Bill—this one five and a half hours long. We've ironed out all the problems, and Bill has proved surprisingly agreeable. He even persuaded Matt to consider changes that would not embarrass him about revelations regarding their relationship. Matt joined us in

some of our discussion and then went off to rewrite a compressed version of the circumstances that brought him into Hutt's home.

Bill spoke at length about Larry Aubrey, Blaine Parker, and assorted topics. He's still mad as hell about Aubrey, and does not want his name mentioned at all in the manuscript. When I said that Aubrey also wished to remain anonymous, Bill cracked: 'In that case, publish his name but misspell it!'

He has not forgiven Parker for undermining his contribution at Theatre London. Portrays him as an opportunist who calls only when he wants a favour.

(Bill forgave Aubrey eventually, and the two had a very congenial friendship that endured till Bill's death. Parker remained beyond Bill's forgiveness.)

April 7: His ego is his complexity. It feeds his genius, protects his vulnerability, contaminates his sweetness, alienates him from many others, distorts his perceptions of reality. He is not quite the big star he thinks he is—though he may well be a greater actor than I sometimes think he is.

June 10: ... had a rather dim message that a Ms. Moffatt of Actors' Equity had called to say that according to Hutt, all solo shots would have to be paid for, but that all cheques should be made out to the author! I was flabbergasted—even more so when I reached [Dan] Ladell and he repeated this information. 'It's a lovely gesture,' he remarked.

A mixture of astonishment, confusion, gratitude, and love in my soul.

June 13: Shortly after Equity confirmed Hutt's generous offer to waive his fees in my favour, Bill's letter (dated June 10) reached me. In addition to being a warm message, it was stunningly generous—confirming one of the best sides of the man: 'I have always realized and gratefully acknowledged the touching admiration with which you write of me, and have fully respected your intent that the biography will, as you put it, "do me honour"—but I have no intention of accepting monies (especially from what should come to you) to prove my point.' Then, after outlining the chief Equity regulations re. photos, he adds: 'I do not waive any fees owing to me and have instructed Equity to that effect—adding that I want Equity, on my instructions and with their backing to see that Mosaic Press pay all monies owing to me from the use of photos DIRECTLY TO YOU AND FOR YOUR USE ONLY. In short, I waive the fees in your favour—I want you to have the money—I want none ... and that, my dear Keith, is my final word.'...

Looking back over some of my diary entries on Bill, I feel guilty of excessive choler and hyperbole. Just how much was real egomania and how much a mask for his true concerns? It becomes increasingly clear that we have both, at times, misjudged each other and been affronted by imagined things. Deep down there is mutual affection and regard—and on his part real generosity which can be stunning in its abrupt, dramatic, unforeseen manifestation.

June 27: Bill is satisfied that I will keep an eagle eye on galleys. 'I hope the book will be a success for you,' he declared. 'I hope so, too—and not just for my sake or yours, but because it could open a path for more theatre books—which is just what this country needs.'

June 30: Made a photocopy of Hutt's first letter to Aster on March 9—simply because it documents Bill's true opinion of my writing: 'Keith is an articulate writer and a perceptive pungent drama critic. His manuscript on myself is not necessarily the story I would tell if I were writing an autobiography—but then few, if any of us can see ourselves the way others see us!!' Fair enough and, at last, a real recognition that Bill's problem with the book was based on his self-perception.

August 18, 1989: Took Bill for drinks after the *Trelawny* to the Prince of Wales ... There was a lunar eclipse—a beautiful silver moon—and heads turned as soon as Bill and I entered the lounge. Bill, true to form, downed double vodka martinis on the rocks, while I, wishing to maintain my head, kept to singles. Bill revelled in the couples who came up to pay respects and homage, but our conversation was unimpeded ... We staggered out after 1.30 a.m.—the last patrons—or should I say that Bill staggered literally while I kept a close, proprietary watch on him. Before he crossed the street to his car, he unbuttoned his shirt and parodied Deborah Kerr's line to John Kerr in *Tea and Sympathy*: 'When you remember this night, be kind!'"

"The essence of being a Canadian actor is the fact of being mistaken for somebody else!" joked Richard Monette, who had the longest tenure of any artistic director of the Stratford Festival. Hutt was sometimes confused with William Hurt, the American film actor—much to Hutt's displeasure. He liked to receive adulation and he liked to be thought unique. He once complained to veteran critic Herbert Whittaker, "This country lacks the audacity to adore." He liked reading reviews of his own work, and he liked to know what others thought of him. At home, he liked to sit in a large peacock rattan chair, sip his deadly vodka martinis, and gossip with colourful anecdotes or wicked epigrams around diverse topics. As a devotee and expert mimic of Noel Coward, he loved wit and could not help being witty, though the range of his humour spanned the light and sweet (about those he liked) as well as the dark, bitter, and acerbic (about those he disliked). As he cracked a joke, he would watch carefully to note any reaction to his quip. His manner reminded me of Laurence Olivier, of whom Peter Brook remarked that "even his laughter was acted, as though he never ceased remaking and polishing his mask."

Though I enjoyed his wit and hospitality, I was cautious about his apparent openness. Were his feelings true or merely feigned? Was he putting on a performance for my benefit? He was a man of many secrets, and while he seemed to be open, he was quite possibly organizing his secrets to guard one against another. He was an extraordinarily generous host, but cunningly self-serving in his reluctance to share the full range of intimate correspondence he had with family, friends, and ex-lovers. He allowed me access to his wartime diary and field journal, but never to private diaries (if these existed) or daybooks. Although never priggish, he was discreet about his sex life, and always seemed to be looking over my shoulder as I developed his biography. Though I was never part of his inner circle of friends, he confided in me more than he had ever done with another writer, apart from his beloved friend Timothy Findley. When he spoke of his parents, his conflicted relationship with his older brother, and his participation in World War II, his face became a map of intimate emotions. There was nothing fake about such moments.

However, he did turn apprehensive prior to the publication of my first biography of him in 1988. Director Peter Moss recounts: "When we were in London rehearsing *The Man Who Came to Dinner*, he was very nervous, but we said, 'Bill, after Liberace and Rock Hudson, you have nothing to worry about.'" At the end of our formal discussions about alterations or cuts, he served tea in a silver teapot on a silver tray, then walked me to the front door, where he sighed, "You know, Keith, the wonderful thing about this is that I won't ever have to talk to you again." Then he exploded into laughter.

When *William Hutt: A Theatre Portrait* was published, he sent me a handwritten letter of thanks, apologizing for the roadblocks he had erected in my path after he had developed cold feet:

In retrospect, Keith, I suppose that my reservations were not so much about revelations of my life which I would like to have kept to myself (much as I realize that a 'bio' has to be revelatory in some areas)—but the simple fact that once the project was under way and I actually began to *read* about William Hutt, I somehow resented the 'invasion of privacy' because you know that basically I am a very private person. This in *no way* is to be interpreted as accusing *you* of the 'invasion,' since had I not wanted to be invaded, I would never have allowed the process to begin at all.

Here was recognition that a biographer is a voyeur and eavesdropper.

Almost impossible not to love such a person, an actor to the core, egotistical, vain, a bundle of anomalies (aren't we all?), the soul of generosity to many, and a man who brought life to art and art to life. I thought highly enough of Hutt to produce three books on him— two biographies and a book of tributes in honour of his 75th birthday. In the course of interviewing Dawn Greenhalgh for *William Hutt: Soldier Actor*, the actress asked: "Were you in love with William Hutt?" "No," I replied in a flash. "I was in love with his talent."

I did not hear of his death on June 27, 2007 until I played a voice mail message from the CBC, requesting me to call back. When I did, I was informed I was too late because the station had already gone with commentary from another theatre critic. A huge career bejewelled with rare honours and distinctions was unworthy of more praise outside the CBC's narrow time slot for a noteworthy newsflash. So little for so much greatness.

Hutt had planned his own elaborate funeral service which was held at St. James Anglican Church, Stratford, on a sweltering day in July. The speakers were mainly family relatives and members of the Stratford Company, and the occasion was memorable, but so was the interment service two years later at Avondale Cemetery on June 27, 2009. The tombstone was a massive white dolomite, over eight feet high, resting on a thick concrete foundation. A rectangular plaque of black marble (from India) bore the memorial inscription, with two engraved Shakespearean quotations. As my mind moved in the relative hush of the gravesite scene, I thought of his enormously supple voice—Hutt had been very lucky in that it had been nature's gift to him. But now it was gone, and that loss seemed cruel, though I would always carry its imprint in my mind. I thought of the various William Hutts: the solemn hero, the farceur, the prankster on tours, the uproarious mimic, the vain lead actor, the warm and generous ensemble player, the shy Bill, the flamboyant show-off, the vulgar clown, the bitter forgotten star, the feminine Dame Hutt (especially when he posed hands on hips in his kitchen as he worried about a baked salmon with fresh dill), the very masculine, lordly, and intimidating Mr. Hutt, the conflicted son and brother, and the courageous pathfinder. The images flooded my mind as the sun beat down from a quiet sky.

The Reverends Lorne and Lynn Mitchell used the *Book of Alternative Services* for the ceremony, including a recitation of Psalm 121; but when Reverend Lorne asked if there were any who wished to speak in commemoration of Hutt, an awkward silence descended. What was there left to say? My mind dwelled on the words "Soldier—Actor" on his massive monument: two words that summarized a long, distinguished life and service. Two words that compressed wholly separate worlds, yet both words somehow intersecting within the miracle of a great actor who had allowed his experience as a soldier to enrich his craft as an actor.

However, he never allowed his military service to push itself to the forefront of his life after the war. He was typical of those heroes who had experienced so much horror that they subsequently boxed up their feelings. They actually hated war, equating it with ignominy, inhumanity, and death, and Hutt was of their number. When Michael Therriault asked Hutt if he would see the hit film *Saving Private Ryan*, he replied: "No, no, no. I've seen enough of that. I don't need to go back to that." In all my conversations with him about the war, he never romanticized or enlarged his own exploits. He had looked on the life of the actor as another kind of national service, a bond with the culture of his nation.

As I summed up decades later in *William Hutt: Soldier Actor*:

The country did offer him many rewards in the form of honours and titles, but a case could be made that he was too big for his time and culture ... No matter: he will be remembered for as long as there is cultural memory because he kept all his appointments with duty or service for the nation, ascended the brightest heaven of invention, and signed his name with imperishable honour on the vivid air.

Heath Lamberts was another genius, whom I befriended in Niagara-on-the-Lake where he was packing theatres with fans madly in love with his comic skills. A premier farceur who ricocheted off walls and furniture, zipped in and out of doors, revelled as Gunga Heath in a tour de force one-man comic anthology, and reached an artistic summit as broken-hearted and heart-breaking Cyrano de Bergerac, he occasionally infuriated rivals and directors by occasionally breaking through the imaginary fourth wall to engage in repartee with an audience. Born James Langcaster in Toronto in 1941 to working-class parents (his father was a labourer; his mother a department-store employee), he loved singing for audiences at home and at parties. He loved the applause and laughing faces. Church choirs, rituals, and liturgical vestments stimulated his senses, and at one High Anglican celebration where he was part of a procession, he dragged himself around like Richard III. Bored with school, his school gave up on him, its principal advising him dismissively: "If you want to go, go! Go and you can sell fish in Kensington Market. You're good for nothing else." It wasn't the first time a school could be wrong-headed. Even the National Theatre School in Montreal hardly knew what to do with him. He was already practising the dictum: "Laugh and you are free." Ironically, his excruciating self-consciousness, physical awkwardness, and antagonism toward his father made him feel separated from his family and sometimes even from the world. He once confessed to me: "We try to heal this in many ways. Neurosis can develop out of it, and it's a matter of a lifetime's spending time trying to get home. By 'home' I mean to be at peace with yourself."

He turned to Buddhism to find inner tranquillity, learning to accept the cosmic scheme of things. His true home was, of course, the stage, where he made his chubby, puff-pastry face, and dumpling nose create a doughy benignity. His physiognomy seemed more suited to custard-pie comedy than to sophisticated farce or artful satire, and yet, he was magically plastic on stage. He could propel himself on busy feet, his eyes enflamed by some inner mischief, his mouth caught in its own pantomime, and his hands playing charades on themes of timorousness, anxiety, and narcissism. As Monsieur Jourdain in Moliere's *The Bourgeois Gentleman*, he was not simply a foolish tradesman deserving of a pratfall or public humiliation, but a human being with tight shoes, runs in his stockings, and a heart that was much bigger than his mind. He was the child eternally seduced by fantasy, a fool bubbling with faults but also one who was endearingly vulnerable. He was the Jourdain for our time—the Jourdain in everyone who wants to be on par with his betters, the Jourdain who is bound to be found out as an overly romantic self-deluder, the masquerading child trapped in the awkward body of a pretentious social-climber.

Plasticity is often what defines physical clowning, and it is one of the many things that Lamberts had in abundance. When he essayed a minuet, he went up on his toes, but his heels and elbows were so out of joint that he seemed to be a moving compendium of disparate limbs. He skittered, slid, tripped, and lurched, but kept enjoying the attempt and energy of his own dancing. In his fencing lesson, his heels locked together and his torso bent perilously off centre, putting his entire body at risk of collapse. Plasticity extended even to his voice. He stretched his mouth, pulling on his lips, and the breath came out as a whine or gasp. His lesson in vowels and consonants degenerated into atonal dissonance.

I tried to convince him to play Falstaff, but he resisted, claiming that he was not a natural fit for Shakespeare. He did not mean just the matter of physique, because whatever he lacked in height, he more than made up for in comic weight. Lamberts certainly had expert facility with farce, and he could easily manage the down-at-the-heel dignity of a recklessly energetic corrupter. As he showed amply in his Cyrano, he could be spry, elastic, wise, noble, melancholy, and heart-breaking, even as he made an audience laugh with him. Not blessed with a handsome physique, his Cyrano lacked the sort of physical glamour that distinguished the Cyranos of Christopher Plummer and Derek Jacobi. Heath showed Cyrano's soul under what Anthony Sher called "the casual dress of flesh." I was certain that Heath's Falstaff would be not just an overgrown, aging, corrupt jokester, but immensely pathetic: Heath would vividly register Falstaff's devasta-tion at Hal's rejection, and in so doing, would reveal the hubristic pride within the corporeal mass of wild comedy. Perhaps, he feared that not being an actor for whom eloquent rhetoric was a cachet, he would not handle the fat rogue's monologues well enough to please old-fashioned critics or English directors such as Robin Phillips, one of a distinct minority who disapproved of the actor's Cyrano, fault-ing it because he deemed it badly-spoken, and dismissing the per-formance with, "I couldn't hear the verse, and would wonder from time to time, was that a line of poetry that just passed by?"

Lamberts had hordes of fans, but he made numerous profes-sional enemies because of his own driven urge for perfection that made him seem extravagantly egotistical at times. He remarked to me, "If you can be the vehicle to put yourself in the hands of God, to be the act of God itself, then this is not an assumption. When you abdicate your ego to the service of God then you find that God is in your heart, so that whatever you're doing is actually an expression of God." It was his custom to bow in humble silence to the theatre while leaving it after a performance as an expression of respect and gratitude to the place of his vocation. However, this humility did not negate an ambition to be perfect on stage.

Some theatre gossip concerning his egotism was justified; much was not. His special genius needed extra space to flourish, and many peers found this to be unacceptable, especially as he was wont to mutter directions under his breath while acting. He confessed to having gone through bouts of heavy drinking and neurotic discon-tent. "Collectively and individually, we can live in such a state of fear that it can make us greedy. When I become greedy, I can justify any behaviour in order to get whatever I think can satisfy my instincts." His Buddhism was a way of making peace with himself. Offstage, he was very sweet to my son Michael, whose active imagination was in full throttle at the time, spurring Michael to mimic everyone from Bible-thumping televangelists to his own father's accent. Michael had seen Heath play four roles in *One for the Pot*, and relished the spectacle of Heath multiplying himself without ever blurring identities or missing a wild entrance or exit. Heath bought books for Michael, gave him a prosthetic nose he had worn as Cyrano, and invited him to a film set in Toronto (which my son was too shy to accept). His generosity extended to me, too, as when he treated me to lunch at Sardi's in New York when we re-established communication after a lapse of several years, and then gifted me orchestra tickets to see Ralph Fiennes's Hamlet.

Even when I engaged him in serious chats, his comic side could not be obscured—as when he revealed one of the lessons he had learned about the illusion of fame and celebrity. During his Royal Alexandra engagement as Cyrano, he was feted by Ed Mirvish in the company of Eartha Kitt and Barbara Rush. Honest Ed requested an autographed photo of Lamberts for wife Ann, and Heath responded in silver ink on a large black and white glossy. Only to discover in a later season that this photo with its personalized message to Ann had been nailed to the wall above a Fruit-of-the-Loom underwear bin!

Heath was forced to move to the States after finding it almost impossible to get work in Canada. But he got to play roles no Canadian theatre would ever offer him. Canada clearly did not know how to handle his genius, but the United States did—as that country has shown numerous times when some of our best theatre talent has migrated there.

He died too soon. But even as he suffered incredible pain from cancer, he didn't complain of his affliction. He didn't tell me in our final brief exchange of emails that he was dying. I heard about his death only when I happened on an obituary notice in a Canadian newspaper. Alas, it contained vitriol from Christopher Newton, famed Artistic Director of the Shaw Festival, who had claimed to have made Lamberts a star and who sounded off on Lamberts' egotistical misconduct. Newton was certainly entitled to his opinion, but it was indisputably the wrong time to make it because it disrespected a family's mourning.

It seemed as if Canada cannot abide real genius when it dares to intrude on art and life. But genius does not intrude on anything. It enlarges both art and life.

Nonnie Griffin (born Lorna Margaret Jean) also found it difficult to get work in Canada, after her struggles with alcoholism and her imperious sense of artistic excellence. Her diary-memoir, *Showbiz and other addictions*, is a genuine classic of theatrical and existential triumph over loss, unhappiness, and pain. Alas, it was published by Mosaic Press, so the book never gained the importance it deserved. After she read a few of my Broadway production histories and my first biography of William Hutt, she became a fan—or, to put it more accurately, we became each other's fans. She was delighted to learn that I knew her name and had, in fact, seen her perform on stage, though I had not experienced her highly praised radio work or voice-overs. Her voice was her fortune in many ways because she was able to change accent, register, tone, and pitch with great facility. Citing the late John Drainie as evidence, she asserted that voice was the basis of acting because it issued not just from the actor's mouth or throat but from the soul, as it were. She had the ability to sum up a character by voice alone, and her oral genius is what made her something of a radio legend.

Although not a tall lady, she was a definite presence on stage and in any social gathering because of her glamorous face, wavy brown hair, sparkling blue eyes, strong bone structure, immense charm and warmth, an enviable facility with mimicry, and a healthy appetite for humour. She also had a hearty appetite for food but always turned down any form of alcohol because she was a recovering alcoholic. She could easily mimic accents, multiplying comedy with malaprops

("He spent many years working on a caboose in Israel"), or adding a whistle to where a lisp might do, as in her imitation of one of Carol Channing's famous comic routines. I can still hear her peals of laughter at parties, where she always wanted to perform, not simply to be the centre of attention but because she genuinely wanted to spread good cheer and be the life of the party. Perhaps, too, party pieces were her way of being seen and heard again as an actress, given that she no longer had solid acting jobs at any establishment theatre. A headline for her diary entry of January 26, 1977 reads: "Actress's Life—No Work, No Money." A hard lesson, but she was never one to give up her inner flame. She turned to writing her own plays, creating leading roles for herself, and appeared at the Edinburgh Fringe Festival and the Spring Works Festival at Stratford. And she never let false pride get in the way of work, wherever it turned up— which it did mainly in television commercials. "You have to be a very good actor to do commercials," she contended. "At the audition, you have one shot. It's fun and pays quite well." Once chastised by a friend for doing a bra commercial beneath the dignity of a classical actress, she shot back, "Are you going to pay my mortgage? I have a lovely house, but nobody handed it to me!"

Nonnie's great grandfather was Sir William Mackenzie, builder of the Canadian National Railroad, but her family fortune was lost during the war. She grew up in a large Catholic household teeming with siblings. Music, singing, and poetry kept them going, she used to claim, but there was a shadow of tragedy when a brother committed suicide at 25, a consequence of suspected sexual abuse in the Jesuit seminary he had joined. She wrote *The Piper's Son* about him, a sensitive memorial somewhat marred by her failure to probe the deeper, darker corners of the tragedy. Her deep-rooted Catholicism also served as a self-censoring filter in *Sister Annunciata's Secret,* a much later play, also about sexual sin, though her performance in what was, in fact, a solo show with her playing multiple roles, brought her acclaim from Toronto to Edinburgh.

She thought the world of my theatre writing, praising me for my ability to bring a production or performance alive on the printed page, and for my biographies of Hutt that focussed on the actor's perspectives on art and life. She also liked how I wrote and spoke my poetry, often addressing me as "Poet," and enthusiastically suggested that we perform scenes from plays together at parties or art soirees. I could feel the electricity we generated together as we enacted scenes from *Macbeth* at a soiree in a private home, our audience thrilled by the dramatic intensity we achieved. This "partnership" worked well, unless I drew more laughs than she did in comedy—as I did in a scene from Neil Simon's *California Suite*, playing the wryly under-stated husband of an egotistical actress. Nonnie never sought to imitate Maggie Smith's nasal interpretation of the same role, but realizing that my dry underplaying was earning more laughter than her emphatic comic exaggerations, she remarked: "Well, we don't need to do this one again."

I often felt privileged being in her company, sharing time with her at her comfortable cottage in Scarborough, at my condo apartment in Mississauga, or as a theatre companion. At shows, she was never shy to react spontaneously by laughing uproariously when something was truly comic or applauding a good performance at the end. It was her way of lending support unabashedly. Off stage, she allowed ego and an abiding sense of entitlement to blind her in friendships. She made friends easily, but she didn't always judge friendships well, leading to bitterness on the parts of those she had carelessly taken too much for granted. This was, sadly, how her friendship with Fern Densem (a most generous supporter financially and socially) ended, and why *froideur* descended on our friendship.

Nonnie had her favourites and villains in the theatre. Although she was never one to let her own ego be quelled, she could be utterly generous when she really believed someone had talent. Meryl Streep was one of her favourite contemporary actresses (but not, for some vague reason, Cate Blanchett), and Nonnie agreed with me about the incomparable genius of Vivien Leigh and Vanessa Redgrave, just as Olivier, Hutt, and Plummer drew her greatest praise on the male side. Problem was she could sometimes allow nostalgia to colour her professional relationships, solidifying her biases and refusing to accept direction from those she considered inferior or not fully up to her mark. She had worked with Hutt in his early years and quickly recognized his innate talent, as well as his vulnerability. She also worked once with Heath Lamberts in an English farce about acting farce, and recorded this in a diary entry, March 1987: "I've heard what a difficult customer Heath can be and I hope I can manage without wanting to kill him. Already he's giving me hints and directions about what to do with the part. Pardon me, Mr. whatever your name is. I'm a seasoned professional and could tell *you* a thing or two!" She was never one to bite her tongue.

She kept the performing flame burning with special fervour into her 80s. Having experienced ill-fated relationships in love, she transcended her feelings of inner loneliness by an extroversion that was infectious. Age didn't seem to wither her enthusiasm the least bit. She bravely brought Marilyn Monroe back to life in a one-act play of her own making (*Marilyn—After!*), and there were moments when audiences believed they were seeing and hearing a reincarnation of the silver screen's sex goddess. Although her stage acting was old-school in technique, she could be stunningly effective, particularly in solo poetry recitals, as she showed when she recited Tennyson's "The Lady of Shalott" for a fund-raiser in Toronto. Because of her never-dwindling enthusiasm for performing, she often seemed the youngest person in the room or audience. Generally robust, she did have a warning sign in 2018, when she had to spend a week in hospital over damage to her aorta. She did not allow this setback to get her down, however, and she was deep into plans for yet another show, *Before Scarlett*, in which she was supposed to be Margaret Mitchell, author of *Gone with The Wind*. She went out bravely and calmly in June 2019, owing to an aortic aneurysm, after refusing to be kept alive with machines, comforted by family and friends who had the privilege of visiting her bedside.

The memorial service on June 27, 2019 at Jubilee United Church, 40 Underhill Drive, North York, was on a day filled with sunshine. A framed photograph of Nonnie was prominently displayed, and a video of clips and stills played on a ceaseless loop as celebrants gathered inside the big hall. Nonnie had always been a Catholic of deep spiritual conviction, but she had had a special fondness for Jubilee United because it was welcoming of all people, no matter their religious differences or sexual preferences, and Reverend Norm Seli had ministered to her in moments of personal need. The gathering was not large, with most attendants being family and close friends. There were only two professional actors I counted, Derek Boyes and his actress-wife Arlene Mazerolle, who had been close to her, though even they confided that they had found her ego to be a problem at times. The memorial program included a stirring bagpipe lament (played by soloist Patrick McDonald) for the processional, in which Nonnie's ashes were carried to the table where a single white candle stood like a silent sentinel beside her framed photograph. Two exquisite floral bouquets set off the small box of ashes, the candle, and the photograph. There were psalms and hymns, prayers and memories. Music and more music. Classically trained bass singer Michael Rogers performed two solos (one being the gospel favourite "Swing Low, Sweet Chariot"), and Nonnie's niece Jennifer Griffin sang "Over the Rainbow." I felt transported to my own private place of heart-stirring gratitude for the memories. Nonnie was uniquely unforgettable.

Unlike the vast majority of actors and actresses I have known, Griffin, Hutt, and Lamberts had wide areas of interest, though their deepest interest was always in people, usually people of some estimable talent. Aware of their own human vulnerabilities, they had empathy for other vulnerable figures. Hutt, Lamberts, and Griffin, three creatures of theatre with immense egos, talents, and acts of generosity. All whom I felt privileged to know on and off the stage. All dearly missed, though their shadows remain immortal.

I have never canvassed my fellow-critics on the matter of fan-letters, but I have written a few. It is not a habitual thing because if it were, it would be damnably cheap. Genius is rare, and so are my epistolary tributes. However, there are times when I feel compelled to make them. One such instance occurred in August 1993, after I had seen Brent Carver playing Molina (the gay window-dresser) in the musical version of *Kiss of the Spider Woman* at the Broadhurst Theatre on Broadway. I had already seen Brent's extraordinary performance during the Toronto run, but on Broadway, it seemed to have reached the highest level of inspiration and genius—larger and more flamboyant than it had been earlier. "How does it feel to be a legend in your own time?" I asked him in his dressing room. He hugged me warmly, but I had to cut short the visit because he had two shows ahead of him the next day and hordes of fans awaiting him outside the Stage Door. Meeting producer Garth Drabinsky, I remarked, "I hope you're paying him buckets because he's worth every penny." Brent's performance ranked with Colm Wilkinson's in *Phantom of the Opera* and B.D. Wong's in *M. Butterfly*, and I sent him a letter from Toronto, putting in words what I didn't say to him backstage at the Broadhurst. Brent replied with a handwritten card, dated August 26, 1993:

Dear Keith:

I am humbled by and in awe of the beauty of your gracious letter. I will ever hold it dear to me and my experience with this show. You have given my work some invaluable light. I thank you for giving of your talents, your generous observations, and positive ideas of what this fragile world of artistry is about; of what we must continually strive for and believe in. I am so grateful to be a part, some small part of that world, from time to time.

I wish you all goodness.

I hope to express my sincere gratitude to you, in person, some day soon.

With warm regards
Respectfully
Brent C.

This card sums up Brent's sweet nature and his modesty as an actor. Alas, he passed on August 4, 2020, his career no longer emblazoned by the sorts of roles he had once played to the hilt. The Stratford Festival had cast him in relatively small roles in recent years. And I wonder if he ever regretted turning down lucrative offers from Broadway, where Hal Prince had become one of his greatest champions.

Another fan letter I composed may never have reached the object of my admiration. The occasion was an October evening in Manhattan, 1989, at the Neil Simon Theatre for a performance of *Orpheus Descending*. A generally bad production by Peter Hall, overwrought, wildly mixing expressionism with film noir technique, unevenly cast, but with a staggering central performance by Vanessa Redgrave as Lady. Not a Deep South small-town wife, but an Old-World Italian, full of fire, humour, and desperate longing. What I got was a performance that transcended all questions of accents and technique. She was powerful, rapid, deep, delicate, bruised, and moving. Worthy of the huge standing ovation that greeted her at the end. I had left a brief scrawled message for Tammy Grimes (who was Vee Talbott in the production, and whom I had interviewed for my 1988 Hutt biography), to which Tammy had responded: "Dear Keith—Bravo— give that great actor Hutt my love. I don't know what Vanessa's up to but come to me first. Best best, Tammy Grimes." I made pleasantly innocuous conversation with Tammy in her dressing room, before she (sensing my eagerness to meet Vanessa) led me on her bare feet to Redgrave's room. The door was open, so I was able to overhear Vanessa say to Sigourney Weaver, "You must tell me if it was too much." Weaver nodded it wasn't, at which point Tammy introduced me to Vanessa as a Canadian critic who had just published a biography of William Hutt. I could plainly tell that Vanessa hadn't a clue about Hutt, but Sigourney Weaver, strikingly tall and beautiful, turned to me and remarked, "Oh, William Hutt, he's such a wonderful actor!" I responded rather awkwardly: "Oh, I like your work, too, Miss Weaver," before paying a gushing compliment to the real object of my devotion, who autographed my program. I left, my beating heart as big as Manhattan, my soul magnified by what I had witnessed on stage.

I found a good eatery where I ate and drank profusely, as if some unearthly appetite had been provoked, and having an extraordinary urge to commemorate the night, I composed an untidy, three-page letter to Vanessa. I finished it at closing time (1 a.m.) and when I returned to the Pickwick Arms Hotel at East 51st, between 2nd and 3rd Avenues, I rewrote it as neatly as I could:

Dear Vanessa Redgrave,

Even with having met you briefly backstage (through the kind graces of Tammy Grimes), I cannot leave New York without writing you this unabashed, fawning letter. As a not-so-humble drama critic, I always feel humbled in the presence of greatness. And you, La Pasionaria of the stage, are indisputably, unequivocally, and gorgeously great.

As a boy with 'divided blood' in Bombay, I had my imagination and artistic sensibility first fired by Laurence Olivier who, apart from Shakespeare, was the only theatre idol I had. Olivier did more to re-create me—as an aspiring actor and forever a creature of the theatre—than almost any other being I could imagine. His acting was often a super-reality— an art so immense, so excitingly poetic, so sensuously beautiful, so imaginatively bold that it was about art itself.

And you, like him, can move me in any role you play. I have witnessed your artistry in film, on television, and, now, at long last, on stage.

I confess that when I re-read *Orpheus Descending*, I could not see how you could make the role of Lady your own. I knew, of course, that your imagination, power, and technique could find ways to the essence of the character, but I did not anticipate how you would present such a richly detailed portrait. Your Lady is vibrantly real—a creature whose sunny sensuality and hope are darkened by the pain from her shadow world. You make us feel the woman's painful losses and touching vulnerability, even as you make the blood bubble with your acid revenge. I cannot now imagine another actress who could hold this spotty production the way you do.

Your Lady is both young love lost with forlorn memories, and a dream that can't quite find its way. Your acting is a supreme test of an audience's complicity because you do not have a Val who is strong enough. Nor do you have a supporting cast able to establish the tone of ominous morbidity to counterbalance the more obvious black humour. And yet this is of little matter when you give us Lady's bone-dry orchard of hate and the wine-orchard of defiant, mocking, and audacious hope. And when you die with a grotesque kiss that seems to suck the very cosmos into your torn body, you seal this epiphanic moment by a shrug and a final dance of twitching limbs. The world of blow-torch cruelty and growling, bestial fury somehow seems a peripheral reality to the spectacle of your character's fate. You were like the exotic transparent bird spread wide in the high blue sky, only to be burned by the sun.

I left the theatre in ineffable excitement. I did not want the night to end. I wanted to share with someone, anyone, the kind of exhilaration that great art brings. As a critic, I am always greedy for genius—which I celebrate with the gratitude of one who feels blessed and born anew. You make an audience see, feel, and believe more than most mere mortals have the capacity to bear. I applaud you and I love you for your genius.

I left the letter at the Stage Door, but I am not at all certain whether Vanessa Redgrave ever received it. She was still *persona non grata* with many, especially rabidly partisan Jews who never forgave her for her denunciations of Israeli barbarity against Palestinians. In fact, I remember seeing in her dressing room a muscular security guard who looked Middle Eastern, so she must have still been receiving death threats.

When I read my son a copy of my letter, he remarked: "It sounds more like a love letter."

I agreed. Love for her brave genius.

CHAPTER EIGHT

FREELANCING

began my freelance writing career in July 1975, searching for book review commissions (usually paltry and often paying less than the minimum wage for workers at fast-food chains). I dutifully plowed through many deadly dull books without trying to make the reviews themselves sound like fast-food, by celebrating good books, but worrying about copy-editors who might misspell my surname. The very first book review I published in a local newspaper (*The Montreal Gazette*) did misspell that name, which was not a harbinger of good things. I was paid the grand sum of $30 for a short review of *Horse d'Oeuvres* by the Four Horsemen, but even the longer reviews did not earn me much more than this in the 70s. I earned $595.34 for fifteen pieces in the six months of my first year as freelance book reviewer, which averaged less than $40 a review. The next full year my freelance income jumped spectacularly to $1145 (for 27 reviews and a feature), and it took me another two years to break the $2000 mark—only because I wrote theatre reviews, three poems, two columns on LP recordings, and was paid an exceedingly small fee for permission to be quoted from one of my scholarly articles.

My richest years came much later, with earnings of $17,146 in 2003; $13,786 in 2005; $22,971 in 2009; $38,030 in 2011; and $33,000 in 2014. The last two bountiful years were only because of pay-outs from a 1996 class-action suit brought by freelancer Heather Robertson against the barons of The Thomson Corporation (now, the Thomson Reuters Corporation), Thomson Canada Limited (now, Thomson Reuters Canada Limited), Thomson Affiliates and Information Access Company (now, The Gale Group, Inc.) and Bell Globemedia Publishing Inc. (now, CTVglobemedia Publishing Inc.). Over 350 Canadian publications were cited in the case, including *The Globe and Mail*, *Maclean's*, *Chatelaine*, *Canadian Geographic*, *Toronto Life*, and *Saturday Night* magazine. The issue was unpaid compensation for digital use of reviews and features, and the upshot was an $11,000,000 settlement. Following deductions for professional fees and other court authorized distributions, the copyright settlement fund available to eligible writers amounted to roughly $5.5 million. The settlement stipulated that a writer could recover up to a maximum of 1% of this amount, which was estimated at $55,000.

"We are pleased to have achieved this settlement agreement and agree that it is a fair one," conceded Sue Gaudi, the Globe's vice-president general counsel. "It is primarily a historical matter from the days before *The Globe and Mail* entered into written contracts with our freelance contributors. We value our relationships with our freelancers and are happy to move on."

Corporate doublespeak. If she or her clients really felt that way, the lawsuit could have been settled promptly, without being dragged out till 2009.

That was then. As I write this chapter, it is August 2020, and not much has changed in the world of freelance book reviewing. A review of poetry in a respectable Canadian literary journal can fetch anywhere between $25 and $100 for at least 500–1000 words. Sometimes (a lot of "sometimes") there is no fee—though the reviewer can depend on a complimentary copy of the edition carrying his or her review. A book review for a national newspaper can bring in around $200–$250 a piece.

It is eminently clear that book reviewers are fortunate to find a place on the final lifeboat of the sinking ship of Canadian journalism. The prevailing ideology is Capitalism, the underlying credo is Profit. Newspaper advertising is expensive and, apart from the large publishing houses, few publishers could afford to run ads in the papers. The return on book sales is abominably low. And serious readers of newspaper Book pages are a tiny minority. Hence, the draconian slashing of space allotted to book reviews which are frequently no more than a paragraph of two (often sloppy) about a book that usually took over a year for the author to produce. And that is only if an author is lucky enough to get a print review. John Metcalf, who knows a thing or two about freelance writing, once asserted "Canada will not read you unless you are validated elsewhere."

Some newspaper Books editors cringe at the very thought of a sophisticated book review. During my Montreal years, after Sheila Fischman was appointed Books Editor at the *Montreal Star,* she invited me to lunch. A few years earlier, at some conference or workshop in Montreal, she had complimented me on my reviews, so she apparently appreciated my writing. However, the real purpose of her invitation was not to bestow additional praise. She did begin with a casual compliment, "You write well," following this with "But we are not the *New York Times*, you know." I bit my tongue, while thinking "Whoever would ever confuse you with the *New York Times*?" And that was the end of my freelance work for the *Montreal Star*—at least for the duration of Fischman's tainted tenure, during which she (celebrated as a French-to-English translator) gave French-Canadian writing primacy of place, much to the bitter resentment of major English Canadian authors. She did not have a long tenure.

Fischman was but one questionable luminary on a list of newspaper books editors. There were others who were more colourful. One such was John Richmond of the *Montreal Star,* an expatriate Brit who was once dubbed "more-British-than-Jeeves." Tall, with a mild stammer or hesitancy of speech, he showed a fondness for books by ex-Major Generals or Colonels (usually British), and his favourite buzz words were "rebarbative" and "non-rebarbative." I was invited to his office after I had pitched him my service as a reviewer. He was courteous, though tentative, almost reluctant in offering me a drink. "Oh, I don't suppose you could have a drink, given that you have to drive back to NDG." He hemmed, he hawed, and finally failed to offer me a commission, remaining true to his rigid British self.

Richmond's claim to fame rests on devastating satirical carica-
tures of him by John Metcalf and John Mills that reportedly rendered him apoplectic. His name no longer brings up appreciable
"hits" on Google search engines.

Doris Giller was quite a different kettle of fish. Her throaty,
boozy voice was the stuff of legend, rivalling the deep "mannish"
voices of Tallulah Bankhead and Lauren Bacall. She had the reputation of a hard-talking, hard-dealing, tough dame. "I used to think
Jaqueline Susann was the best fiction writer, when I was young," she
disclosed at one of our very brief meetings at her office. Whether she
meant to be slyly ironic or not, I believed her immediately. Nothing
she ever did editorially persuaded me to think her taste had changed
radically or that she was a deep lover of literature, despite the testi-
monials of close friends to the contrary. When she became Assistant
Books Editor at the *Toronto Star* and wrote a column called "Reading
Habits," she interviewed celebrities about their reading habits—
nothing to do with her own. The last time I saw her was at a theatre
opening-night in Toronto where we exchanged very brief pleasant-
ries. I asked her what she was doing of late and was startled to hear
that she was working on a film script. I resisted the temptation to do
a double-take in the manner of Marie Dressler in *Grand Hotel* when
Jean Harlow announces she's been reading a book.

After her unfortunate death from lung cancer five months after
her final column, her reputation increased. A *Toronto Life* article
claimed that she was an Auntie Mame because she was outspoken,
always ready with a one-liner, and frequently with a drink in hand.
Grief-stricken husband Jack showed his undying love of her by insti-
tuting the Giller Prize, with the largest purse for Canadian fiction
in all of Canada.

A far more modest figure but a much larger talent was Ken
Adachi, books editor at the *Toronto Star*. Though we were never
close friends, Ken supported my freelance work by passing along
many books for me to review. Perhaps he appreciated the struggle of
all freelance reviewers; perhaps (being Japanese-Canadian who had
been incarcerated in a wartime detention camp in British Columbia)

he understood the tensions in my own mixed-racial life. Ken's dark moustache and goatee combined with his elegance, courteousness, and soft-spoken manner made him seem mandarin. When he offered me a huge Iris Murdoch novel, challenging me with a rather narrow deadline, he suggested that I scan much of it. "You don't read every word, do you?" he asked. When I told him I did, he retorted: "Oh, you'll never do for newspaper work."

He was correct.

When ECW Press published *Carry on Bumping*, edited by John Metcalf, and in which I had a long review-article of Elspeth Cameron's controversial biography of Irving Layton, I was concerned that Ken might feel I was disloyal to him in my attack on the Establishment figures who had praised the biography with hyperbolic adjectives. Ken was named, but not dismissively. I had too much respect for him as editor and author of the remarkable book *The Enemy That Never Was* about wartime Japanese-Canadians humiliated and virtually destroyed by the Canadian Government. "I hope you don't think of me as one of those Establishment figures," he remarked.

Not at all, Ken, not at all. I knew he respected writing and writers, and that he had been instrumental in promoting the work of David Adams Richards, Jane Urquhart, Timothy Findley, and Neil Bisoondath, among others, and that he never sought bad gossip about people. He was the quiet type, quiet at work and quiet in his own psychological struggles. I was saddened to learn of his suicide a year later, following a scandal arising out of charges of plagiarism against him. He died, as Timothy Findley phrased it touchingly, as if "he wouldn't have troubled us for all the world."

Other newspaper editors engaged me frequently, the best being Dan Garret at the *Montreal Star*, and, later, Martin Levin and his assistant books editor Jack Kirchhoff at the *Globe and Mail*. Dan, Martin, and Jack valued books and writers, and they allotted me more than the standard space and word-length for my reviews and columns, though their papers were far from generous in their payments. Levin and Kirchhoff were newspaper editors who did not necessarily indulge in the usual practice of matching authors with their adversarial critics—as when the *Globe* assigned comic writer Donald Jack to review Findley's *The Wars* (October 15, 1977). Jack had published a series of novels about the misadventures of Bartholomew Bandy during the First World War and had twice won the Stephen Leacock Medal for Humour, but Findley's novel was no slapstick comedy. Jack's review was a total fiasco, compelling Margaret Atwood to point out that matching him with Findley was tantamount to getting Red Buttons to review *Hamlet*.

When Martin Levin set up a symposium in print (January 12, 2008) with me and American journalist and archly conservative Claire Berlinski, it wasn't because I had an axe to grind about her personality. Berlinski (daughter of author and academic David Berlinski and cellist Toby Saks) had read Modern History at Balliol College, Oxford where she earned a doctorate in International Relations. She had worked briefly for the United Nations Development Program and in Istanbul as a freelance journalist. She had also authored two books of non-fiction about European menace (or menace in Europe) and why Margaret Thatcher mattered (positively, I am guessing), so her American Conservatism was very much to the forefront in her writing. The issue was Berlinski's review of Orhan Pamuk's essay collection *Other Colours*, which called the book faddish and Pamuk's melancholy wearisome. I found her review to be politically biased and literarily unsophisticated. We aired our dissenting views at more than the length usually allowed in Letters to the Editor. I asserted that Pamuk's essays showed us a writer "who wisely refuses to have his sense of national identity manipulated by anyone—including Americans and Turks—while he continues to find a different style to suit different subjects." My essential point was that "Berlinski's self-satisfied superficiality produces puerile perversity—not a valuable book review."

Berlinski did not think that she and I were in substantial disagreement, though clearly what rubbed her the wrong way was my tone: "I do not know what Garebian means by the 'vagaries of impersonation.' As for these themes being beyond the ken of the chic café society along the Bosporus, I am guessing that he intends to suggest that they are beyond my ken, but it is, of course, Pamuk who emerged from this milieu, not me. I grew up in Seattle." A fair point but a disingenuous one. She was, after all, living well in Turkey, whose human rights violations were exceeded only by the country's obscene practice of genocide against Armenians in 1915, the sequel to an even earlier one against the same subject-people.

But whoever was deemed to have prevailed in our debate, the main point is that one of Canada's major newspapers—and not a literary journal or academic quarterly—offered generous space to two opposing writers about a book and author rather than to a trivial discussion of NHL games or media celebrities. And I was paid for my contribution. However, I never saw another such symposium again either at the *Globe* or in any other Canadian newspaper.

Martin Levin also commissioned me to write a substantial review in 2009 of Grigoris Balakian's *Armenian Golgotha*, a massive memoir first published in Armenian in 1922 and now making its debut in English via the graces of Balakian's distinguished great-nephew, author Peter Balakian. I found the author's prose "hot," in contrast with Primo Levi's in *Survival in Auschwitz*, "which is as cool as a scientist observing laboratory test tubes and chemicals." Balakian's chronicle had wrenching moments: a scene of schoolboys pleading with him to be rescued from Turkish mobs; a train ride generating tormented anxiety and melancholy; a German nurse who embraces the decapitated body of a six-month-old infant; Armenians kissing skulls of the dead; four elderly Armenian women uttering a vehement curse worthy of a tragic Greek chorus." The prose was not overheated, however, except when Balakian was piously quoting from the Scriptures or sentimentally indulging in purple prose or paeans to nature. The wrenching horrors found a reservoir in Balakian's prodigious memory. The book was "not a scholar's history, of course, but an educated prelate's [Balakian was a bishop of the Armenian Apostolic Church], with an enviable grasp of Ottoman and European history." It explained German and European imperialist designs on Turkey and Turkish resentment, and how Turkey exploited the chaos of war.

Noting that some good-hearted, sympathetic Turks had come to his rescue and to that of other fortunate Armenians, his book was, therefore, "not a wholesale condemnation of Turks." I felt, however, it probably would not be read by most Turks who still couldn't accept responsibility for one of history's greatest crimes against humanity. I concluded with a rhetorical question: "How could a people be expected to understand and atone for a story they have never been officially permitted to know?" A question also echoed by Atom Egoyan.

Turks were outraged by the review-article, flooding the paper with their usual venom, while rehearsing their customary farrago of political and moral garbage: the reviewer was Armenian [only partially] and was therefore biased; the Turks also lost thousands during the First World War; there was no genocide, merely an unfortunate series of events resulting in many fatalities [perhaps like a flu epidemic?]; the whole question of this genocide needed objective examination by a non-biased historian; and so on.

Perhaps appreciating the volume and vehemence of reader comments, the barons at the *Globe* did not silence me.

Things were different at the *Toronto Star*. Dan Smith was Books Editor with no discernibly strong literary taste or prejudice, but he betrayed the normal newspaper editor's ultra-sensitivity to the smallest criticism. An otherwise harmless man, he exploded in rage at a correction I made in a satiric Letter to the Editor. The backstory was simple: perplexed by the word "ludic" I had used in a review of a Leon Rooke novel, he revised it to "lucid" without consulting me, thereby changing the meaning of a sentence. And I, in the spirit of light satire not intended to wound anyone, had pointed this out in my letter. If Dan had been around when I called his office ahead of my letter, we might have had a civil conversation, but he was away. However, when he returned and read the letter, his umbrage was a Vesuvius of eruption in a telephone call to me: "I checked around the office and nobody knew the word!" Before I could pronounce the name Johan Huizinga or the title *Homo Ludens* as a helpful allusion, or point to the readily available resource of an English dictionary, Smith declared me an arrogant brute (I am paraphrasing) for my daring to criticize (in a private, off-the-record call to him) other *Star* staff reviewers for their lapses of critical judgement and literary style. And that brought to an end my book reviewing at the *Star*, except for one or two brief stints when a new editor apparently had forgotten the injunction against me.

A corollary to this event was that *Quill & Quire*, for whom I had also been doing a vast amount of book reviews, stopped commissioning me. I had not suspected the incestuous connection between the *Star* and *Q&Q*.

My freelance book reviewing did earn me a few admirers from the Canadian literati, one of whom was Ralph Gustafson (a poet I had never met) who sent this pithy note to the *Montreal Star* on December 17, 1977: "*The Star* has got a critic of poetry of intelligence. Congratulations." Irving Layton, a poet who should have been every aspiring young poet's model, was also a fan, praising me in a letter from November 1977 (bearing a striking black-and-white drawing of his head on the envelope) for "an excellent review" of a George Bowering book (whose title I forget), though Irving's inclusion of three inferior new poems was an embarrassing misjudgment on his part. When I sent him my review of the bad Véhicule anthology of Montreal poets in 1978, he responded, once again with the same black-and-white headshot on the envelope:

> I very much enjoyed reading it, for its wit and sprightliness as much as for the shrewd criticism that went along with them. I'm glad you picked out Solway for praise from the general welter of failure and pretentiousness. He's the real thing, a genuine poet whose legs or lines get stronger with every step he takes. I've watched his progress from book to book and his last one was unanimously given the York Poetry Workshop Award. You're so right about the heavy breathing and imitations and formlessness and the maniacs in juiced-up speedcars [sic] careening all over the place, an intellectual menace to themselves and others.

. . .

> I especially enjoy your hammering of the Tishites and
> Bowering. I hope one day you'll hammer them completely
> into the ground from which they will emerge transformed
> into flowers smelling more fragrantly than they do now.

Aside from Bowering (whom I came to appreciate more in time) and a few others, I did enjoy hammering what I believed was pretentious crap, though this particular review made me enemies in Montreal. I discovered this when I made one of my periodic visits to The Word, a marvellous bookstore of second-hand books, owned by Adrian King-Edwards and wife Luci, on Milton Street. The couple were known for their strong support of local writers, and Luci made her displeasure eminently clear, though I found her reason appallingly partisan. She implied that it was wrong to attack serious local poets, though as my review had indicated, it was not at all clear that most of the anthologized writers were, in fact, poets of quality, because many of their poems were woefully amateurish. I was all for supporting Canadian writers if they were deserving of literary support. Partisanship was hardly relevant to the question of criticism, but in this particular instance I was the prick my enemies were kicking against.

I did have Irving Layton on my side. When I met him in person for the first time at a delicatessen, he was everything I imagined he would be in terms of physical appearance. His powerful head, crested with thick curly hair, and stocky body made him seem leonine. He spoke volubly but never arrogantly. In fact, he gauged that I was shy and almost embarrassed to show him a couple of my recent poems, but he was pleased with what I had written, and encouraged me to write more. "Irving, I'm not a poet," I said sheepishly. "I'm a literary and theatre critic. I've written very few poems." "No, no, I think you should write more poetry," he said, sounding not in the least insincere. "I'm going to show the poems you have handed me to Aviva, especially the one about Patrick White's Voss in the desert." What did the great Irving Layton know of my poetic potential that I didn't? It seemed to me that poetry was not simply a vocation but a way of life for him, and he believed in a real community of poets. He continued to be an epistolary friend, sending me a post-card (no self-portrait this time) with his thanks scrawled in red ink when I congratulated him on his being nominated for the Nobel Prize: "I warmly thank you for your congrats and good wishes. The nomination has given me a great lift, but since it's for 1982, I have another whole year of nail-biting ahead of me. I'm glad Canetti got the Nobel Prize this year—it removes him from the competition."

Irving never did get the Nobel, but our friendship endured, especially when I panned Elspeth Cameron's biography of him in a review-article prepared for Metcalf's *Carry On Bumping*. Reading a draft, he sent me a long letter of gratitude (September 11, 1987), though in it he had one ringing caveat:

> You seem to have found the winged words to articulate every honest man's indignation and disgust. There's not a word I would wish to change. How perfectly marvellous when truth and justice find their eloquent spokesman.
>
> Wonderfully, you were able to spot not only the bogus scholarship, the shoddy writing, the malevolent bias, but also the blatant antisemitism which, to do Cameron justice, she made no effort to conceal. You haven't left her a single rag to cover her nakedness, not a single hole into which she might crawl with her disgrace. If I were she I'd think seriously of emigrating ...
>
> Bravo, and again, my warmest thanks. So I hope you won't think me churlish that I must enter one caveat. I simply fail to see your grounds for saying that I or my politics are reactionary. Reactionary? Because I demand freedom, human rights and democracy? All my adult life I've supported left-of-center causes and championed the poor and oppressed against their exploiters, have been a member first of the CCF, presently and ever since its foundation, of the NDP. Yes, I

approved of the War Measures Act. So did F.R. Scott, so did
Ralph Gustafson and Hugh MacLennan. Would you call
any of these reactionary? My stand during the Vietnam War?
Very early I said the Americans were fighting the wrong war
at the wrong time and in the wrong place. But I also said I
saw nothing immoral in the Americans attempting to defend
South Vietnam from a Communist takeover. I still don't. I
disagreed with Canadian leftists, many of them old friends
of mine,.who pictured Uncle Ho Ho as a progressive and
benign agrarian reformer. I thought they were all living in
cloud cuckoo land. Time and events have proven me to have
been correct. Even Jane Fonda must now realize how utterly
naïve and stupid she was in her estimation of the strategy
and goals of the Viet Cong. The bitter epic of the Boat
People and the savagery which the victorious Viet Cong
unleashed has undoubtedly contributed to her political
maturation and that of her propaganda-blitzed confederates.
At least, I hope so.

Well, so much for now. We can leave a fuller discussion
of these matters for our meeting which should not be too far
off. I will be giving a reading in Mississauga on November
8th and hope to see you then.
Avanti and best wishes,
Irving

Such vigorous feistiness is something to be admired, even if in this
case, it was in response to a single sentence suggesting that Irving's
"political views are staggeringly reactionary." The lion's roar was
audible, indeed.

I conducted brief but telling interviews with the likes of Hugh
MacLennan and Mordecai Richler. MacLennan cut the distinct
impression of an old-guard Establishment prof, elegant in phrase,
superficially liberal humanist, but with a palpable disapproval of
students called "new immigrants"—students, as I gleaned, who were
from Third World countries. He did not specifically mention the

"threat" to received ideas of the Canadian mosaic during our short interview in a rather dimly-lit office at McGill University, but his thinly veiled distaste shook me somewhat, especially as he had been celebrated for promoting a radical rapprochement between French-Canadians and English-Canadians, the "two solitudes" of one of his famous novels.

Richler left a more lingering impression on me, perhaps because of his satiric writing that was pithy, perverse to the point of being often screamingly comic, and utterly non-compromising. I interviewed him at the Montreal Press Club in Montreal where he seemed to be already working on a Scotch, his hair rumpled, his attitude calmly casual, polite but certainly not gregarious. I had read of his utter inability to make small-talk, and recent sensational headlines about his mother Leah's memoir raised an imaginary red line I could hardly dare to cross. *The Errand Runner: Memoir of a Rabbi's Daughter* made little of Leah's decision to end her marriage to Mordecai's father or of her own wretched conduct as adulterous wife and abusive mother. As Charles Foran's exceptional *Mordecai: The Life & Times* would later show, Richler had sent Leah (Lilly) a strongly-worded 2400-word letter (written in August 1976) that mixed scorn, fury, tenderness, and sadness in its excoriation. The second paragraph read in part: "If your old age tastes of ashes, if you are wretched, lonely, worried about your health, money, I am sorry. I am very sorry. For certainly, it is sad." But Richler forced her to grasp that she had brought most of her misfortune on herself. Perhaps nobody but his wife Florence and his closest friends knew the great pain in his psyche. Her memoir revived this ulcerous pain, and I was forewarned not to probe the ulcer. I didn't really want to. He was soft-spoken, courteous, and laconic. I tried to lure him out of his apparent taciturnity by asking soft questions, to which he gave brief answers. It was clear that he had little time for cultural nationalists or literary jealousies. But the interview was one of the least substantial ones I have ever done, one reason being that the *Montreal Calendar Magazine* (that had commissioned the piece) was the wrong place for a probing interview. Nevertheless, I left, still an admirer of his witty writing because of its twin underpinnings of seriousness and honesty. It was many decades later, when I read Diana Athill's memoir *Stet*, that I appreciated the nature of and motive for Richler's understatement. Athill (along with Andre Deutsch) had taken a risk publishing his first (messy) novel *The Acrobats*, and its very successful successors. She wrote: "How could one tell that someone was generous, kind, honest and capable of being very funny if he hardly ever said a word? I still don't know how, but it happened: I was always sure that he was all of those things, and soon understood that his not saying anything unless he had something to say was part of what made me so fond of him. He was the least phoney person imaginable, and still is today (though he has become much better at talking)."

I remain amazed that Richler ever agreed to being interviewed by me. I surely was an outsider to him, but was it possible that he had read my numerous book reviews in the *Globe and Mail* and *Montreal Star*, and had observed that I was never an apologist for inferior writing or mere cultural nationalists? I wish we could have met years later, when I had by then shed any reticence. Perhaps, I could have honed in on the important thing we had in common: our separate existences as persons we wanted to be.

CHAPTER NINE

MY BOOKS

Twayne Publishers in Boston launched my first book, *Hugh Hood*, in 1983. Edited by Robert Lecker, it certainly put me on the literary map in Canada. In a small corner. While this book is not part of a cluster that would define me as a writer, it was ground-breaking because it attempted to explain how Hood's fiction is a secular analogy for Scripture. The book could not help but be an interim report, encompassing his work only till 1982's *Black and White Keys*, yet it stirred up controversy for those critics who felt that it invoked too much Catholic theology in its interpretation of his fiction. What these critics seemed to forget was that Hood's Catholicism infused his writing, and whether he was a moral Pollyanna or not, his Monotheism allowed him to see life and art as a continuous relationship shot through with trinitarian structures. The three highest forms of human activity for him were religious worship, art, and love, and all his fiction made a single tapestry of these interrelated motifs. My claim did not make me a Catholic propagandist. I was merely reading Hood the way he showed that life was a human comedy held by a glorious creative force.

Although I went on, at ECW's invitation, to write a long essay on Leon Rooke, my radical interest in theatre is what led me into writing books about it. Jack David and Robert Lecker invited me to draw up a list of titles that would have a wide appeal to those who loved Broadway musicals. At the time, I was not a real fan of the genre, but it did not take me long to draw up a short list: *My Fair Lady*, *Gypsy*, *West Side Story*. Not exactly surprising choices, given that the first ran for over six years on Broadway; *Gypsy* compelled a serious measure of art in the American musical; and *West Side Story* was the first great example of a movement musical where story, characterization, music, and dance were merged into a seamless unity. Not being a musicologist, I could not tackle the music analytically, except in a very rudimentary manner. However, my strengths as a theatre critic enabled me to trace each show's genesis and development from initial idea to production concept, casting, design, rehearsals, opening night, and beyond. I decided to write each book differently, if no other reason than to challenge myself. ECW and I settled on an umbrella title for the series: *The Making Of* _____.

Being a novice in the field of American musicals, I was far too reliant on secondary sources for *The Making of 'My Fair Lady.'* I had vast gaps, more like yawning chasms, in my knowledge of musicals in general, and because the series was not going to be academic in manner and without a generous budget, I could not opt for interviews with the production team or cast members. All I could do was read a great deal of books about Broadway musicals, and steal loads of information from seminal books such as Moss Hart's *Act One*, Gene Lee's *Inventing Champagne: The Worlds of Lerner and Loewe*, Alan Jay Lerner's *The Street Where I Live*, and Valerie Pascal's *The Disciple and His Devil*. To expand and embellish my discussion of sets and costumes, I had Cecil Beaton's diaries and his book on the musical. For details on the music, I turned to Joseph P. Swain's *The Broadway Musical: A Critical and Musical Survey*. There were scores of books on Shaw, of course, and when I visited the New York Library for the Performing Arts at Lincoln Center, I had a treasure trove of reviews, feature articles, interviews, and video material at my disposal. The book received good reviews, but I was radically dissatisfied with my own work. I felt that I had not invested deeply of myself and was too dependent on secondary sources. I decided that each successive book in the series would take a slightly different tack from the others, with a special emphasis on a different element, such as a central performance or production concept or a socio-political persuasion or shaping emblems.

The Making of 'Gypsy' became a portrait of Ethel Merman in performance as hardboiled Rose, the ultimate stage-mother, and of the show itself as a fable of metamorphosis. *The Making of 'West Side Story'* made a case for the concept-musical while providing a sense of the collaborative excitement. All three books did well in sales and critical response, and ECW was able to sell them to book clubs in the States. But wanting an even greater market and much higher sales, ECW did not want to continue the series. Howard Aster of Mosaic Press promptly accepted a transfer of publication rights, without having to pay a single dollar, but Mosaic and Aster proved to be absolutely the wrong publisher for me in terms of proper publicity, professional editing, and honouring contractual obligations, especially the matter of royalties.

There are precious few reputable publishers of theatre books in Canada, and the readership of such books is small, indeed, but almost none of these publishers really knows or is willing to learn how to promote theatre books. With Mosaic, I frequently had to personally deliver review copies to review editors of the Toronto dailies, arrange my own radio interviews, and muster up coverage from other sources—all at cost to my own pocket. Aster probably believed that sponsoring me for OAC Writers Reserve Grants would compensate for not paying full royalties. He developed a real art of phantom statistics when it came to royalties. Intriguingly, while bemoaning low sales, he did not remainder my musical production histories. In fact, he published two more in *The Making Of* _____ series, though as cheaply as he could.

My dealings with Mosaic ended after I was contacted by Stacey Wolf, distinguished American and author of the highly-regarded *A Problem Like Maria*. She reached out to me to complain that the *Cabaret* book was difficult to order for her courses on the Broadway musical. I was not surprised. Aster often travelled to international book fairs, and the small, underpaid staff did not attend to orders with urgency. When I unloaded my own complaints about Aster,

Stacey offered to advance my name to Norman Hirschy at Oxford University Press, New York, which is how I obtained a major American publisher. All Oxford manuscripts are refereed by at least two or three academic readers before making it to publication. Unlike Mosaic, Oxford had a significant budget for use of photographs from Photofest or the New York Public Library, a team of expert editors, and layout specialists, so all their books have a professional look.

The Making of 'Cabaret,' Second Edition was published in 2011 to excellent reviews in American and Canadian journals, easily establishing itself as the most detailed production history to date of the original Broadway version. Americans appreciate stage musicals, and many of their universities offer courses on the genre. In Canada, too many universities and theatre directors simply frown on or shun the Broadway musical, despite the fact that the highest achievements in theatrical production are enriched by the highly gifted contributions of Stephen Sondheim, Alan J. Lerner and Frederick Loewe, Frank Loesser, Andrew Lloyd Webber, Lin-Manuel Miranda, Hal Prince, Michael Bennett, Jerome Robbins, Oliver Smith, Irene Sharaff, Patricia Zipprodt, Jo Mielziner, Jean Rosenthal, Boris Aronson, Bob Fosse, *et cetera.*

Unsurprisingly, my theatre books are more highly and widely regarded abroad (especially in the U.S.) than they are in Canada. *George Bernard Shaw and Christopher Newton: Explorations of Shavian Theatre, The Making of 'West Side Story,'* and *The Making of 'Cabaret'* (Second Edition) are on reading lists of several American universities. Even my first biography of William Hutt (miserably copy-edited by Mosaic Press, with a jacket that didn't fit the size of the hardcover edition) was a way of introducing one of our greatest stage actors to Americans and Brits for whom the world of theatre is limited to Broadway or the West End.

This biography made some folk at the Stratford Festival edgy. One of these was John Hirsch, only the second Canadian to be appointed that festival's Artistic Director. Hungarian-born, he had an inflated reputation as director and ultra-nationalist. When I consulted

the archival records of the festival, it became clear that for all his denunciation of foreign or colonial (meaning British) influences, he
never staged a single Canadian play on the main Festival stage during his tenure (1981–85). He did have his lover Michael Schonberg
serve as Production Manager of *A Variable Passion*, co-written by
Elliott Hayes and Nicholas Pennell, but that was essentially a one-
man show for Pennell (a brilliant actor) and it was given only six
performances at the Third Stage. I avoided Hirsch as much as I
could, not having much respect for his directorial craft that often sank
dangerously into the cheapest melodrama or *Kitsch*. His *Mary Stuart*
had an inept supporting company; his *As You Like It* was a representation of the Sick Soul of Europe; his *Tartuffe* was sour and narrow;
for A *Streetcar Named Desire* he took hammer and anvil to the sym-
bols; *The Glass Menagerie* featured an Amanda who barged through
the role, capsizing the pathos, ramming the satire with her nagging
humour; and his *King Lear* turned the title role played by Douglas
Campbell into a ruined piece of ham. I kept my critical distance
from his bad taste, but one day, while I was making copious notes in
the Administration offices, he happened to pass by. "Vhaat are you
dooing?" he inquired in this thick Hungarian accent. "Oh, I am
working on a book about William Hutt." He nodded and moved on.
He and Hutt had had a falling-out.

As it turned out, Bill Hutt had more enemies than even he had
suspected. Several actors turned down my requests for interviews,
with Douglas Campbell eventually admitting that it was Bill who
had provoked his unforgiving displeasure. I soldiered on, writing a
book that sought to honour its twin subjects: Hutt and the development of classical (especially Shakespearean) theatre in Canada. But
the book was almost sunk prior to publication when Hutt developed
cold feet, fearing that I might reveal intimacies he had guarded most
of his life. His older brother Bud was dead set against the book,
charging that it would dishonour the family name, even though I
assured him it would not. I wasn't a Kitty Kelley, intent on writing
a sensational, scandal-unmasking tell-all. My interview with Bud in
his Stratford home was one for the ages. After making brief small

talk, I started to tape what devolved into one of the weirdest non-interviews imaginable. I would ask a simple question, there would be a long pause as if Bud was mulling the question, but the pause would continue as the tape-recorder kept recording silence. I would ask a second question, and there would be more silence, with the recorder still running. After a third or a fourth question with a similar pattern of non-response, I decided that there was no point continuing. Bud disappeared without apology, though his wife Barbara, palpably embarrassed, stepped forward to give me as candid an interview she could manage under the circumstances, filling in a lot of Hutt family history, the war years when she first met Bill, and continuing with Bill's university days and his early acting career.

Bill had been the very picture of sweetness and cooperation at the outset, welcoming me into his Victorian home on Waterloo Road, unburdening his heart about his parents and siblings, recounting his war years, his training under Robert Gill at Hart House, his experiences with various theatre companies around Gravenhurst, Peterborough, Niagara, and Toronto, and much more. When he recalled his wartime years, it was clear how scenes of the wounded, the dying, and dead had seared themselves in his memory, and when he recounted the death of his mother, his eyes brimmed with tears. This was not acting for a biographer's benefit. It was genuine emotion, and it revealed his vulnerability. I was moved to silence, allowing him to recover. And, then, there was his sharp wit, and his magnificent way of spinning an anecdote, calibrated to his expert sense of timing.

One of his idols was Noel Coward, and when he delivered a reminiscence of Coward, he brought the memory vividly to life by an expert mimicking of the master's voice and manner. He was generous in his compliments and praise for people he admired, but devastatingly dismissive of those he considered superficial or fake. His unspoken fear was that I might choose to write about William Hutt in the bedroom, or delve into his complex relationship with his loyal, live-in companion Matt Mackey, a much younger man with an extraordinary talent for creating gardens and doing home renovations, in addition to possessing a philosophic curiosity. Matt did not know me well at the time, and he preferred staying in the shadows. And Bill was already widely known inside the profession as the Duke of Dark Corners. Matt wanted to remain in the shadows; Bill decided to withdraw his participation. I was stymied.

Until it became clear that I was determined to publish the biography. When Bill finally decided to re-participate, inviting me to visit his Stratford home again and give him the opportunity to make final revisions or cuts, I discovered why he had suddenly gone cold earlier. He had heard false reports from close friends that I was more interested in his sex life than in his career. He had also felt that the first bulky draft did not use his personal voice very much, and that there was too much of a distance in the writing between me and him as the subject. He did comment to me: "The book seems to reveal more about you than me." Looking back at what I had attempted, I have to agree with his assessment. Perhaps, I had been too respectful of him; perhaps, I was too clenched in the writing, the narrative not spontaneous enough. He also was under the mistaken belief that the book would never find a publisher. When I reported that I had lost at least two potential publishers because of his dithering, he was surprised and apologetic. He made gracious small talk, insisted on cuts that I agreed to, and then made one unnegotiable demand: that I allow Matt to draft his own version of their relationship, without any editorial modification. "And that's that!"

After his death in 2007, matters changed considerably. I was free at last to create the biography I had always wanted to write. Matt Mackey had become a trusting, respectful friend, and gave me access to letters to and from Bill, while describing his own role in Bill's life. Wanting a fitting memorial to his great friend (and surrogate father), he was willing to fund a massive biography, embellished expertly by Scott McKowen with a huge stock of photographs (most in colour). The book became the basis for *William Hutt: Soldier Actor* that Guernica Editions published near the end of 2017, almost three decades after the first biography. I built on the portrait I had first sketched in the 1988, and I take immense pride in the fact that

I was able to relate the history of professional Canadian theatre while tracing the life and career of one of its immortal shadows. I gave ample space to William Hutt to speak his mind on anything, without necessarily agreeing with all his views or insights. Using family history, documentary evidence, anecdote, close analysis of many of his great roles, and adversarial counterpoint by nationalist critics, I created a multi-layered biography to establish why he mattered to Canadian culture. And, yet, this massive biography did not get a single print review in any national paper.

Perhaps William Hutt's memory is fading faster than I had anticipated. Perhaps his occasional displays of massive egotism or arrogance lingered in the minds of rivals and enemies. Perhaps the Stratford Festival, to which he had committed much of his art, craft, and dedication, resented the fact that I was able to produce a book that did not soften criticism of several of its past Artistic Directors or Boards or actors or productions. Antoni Cimolino, Artistic Director, had initially applauded me for undertaking the biography ("I'm so glad you are doing this book"), and Anita Gaffney, Executive Director, had seemed to be equally supportive, arranging for me to meet with her and Michael Levine, Entertainment Lawyer and Literary Agent, at his imposing office in Toronto. Levine was not keen on my idea of an exhaustive biography, and he suggested that I write a much shorter biography that could join Random House /Penguin's list on Extraordinary Canadians (Maurice Richard, Tommy Douglas, Glenn Gould, Pierre Trudeau, Stephen Leacock, Norman Bethune, Emily Carr, Louis Riel and Gabriel Dumont, and other Usual Suspects), because this could possibly lead to television and film rights. I declined, though I was grateful for the festival's gift of a little money up front and its permission for free use of the Archives and production photographs. Perhaps I did not sound grateful enough. Whatever the reason, neither Antoni Cimolino, nor Anita Gaffney attended the launch of the biography at Revival House (the newly named Church Restaurant, once owned by Joseph Mandel, life partner of Robin Phillips, the arch enemy of just about every Canadian ultra-nationalist). Nor were other staff represented, apart from wonderfully witty, Lisa Giffen, super-efficient Head of Archives. Nor was its acting company largely or even moderately represented. I knew that the situation would have been quite different had Bill Hutt still been living, with scores of sycophants from the festival rushing to get his autograph or congratulating him for a book he did not write.

This book was praised by Howard Loxton, Chair of the Society for Theatre Research's Theatre Book Prize in London, England. "You should be very proud of your book," he commented after reading the work that made the Long List that year, joining books by (among others) Jonathan Miller, Peter Brook, Stephen Purcell, Garry O'Connor, Tim Pigott-Smith, and Michael Coveney. I was proud, indeed, though the award eventually went to Nicholas Hytner (a Brit, of course) for *Balancing Acts*, a behind-the-scenes story of twelve years at London's National Theatre.

I did undertake another book on Canadian theatre, out of respect for some of the best Shakespearean actors in the country. Anita Gaffney had not sounded very eager to circulate my request for interviews among the actors and actresses I had named. "I have had complaints about you from actors," she claimed, but when asked to name names, she was silent. "I would appreciate your telling me who feel offended because I would be more than willing to strike them off my list." I may have sounded like Gilbert and Sullivan's Lord High Executioner, for she was silent again. Though there were several Stratford actors and actresses I genuinely liked, none of these was a god or goddess who deserved unconditional praise. The ones I liked were all hardworking, talented artists, humbly putting their skills at the service of history's greatest playwright. I had enjoyed many of their performances (not just in Shakespeare), and appreciated their genuine modesty and humility in the course of our interviews for *Colours to the Chameleon: Canadian Actors on Shakespeare*. Nancy Palk, Joseph Ziegler, Albert Schultz, Ben Carlson, Moya O'Connell, Tom McCamus, Juan Chioran, Chick Reid, Tom Rooney, Graham Abbey, and Lucy Peacock all agreed to be interviewed. Most of them were secured by me privately, although Gaffney and Marion Burr did arrange scheduling and venues for the interviews. Who could possibly object to the ones available, when they represented some of the cream of Shakespearean acting in Canada? Of course, I had wanted others as well: Ben Campbell (who has never had the honours he deserves), Seana McKenna (who had agreed a year earlier before being swept away on clouds of further glory and business), Jonathan Goad (who had agreed to be interviewed till he became a first-time parent), Maev Beatty (who had also agreed to an interview in Toronto before some other theatre business put an end to that idea), Yanna McIntosh, Brent Carver, Colm Feore, Geraint Wyn Davies (who was soon to set off on an ambitious trip to several continents), Stephen Ouimette, and Sara Topham. But none of these was available.

Evan Buliung had agreed to an interview, and I looked forward to discussing his dual roles as Oberon and Titania at Stratford, but once he objected to my including Albert Schultz in the book, I decided that he was quite dispensable. I had known Albert for decades, and admired how he had steered Soulpepper into being the best actor-led company in the country. But he had just been the centre of a nasty storm over allegations of sexual exploitation or abuse or God knows what at Soulpepper. I was simply not interested in his alleged sexual misconduct, nor in the shady theatre politics at work at Soulpepper. I was interested only in his views on acting and directing. I detest the Piling-On syndrome—that common, cheap, claptrap business of selecting a whipping-boy or cause for whatever is the prevailing "Woke" business of the day that proliferates into an irrational rapture, while piling on accusation after accusation, often on the flimsiest or silliest of evidence. Theatre is hardly the province of the sacred or the morally righteous. It has never been—not in Shakespeare's time, not in our own. It is not Theatre's business to become another Salem, to go witch-hunting or to find moral fault in an artist. I prefer to judge artists by aesthetic criteria. I leave the rest to Heaven or any similar religious fiction.

I am in a minority of Canadian authors who specialize in Theatre and Poetry, two genres I cover in very short essays in *Mini Musings:*

Miniature Thoughts on Theatre and Poetry. The miniature essays are a mix of observations, anecdotes, and reflections, intended to be a kaleidoscope of topics and angles of vision, coloured by my inner mischief.

Unlike Theatre, Poetry (or the practice of it) came to me late, but my poetry collections are ways of catching up with the past in order to catch up with myself. After *Reservoir of Ancestors* came *Frida: Paint Me As A Volcano* in a simultaneous French translation by Arlette Francière (*Frida: Un Volcan de Souffrance*). John Buschek published this bilingual volume, forewarning that bilingual poetry books were a hard sell. But neither Arlette nor I was dissuaded from a collaboration. Her French translation showed how the original poetry can undergo a transformation in a new language. I was happy with my poems, because they had achieved what I had intended: a sequence of monologues meant to be primarily sonorous, lyrical, and dramatic in the imagined voice of Frida Kahlo. I had read many books on Kahlo and Diego Rivera, primarily Hayden Herrera's authoritative *Frida: A Biography of Frida Kahlo*, and my personal library swelled with new acquisitions about this superb, conflicted artist whose self-portraits were an unparalleled psychological map of herself. My Frida spoke beyond the grave, a spectre become flesh and blood, recounting her Mestizo heritage, love for Diego, her political fervour and several griefs.

While in the process of composing these poems, I listened to Spanish music, watched Spanish and Mexican films (with English subtitles), and read famous Hispanic and Latino poets (Neruda, Paz, Mistral, Gongora). I made a trip to Mexico City, where I visited the Casa Azul in Coyoacan with its cobalt blue walls and ground floor with eight rooms bearing relics from Frida's life: kitchen, living room, dining room, Diego's bedroom, paintings, pottery, blankets, a dress with dusty hems, her studio with bed and her painful corset, photos of Diego, et cetera. I also toured places associated with her life: the Palacio de Bellas Artes (for a performance of Mexican dances), the floating market of Xochimilco, the Plaza de Toros (where I watched many bulls being killed in a colourfully savage spectacle), and the bustling Zona Rosa (celebrated for its shopping, gay community, and nightlife).

I approached my research as an actor would, probing beneath the surface of Frida's biography, investigating her choices and motives, expanding my curiosity in the interest of reaching her essence as a woman and artist. And then writing poems that would speak in the active present, vibrating like a soul in ecstasy or torment. *Frida: Paint Me As A Volcano* would marry my passions for Theatre and Poetry. And this was borne out splendidly when actress Jennifer Dale (costumed and made up strikingly as Frida) performed a 20-minute selection for a WordStage event at the Cervejaria Restaurant, Toronto, on September 14, 2006 to great acclaim. "I think we should go for it, Jennifer, with a multi-media staging," I suggested, but, alas, even though I assembled a first-class production team (Cylla von Tiedemann for videography; Anne Dixon for costumes; Richard Feren for sound and lighting; Keir Brownstone for music, helmed by Brenda Bazinet as director), the project did not receive funding from either the Canada Council or the Ontario Arts Council.

My next collection was even more daring in its subject matter and approach. *Blue: The Derek Jarman Poems* (Signature Editions) is an elegiac verse-biography that is sometimes virtual cinema, sometimes experimental verse, sometimes randy, always lyrical. Expertly edited by poet John Barton, it gets as close as I thought possible to the core of Jarman (visual artist, poet, sexual rebel, gardener, political militant, AIDS victim) without recourse to demotic or deliberately raw gay terminology. I served as a poet of brooding melancholy, despite my forays into word sonnets, slanted documentaries, and lyrics with surrealistic suggestions. In *Blue*, my voice interacts with Jarman's voice in his art, films, and journals, concluding with poems of loss and grief. The collection received glowing reviews. I was made even prouder when American composer Gregory Spears set one of the poems ("Dungeness Documentary") to music for choir and string quartet in the company of a poem each by Thomas Merton and Denise Levertov. Spears is celebrated for his operas (*Fellow Travelers*; *Paul's Case*), as well as for his *Requiem*, his signature style being a captivating blend of romanticism, minimalism, and early music forms. His thirty-minute composition, entitled "The Tower and the Garden," uses the tower to symbolize technological *hubris* that destroys our natural world, and the garden to represent a place for peaceful refuge. Commissioned by Cantori, New York, The Crossing, Notre Dame Vocale, and Volti, with funding provided by The Ann Stookey Fund, it premiered October 27, 2018 at the Presbyterian Church of Chestnut Hill, Philadelphia, Donald Nally conducting, before opening in San Francisco and New York. My hope of attending the Manhattan premiere on May 11, 2019 was shattered because I was in the midst of intensive radiation treatment for throat cancer, but Spears's score was published by Schott Music, and there is also now a widely-praised CD of it from Navona Records.

Like my chapbook *Samson's Hair*, *Frida: Paint Me as a Volcano* and *Blue: The Derek Jarman Poems* marked me as a poet of masks. Colleague, poet, editor, critic Elana Wolff claimed in our 2013 interview for *Open Book, Ontario* that the two full-length collections situated me on the frontier between self and the world, while embracing the plurality of self:

> In *Frida*, you assume the voice of the artist, and one has the sense that many of your own passions are streamed through her 'I.' Of course, you are telling her story and presenting her emotions, but you've chosen her—in no small part, perhaps—as a vehicle. Thus, the emphatic declarations: 'My body is mad/ My face is mad' (from 'Madness') could very well come from a deep place within your psyche.
>
> Her views and substitutions could be yours too. 'I refuse the collusion of a victim,/ fighting every moment with my heart' (from 'You Say You Could Live in My Hair'). 'I paint myself a mask that won't cry (from 'Earthquake'). Her assertions could coincide with your truths. 'Art is the telling of lies. And the exoneration of this' (from 'The Telling of Lies'), and her sexual expression mirrors your own: 'I touch a woman/ and I am swimming out to sea' (from 'Holy in the Ecstasy').

The role-playing, I'm suggesting, allows you to wear
masks of authenticity.
Or, to use your words:
Surfaces are deeper than they seem.
I paint what they show in creases and folds,
still fruit in bowls, leaves and vines,
tilted heads and curved backs,
animals exposed outside cages. (from 'Beginning')

Like Frida, your collection *Blue: The Derek Jarman Poems*, is
a kind of biography in verse. Even more than *Frida*, though
I would say Jarman presents as a kindred spirit—cineaste,
artist, sexual rebel, and gay rights activist. Brash, bold,
provocative to the end. In *Blue*, you address your subject,
and his subjects, with almost promotional clarity—a
factuality of style that's intense, graphic, saltily honest.

Blue fortified my commitment to creating figures who sound like
real persons speaking words from real life. and the most passionate
of them had a palpable sense of urgency. My quasi-biographical collections (*Frida*; *Blue*; *Georgia and Alfred*) marry fact (biographical,
autobiographical) and truth (authenticity of language and insight).
And it was inevitable that I would write about my own cultural and
personal background. As someone with a mixed Armenian and
Anglo-Indian ancestry, who speaks, reads, and writes only in
English (though I can speak passable French), I am one of a swelling
number of "in-betweens"—that is, persons who can't seem to belong
to one side or another, who cannot find a fixed place. I am between
histories of affliction, between cultures that often misapprehend
each other, between two languages (Armenian and Hindi) that I
don't understand, between a birthplace country that is ebbing away
in memory and another, an adopted one, that is not always firm in
its own identity. I find myself between an attraction to meditation
and an inclination for action, between belonging and not belonging.
I also have an exilic sense, and being half Armenian, I also have an

almost inexplicable sense of melancholy yearning, though I am not sure for what. Perhaps for what has been lost by ruptures of geography, history, culture. So, to quote Gail Scott from her novel *The Obituary*: "Is not the hybrid a melancholic? On a line between appearing + disappearing?"

Because the subject of identity is a permanent project, my mind and heart store subject matter as materials for an architecture I can only sense, even as the materials sink into my psyche. In a radical sense, I maintain a vigilant surveillance of what is real in my life, but because of my obsession with theatre, I use personae in an existential poetic theatre of my struggles, sufferings, smothered screams, successes, defeats, and traumas. I do not create art for art's sake, though I do not dismiss aesthetes out of hand. I don't deny that writing can be a luxury where a writer can exploit himself; I don't deny that poetry is the luxury of dreaming variously. In my most personal poems, which is to say the poems about my family history and my life to date, I try to dream for others, to give voice to the dead. I question my origins, my ancestors, my traumatized father and his blighted history, the uncertain pattern of my own journey through life, while always trying to record music of the ravaged heart, the murmur of tears, the hammer blows of atrocity, the shudder and stammer of the dispossessed.

Some poets breathe backwards, feeling battered by the present. The poet's heart is source, target, terminus. As Joy Harjo contends: "It is in the heart where poetry is born and the place where it enters when it is finished." *Children of Ararat* sprang organically from the Armenian sections in *Pain*, where I represented myself as "a divided river beneath a bizarre zodiac." As a mix of Armenian and Anglo-Indian, there is a leakage of one history into another, but both extravagant in a subcontinent of exotic improbabilities. I recognize that I was colonized. However, there were worlds elsewhere, to which I was not denied entry. I had simply not found my place. And after we did leave India to immigrate to Canada, I experienced the culture-shock of an immigrant, though my sense of voluntary displacement was reduced by a commonality of language and custom.

I had English, the Bible (as mythology), Shakespeare, and the Commonwealth (an historical deception, as I discovered) as my commonalities with Canada. But there were many times I felt like a "resident alien"—to quote Clark Blaise's memorable term which was, in fact, the title of a book in which he wrote: "We are born to strangers we must learn to love, in a town or country we would not have chosen, into a tribe that defines and restricts our growth. We spend a lifetime overcoming the givens, only to return from the distant vantage point … when the parents are gone, to look back and say: this is what I am, something no larger, no freer than they made me." However, I feel freer than my parents made me because I've given voice on the printed page to their histories and mine.

In her poem "The Second Question," Diana Der-Hovanessian summarizes two radical questions Armenian holocaust survivors repeat: Where and How? Where were your people from? How did you escape death?

Children of Ararat is my work of witness or, as Elana Wolff put it so eloquently in the *Open Book* interview, "a document and song of suffering from one who himself has not ascended Ararat, yet carries the burn of memories like yellow flames." In dealing with my conflicted relationship with my father and the obscenities of genocide, I was stung into poetry, and my pain (historical and personal) expressed itself in rage and grief. Poet Mick Burrs (quiet, modest, very soft spoken) edited the poems with extraordinary sensitivity and poetic acumen, urging me on, while showing how I could keep my passion in check so that it did not overwhelm craft. The only time his temper flared was when I titled a poem "Thirteen Ways of Looking at the Turk," obviously a variation on Wallace Stevens's "Thirteen Ways of Looking at a Blackbird." Mick objected to my title, believing that my denunciation of Turks as a group was unfair, tantamount to calling all Germans during World War II Nazis. Grudgingly, I yielded, re-titling the poem "Thirteen Ways of Looking at 1915" while silently regretting this concession to political correctness.

Part of the reason I submitted to Mick's suggestion was out of respect for his innate decency. Born Steven Michael Berzensky in California to Jewish parents (his grandfather had fled Russia), Mick was one of many conscientious Americans who had avoided serving in the obscene Vietnam War. He had fled to Canada, settling for a long while in Saskatchewan where he produced award-winning books of poetry. Of frail health but perfect mind, he moved to Toronto but was compelled to live frugally in a low-income apartment, and remain dependent on the kindness of close friends and on meagre editing commissions. Only three years older than me, he was very thin, bony, and had curly white and grey hair. His poverty and ill health made him look older than he was, and I was saddened to learn of his dementia in 2019. He had moved into assisted living, unable to care for himself. I called him by phone a few times, but was never able to reach him successfully. I left a voice-mail message: "Hello, Mick. This is Keith Garebian. I hope you remember me. I certainly remember you and the wonderfully sensitive way you edited *Children of Ararat*. I am sorry you are not well, but if you have the time and energy, do call me. I send you my best wishes." Mick never did call me back. I am not at all certain he ever heard the message or if he did, whether he remembered me at all, though I like to think he did because he was acutely supportive of my writing, sharing my understanding of what it was to be a descendant of a people who were almost exterminated in their homelands. His name will never leave the stones around his grave.

Children of Ararat was selected as one of ten prize-winning titles in Frontenac's Dektet competition where there were over 250 manuscripts, each read carefully by publishers David and Rose Scollard before a long list was sent to bill bissett, Alice Major, and George Elliott Clarke for adjudication. I had not yet completed the final version, but it was very gratifying to make the final cut and join the literary company of Douglas Burnet Smith (an extraordinary poet), Jannie Edwards, Lori Cayer, Jocko Benoit, William Nichols, transgender S. Mcdonald, and exciting newcomers Nikki Reimer, Adebe D.A., and Laurie MacFayden. Frontenac House earned its amazing reputation in Calgary because the Scollards were the best sort of poetry enthusiasts imaginable. Generous in spirit and of broad intellect, they treated their writers with utmost respect and courtesy, and it was a distinct privilege to be welcomed into their stable of poets. Because 2010 was their tenth anniversary as publishers, they were granted financial support by the Canada Council, the Alberta Creative Development Initiative, as well as The Alberta Foundation for the Arts, and their Dektet launch was an unforgettable experience for me. I finally got to experience first-rate treatment by a Canadian publisher, as well as receiving the opportunity to read in Calgary and at the Edmonton Poetry Festival, run by irrepressible spoken-word artist Sherri-D Wilson.

I allowed the white of the printed page to free my crouching demons, and have recently discovered in the vibrantly intimate French poems of Moroccan Abdellatif Laabi, this short passage (English translation by Donald Nicholson-Smith) that serves to summarize my own exploration:

> *de la lucidité aux larmes* from clarity to tears
> *des larmes à la fureur* from tears to fury
> *de la fureur à l'amour* from fury to love
> *de l'amour à cette étrange folie* from love to this strange folly
> *de croire malgré tout aux hommes* of believing despite everything
> in human beings

Melancholy and lamentation are not qualities that apply only to Armenians, but my poetry has a personal cadence because of my sense of being *odar* or the Other virtually anywhere, of having a surname whose etymological root is probably Arabic or Turkish (*garip*) without exact English translation, and one that connotes apartness, strangeness, or a degree of alienation.

Writing into trauma (my father's, my own) paired grief and anger, and even though much of the tone is elegiac, *Children of Ararat* seeks to illuminate *living* after and despite continuing terror, rootlessness, exile, ambiguities of identity. The collection is an affirmation of survival. Over and above the negative moods and themes, there is *a liberatory desire.* This is made clear at the end of the book, in "Denial—An Afterword," a prose summation of my existential state in 2010:

> Denial can hurt a writer into poetry, but the poet need not disappear so much into imagination as to be absent from the real world. There is a place to bear witness to a devastation of grace and to some hope beyond despair ... We have the right to dream that denial will run to its own ruin. That one day a true mental picture will be summed up in a language that is undeniable, and with a brightness that will, indeed, fall from the air.

Poetry is Blood, expertly edited by brilliant Elana Wolff (a Canadian Louise Glück) at Guernica, continues my poetic self-making, cognizant of historical toxins. This book is informed by my conviction that we are not born to love ourselves and all others every day.

The most difficult poem to write for this book was "Finishing Sentences" because of its impetus. It seems to be perpetually in motion:

> My eyes are grooved with persuasions of
> Shame, which is the spur for
> The writer's rage to order words
> I stand in the impudent ranks
> Anything I say is as partial as
> What was it like when
> To the burning mouth,
> No part was in touch with art,
>
> Is not writing also part of
> Our words for the dead, uttered in
> A room where you are reading
> After you've learned things, you're left
> But we are the Mountain, so

It is a poem that needs to be read aloud, but there was only a single instance when I felt I had done full justice to the poem in a live reading. That occasion was the Guernica launch for the book when I felt what Spaniards call *duende*, that inexplicably mysterious yet exciting feeling of being fully immersed in the moment of "creation" or "performance," while feeling that an audience is fully immersed in the same moment with you.

Robert Hayden wrote in his poem "The Tattooed Man," "all art is pain/ suffered and outlived." *Poetry is Blood* attempts to make its world and my lived life into an art object. It is a celebration of creativity beyond the boundaries of its solemn subjects. In this way, it is an optimistic collection because it suggests how I live inside a story of grief without succumbing to the toxins of history. I am *not buried* in my longing or melancholy. Grief need not be an end in itself, but a site of transformation, a way of achieving a new reality of the self. As with *Children of Ararat*, *Poetry is Blood* is not simply a literature of blame. Like my other poetry collections, it shows that the "lyric me," the one who observes as a bruised poet. Every poem has an emotional core, and the best poems express what is at stake.

Poets such as Ocean Vuong, Jericho Brown, Billy-Ray Belcourt, Richard Blanco, Naomi Shihab Nye, and Mahmoud Darwish have taught me that trauma is who you are, with loneliness, alienation, grief, rage, love, and forgiveness being outbursts of language that can miraculously have beauty. "To write beautifully about unbeautiful matters is a minor miracle," says Billy-Ray Belcourt. Especially when history argues against such beauty. For all its melancholy lyricism, all its melancholy meditation, *Poetry is Blood* is testament to life because in honouring what have vanished, in deepening what we know of loss, it connects with something human. The dead bodies are not emptied things. Even nameless, they live in memory. The walls, monuments, villages, cities that have been destroyed are ghosts that hover over survivors. The book shows that genocide need not lead to poetic linguicide, that poetry is, indeed, possible after historic atrocity on a mass scale. From inside my skin, inside whatever wounds I have inherited through trauma, I can write of a legacy that rescues words within the hush of pillars, pediments, altars, urns, walls, monumental time. The twisted self can sing; the exile can have song leaping from his mouth. What is experienced as a void can also be an unsuspected gift, the hollow to be filled with poems beyond grief or rage or disillusionment. I am a custodian of a fraught legacy, who despite feeling like a wanderer or stranger in any land, knows that my own story is something urgent and necessary.

My own story continues in a narrative poetry sequence *Against Forgetting*, accepted by Frontenac House for Quartet 2019. The wonderful Scollards had retired from publishing and had entrusted their beloved company to Neil Petrunia who recruited Calgary poet and professor Micheline Maylor to edit the series, in which my book kept company with Natalie Meisner's *Baddie One Shoe*, Conrad Scott's *Waterline Immersion*, and Laura Zacharin's *Common Brown House Moths*—three debut collections of impressively high standards. Agreeing with Billy-Ray Belcourt that "no language is placeless," I shaped *Against Forgetting* as a retrospective look at where I was born and where I had my earliest cultural influences. The book's title is the same as that of Carolyn Forché's ground-breaking anthology of witness poetry, though my collection is composed with poems that imply inter-related connections they don't explicitly state. In her anthology, Forché claims, "Our age lacks the structure of a story." As I wrote in my prefatory note, her sentence prompted me to recognize some of the key features of my own autobiographical narrative: progression but incompleteness. My discrete poems in the collection are circumscribed by the larger narrative of my Bombay background and immigration to Canada. The sequence of themes does not make for a tidy closure.

Against Forgetting completes what Elana Wolff calls my "tetralogy of witness." It is a tetralogy that anyone who wishes to understand my literary and psychological sensibility needs to read because it provides a wide, deep exploration of uprooting, diaspora, and identity. Like all my best writing, the tetralogy attempts to balance passion and craft. It is far from perfect as literary artefact, but I always keep Toni Morrison's dictum (from her 1993 Nobel Prize address) firmly in mind: "We [writers] know you can never do it properly— once and for all. Passion is never enough, neither is skill. But try."

Like many, if not most poets, I re-invent myself with each new book. As Roo Borson put it when interviewed by Julie Bruck for *Where the Words Come From*, "different forms, different styles, rhythms and ways of speaking, actually allow you to say different things." Borson articulates what I try to demonstrate in each poetry collection, that whatever I am curious about or wish to explore has to find a form in which it can live. My two most recent collections in 2022, *In the Bowl of My Eye* (Mawenzi House) and *Finger to Finger* (Frontenac House) consolidate my point. *In the Bowl* deals with Mississauga/Etobicoke suburbia, including geography, sociology, characters I have met from this milieu, and meditative reflections on lake, park, and road, whereas *Finger to Finger* is an even more personal, more intimate distillation of relationships, travel experiences, and some realities of aging. *Finger to Finger* is the most compact, concise confessional poetry I have attempted, using Jack Gilbert as my poetic touchstone, and aiming to suggest John Thompson's insight of "how small a poem can be:/ the point of a fish hook." Poet John Wall Barger edited my manuscript, teaching me how less could be more, how discretion can be disclosure, how a good confessional poem needs an explicit gesture to make it more than simply a diaristic recording. The book summarizes what I have omitted in this autobiography: my two failed marriages, some of my other passionate relationships, and my sexuality. The poems are trimmed down to a bare tight fiery edge, but the best of them break loose into something wilder, transcending disappointment and heartache. I have never been a writer of icy intellectual reservation or cryptic codes. I prefer being a poet of fact and feeling, and one who believes in all my pores that one little life can become craft or art that matters.

The two new collections are hardly the last poetic word by me on anything, for to quote John Thompson once more, the poet is "a cinder never quite burned out."

CHAPTER TEN

MORE THAN A
WANDERING OF BODY

"Everyone who is born holds dual citizenship, in the kingdom of the well and in the kingdom of the sick." Susan Sontag's claim exposes illness as "the night side of life, a more onerous citizenship." As one who fought cancer twice in the space of eighteen years, I understand what she meant, though her arguments against metaphorizing cancer or expanding its mythology seem outdated in the light of contemporary scientific advances and the ability of poetry to fight against romanticizing illness. Louise Glück calls poetry "a form/ of suffering" with a defined shape. The shape can alleviate the suffering by precise self-awareness, leading to psychic growth. This truth dawned on me as I was diagnosed with potentially deadly cancer in 2019. Facing radiation and, later, neck surgery, I felt a sudden phenomenal urge to express in poetry the effects of disease on my psyche and perspectives on relationships, creativity, aging, and mortality.

I asked poet/editor/publisher Allan Briesmaster (who has read most of my poems) to serve as custodian of whatever new poems were generated by me during the course of my illness, though I had absolutely no idea of the volume or quality of what would emerge. I shocked myself when in March 2019, the first month of my new creativity, fifty-nine poems took shape. Some poems were unashamedly raw; others were polished meditations. Although I accompanied and fortified my writing by voluminous reading of other poets, my poems refused to be exhortations or polemics, metaphoric flourishes or disembodiments. Some poems were pared down; others expansive. Their rhythms sprang from my moods and attitudes. Sometimes coloured by anger, sometimes by sanguine, wistful recollection, they were about power and powerlessness, light and dark, calm and disquietude, grief and love. No matter what their inspirations or geneses were, their facts and truths belonged to me. Coming from my inner life, they were effluences of the heart, radiations of the mind, not meant as psychotherapy but as truthful, artful responses to existential challenges that are becoming all too prevalent in our time. It was only when reading Joy Harjo's *How to Become Human* late in 2021 that I appreciated how amazing the creative process can be. As Harjo noted, "even as we are dying something always wants to be born."

An early poem, composed in March 2019, began with images of physical distress, portending something ominous, but it veered away into a flight of almost surreal passion, almost abnormally erotic and abnormally apocalyptic. I cannot explain why, and I shall leave psycho-literary forensics to experts in the field. Two other poems written the same day—one refusing to be consoled by the artifices of rhetoric, image, sound, or diction, but acknowledging a "sinking feeling"; the other deliberately exploiting the manipulations of poetry while seeking some "closure beyond the restless mind." The poems were clusters or constellations around familiar themes, but none sought to glorify either bravado or stoicism. They used metaphor not to make false comparisons but to heighten my negative feelings about spring that felt false, its slanted light declining in a hospital ward. My will or heart weighed down with doubt, my mouth drew breaths of poetry. Although some of the poems did not resist metaphors of battle or invasion—what Sontag decried in her book-length essay on illness—they did not gild what was eerily dispiriting. They were a truth-telling, a recognition of my own vulnerability.

I have long known that there is no clearly discernible pattern in life. There is only *living*, with the heart "full afraid of the asking price" (to quote Barbara Kingsolver). Any chronicle is fundamentally a remembrance of gradual dying, because what the mind remembers has already passed in time. The disease was a long-enough misery, a season of radiation with a thermoplastic mask contoured to my face and looking like something worn by a professional fencer. There were also anxiety-producing CTs, MRIs, and neck surgery, where the maps of my body showed a family tree of inescapable burdens— some essentially genetic—making life an existential hazard. But the medical treatment and period of recuperation was an opportunity to take stock of my own life: the too-many lovers, sequences of love gained or lost, an eventual sweet partner, an only son vital to me, and attempts at a philosophic summing-up through the medium of poetry. So, what are we at the end? Any more than a bundle of molecules, a heap of ash, "death's clay" (in the words of Jane Hirshfield), a shadow of being anxious and amazed at the waste of our own salt? The poems were testaments of a year-long voyage through psychic tides. I realized that my life on Lakeshore Road East, Mississauga had crucial emblems of lake, park, road that could be shapes of silences (blue, grey, green, black), where spring could be a false lurch towards good weather, where the ample dog-run in the park could be breath in the shiver of winter, where there was no iconic imagery, only adaptable moments. I longed for my literary vocation to continue, and was in due course surprised that much did continue when so much else did not.

The cancerous cells of my body bloomed against my will, tinted with the darkness I was trying to elude. In the antiseptic chambers of Princess Margaret Hospital there was no time for bravura. Stoicism would have been a deception in an environment of bland blue gowns and tissue slippers, IV's coiling like a long snake, daily medical readings, chronic routines, and an acknowledgement of radical tropes in the body's health and tone, when skin sagged, muscle mass dwindled, bones seemed to become more brittle, ardour drooped, and the body as a whole humbled beyond expectation. Being a poet, it was difficult for me to resist the notion of illness as metaphor.

I became ever more sensitive to my surroundings, my senses more alert than they had ever been before. Even during scans in antiseptic chambers, with magnets clattering, and with the body held still, the mind was free to wander and wonder what was on the far side of existence. Words are a writer's fuel and channel, but no words, however mighty, however accurate, could evade reality. The body's diseased cells had a life of their own, and the monotony of therapeutic treatment liberated the mind to examine what was written on the skin and inside me. With one tonsil and a particular lymph node in the neck identified as prime sites of disease, I envisaged the throat in multiple images, such as beggar's bowl, fire, cup of wine, a wall gathering ghosts. My throat felt drier by the day, issuing sounds that felt raw, parched, wavering in pitch and strength. Not the sounds I liked or was used to hearing. There could be no more sugar arias in my poetry performances or readings, only turbulent sonic waves of weak volume. Christopher Hitchens, who was to die from esophageal cancer, wrote of this loss with acute, penetrating honesty in *Mortality*, drawing a link between the biological "cord" and "chord," the "resonant vibration that can stir memory, produce music, evoke love, bring tears, move crowds to pity and mobs to passion." Admitting that we may not be the only animals capable of speech, Hitchens nevertheless recognized us as "the only ones who can deploy vocal communication for sheer pleasure and recreation, combining it with our two other boasts of reason and humor to produce higher syntheses. To lose this ability is to be deprived of an entire range of faculty: It is assuredly to die more than a little."

I began to miss the best of my body. And there was no euphemism that could be more than a mask for what was really occurring within me. Words or phrases such as "chemo-cocktails" or "pain management" were mere masks for disease and its discontents. What was it like to die? What was it like to survive if the cure seemed worse at times than the disease?

Into the final week of radiation, skin on my neck split open, exposing raw flesh that burned, requiring prompt antibiotic cream applications. I could not use normal tape over the wound, so, light gauze had to suffice. I had been forewarned by nurses and attendants in the radiation chambers that for about ten days immediately following my treatment, I would experience the worst pain and discomfort imaginable. But I never imagined the worst. At home, I was on my own, except for the tender ministrations of my partner who was unable to understand the sort of discomfort I was experiencing mainly in silence, broken at times by groans and soft cries for surcease. Salvation was hardly the point; all I wanted was an end to physical distresses, such as a chronically dry mouth, almost total lack of appetite, physical exhaustion, and a sense of something burning inside my throat. Being an agnostic, I could not pray or even pretend to. Besides, I knew that prayer was self-cancelling because nobody I knew, mortal or immortal, was in charge of my body. I was an unbeliever, or at the very least, a sceptic when it came to churches and God. If there is actually a God, why the need to pray to this being for what it is going to do anyway, regardless of human petition or intervention?

My two assets, pen and voice, were stilled for nine days of this affliction that suddenly disappeared. I had lost over fifty pounds without even trying, and while I was delighted to learn that my waist had shrunk, I was perturbed by the concomitant loss of muscle mass and power. There were signs of age on my face. I looked ten years older than I was, and I wondered what other physical costs and new psychological stress I would incur on my journey back to what is vulgarly called "wellness." One consequence of the radiation was a sense of insecure balance when standing in the shower or even occasionally when one leg seemed to buckle when walking around my apartment. Sometimes my feet misunderstood their purpose and task. I immediately saw this as a metaphor for an imperilled life. Good health was definitely in the past.

But there was a vital boon: sharper perception and insight. Cancer, that dreaded octopus strangling health, could not necessarily kill the mind. It was definitely time to discover the names of my own incomprehension, and (with Jane Hirshfield's poetry in mind) to "scrape from the world its tilt and meander of wonder." I learned to notice things I had previously slighted or ignored. Being at an existential crossroad, my body humbled, I realized that we are the sum of all our choices, and that though summer seemed forever elsewhere, it could return if Hope became the skin to insulate the soul (to borrow poet Barry Dempster's wonderful metaphor).

Neck dissection surgery (sounding more sinister than it actually proved) followed in January 2020—after I had vacationed in Venice in the fall, sailing in a *vaporetto* without benefit of Mahler's melancholy music, except in the mind. Venice, where I walked over water in San Marco, lucky to miss the floods that swamped the city months later. Venice, where the cobble stones were relics of a historic past, and where Murano still boasted its bounty of the finest coloured glassware anywhere in the world. Venice, where the gondoliers still wore their antique costumes but where their gondolas were extravagantly priced and not at all as romantic as I had once believed. Venice still plagued by American tourists yearning for hot dogs and burgers. A Venice of hustlers and shlock artists plying their trade with paintings a step above shopping-mall or Farmers Market art. Venice, where a husky Peruvian busker pretended to be a musician as he caterwauled shrill, atonal sounds that threatened to contaminate all the nearby vendor stalls. Nevertheless, there was a palpable thrill in being able to walk the Rialto, sample much-praised pasta, though the finest red wine proved too much for my damaged throat. Venice, where I simply had to walk and climb, huffing and puffing up old stone bridges, lugging my bulky suitcase, larding the stones with my profuse sweat.

The Old World was always around me, but never much more than at dusk when store shutters rattled to mark the close of day, and where tourists had to walk carefully as night cast its mantle over the city, making it too dangerous to loiter near the canal, especially for those who had a phobia of dark water. Venice was only part of Italy, and Italy only a small part of Europe, and Europe itself far from being a unified giant culture. I have always loved Europe as a place to travel, knowing full well that its cities and countries have been falsified in Hollywood movies—as Rome has been with Kate Hepburn (*Summertime*); Paris with Gene Kelly and Leslie Caron (*An American in Paris*); Greece with Anthony Quinn (*Zorba the Greek*); or Spain with Ava Gardner (*The Sun Also Rises*). I have found it genuinely fascinating and awe-inspiring to explore The Spanish Steps, the Parthenon, Trevi Fountain, the Leaning Tower, the Colosseum, the Alhambra, or to drive past where Robert Graves once lived, where Federico García Lorca grew up, wander where Pablo Picasso was born, or stroll past fossilized human and animal remains behind glass or wire cages in Pompeii, swim in the Aegean Sea and emerge with salt-shine to see and touch what Yiannis Ritsos saw and touched in a confluence of eyes and hands, a meeting as real as our psyches.

Thailand awaited me after neck surgery. It, too, was an old world—but one where the larger cities (especially Bangkok) had the sheen and commercial popularity of modern technology. Modern conveniences are all to the good, but I also savour cultural authenticity in the belief that one should never travel without an open mind and heart. What is the point of travelling without expecting new discoveries, of returning home radically unchanged or unaffected by what one has experienced abroad? I always seek more than the conventional tourist attractions, North American food and drink. Water is my element, so, of course, I thrive in places with warm sand, clear blue water, outdoor swimming pools, but far more interesting than aquatic pleasure are the details of daily life in cities I have travelled in Europe, Asia, the Americas, and Australia. Our eyes and ears can tell us much more than any tourist brochure. Too many of us waste time by not seeing what is actually around us. I produced a few poems to document what I saw, felt, and thought in the knowledge that I was living out a battle between mind or soul and body. Metaphorically, the body is "a story with unwilled plots" and therefore we do not always want this story or its tropes. Sometimes we want more from the story than could be found, and far less when it is rumpled into self-loathing and terror. Perhaps we merely crave the foundational—the power to carve the world as embodiment of a complex heart.

As I voyaged through various psychic tides from 2019 to early 2020, my creative words were an intervention "for undoing some things already done." While recognizing the impossibility of refusing death, they were measurements of how we die, with the end being a release from the pressure of humanness. I conditioned myself to being open-minded about surviving this life-threatening illness—as in my *glosa*, entitled "Hope, the Skin," that takes as its launching pad four lines from Barry Dempster, a poet who has himself battled life-threatening illness. Thanks to expert medical intervention by Dr. Scott Bratman and Dr. John de Almeida at Princess Margaret Hospital, I defeated my disease. And I was fortunate to discover Frog Hollow Press that operates out of Victoria, whose editor, Shane Nielson (poet and physician), accepted roughly two dozen of the cancer poems for publication in a chapbook, elegantly designed by Caryl Wyse Peters, proprietor, for the press's Dis/Ability series. Described by Kuldip Gill as "a book artist" whose bookmaking styles and designs are "clean and distinctive, often minimalist, modern, and occasionally expressionistic," Caryl printed *Scan* in an edition of 100 numbered copies.

Despite many debilitating effects on my body, I learned to appreciate what illness taught me—especially the lesson how Time seems to move with ineffable unpredictability, speeding up my journey to the edge of an abyss, while maintaining its indifference to my literary ambition. In some ways, my illness intensified that ambition as well as my introspection. I realized that as a writer I could no longer afford to pay scant attention to the world of physical nature I usually took for granted. Mary Oliver had something to do with my new perspective, even though I do not like all or even most of her poetry because her writing tends to be unduly sentimental or sugary sweet. Her essays, however, reveal her wisdom, where she claims, "I walk in the world to love it," adding: "We need the world as much as it needs us, and we need it in privacy, intimacy, and surety." While I don't agree that the world needs us as much as we need it, Oliver astutely recognized what virtually every writer requires fundamentally for vocational support, apart from time and money. And so, after the hectic in my blood from the psychic trauma of my Armenian father, my own turbulent conflicts and self-quarrels, I looked more closely at the geography, history, and sociology of my suburban Mississauga world—neither Paradise nor Sahara. My poetry collection, *In the Bowl of My Eye* (published by Mawenzi House), is a radical departure from my previous poetic themes and aesthetic practices. It refuses to sentimentalize lake, park, and road, or to turn away from etching truthful portraits of suburban neighbours in their various anomalies and flaws. Maturity in age and experience have shaped me to be a little more like Wordsworth; in other words, "to look on nature, not as in the hour of thoughtless youth; but hearing oftentimes the still, sad music of humanity."

Nor did I refuse to interrogate myself in this world, particularly in the summative final two poems in the ninth poetry collection. Once more, mortality weighed on my mind, for I knew that life never escapes entropy, and that we cannot cancel or unbecome pain. Thorns and dark shadows remain, but we can still sing as naturally as blood coursing through our veins. There is still much unsaid in my life, songs without words, blue with melancholy, green with hope. Remembering Shakespeare, I know that time wastes us, just as many of us waste time. I have written about grief, love, ecstasy, art, disappointment, disillusionment, disease, knowing full well that whatever I have written are but shadows of real things, real passions. As I advance deeper into old age, I hope I can find a relatively secure place from where I may proudly write another significant book and still make love ardently while discovering that I am, indeed, truly understood for what I write, even though what I reveal are only pieces of my anomalous, restless self. I can truthfully and justifiably claim that because much of what I write arises from the depth of intimate experience, a reader reads *the work inside me*. I will my voice to be more than a wandering of body. I hope the voice's sound waves will reverberate longer than the body's wandering, waning, decline, and death. I wish to test the truth in George Eliot's dictum: "It is never too late to be what you might have been."

The only pattern in my life and writing has been a search for self-definition and the prospect of re-creating myself rather than simply wishing for a different life. As Joan Didion phrases it: "I write entirely to find out what I'm thinking, what I'm looking at, what I see and what it means. What I want and what I fear." Following Yeats's dictum "Out of the quarrel with others we make rhetoric; out of the quarrel with ourselves we make poetry," I have used non-fiction and poetry in this memoir. Hari Ziyad notes in his memoir *Black Boy Out of Time*, "history is, at least in part, what we interpret it to be." And interpretation can lead to healing, though not necessarily to a muting of whatever rage once burned within. But wise folk also learn that if we could replace the bad things in life with good things, what is the best in us shall not die. We do blunder towards what we want.

In theory and in practice, I am a hybrid writer—one who has no strong ties to his birth country, who moved away from it for another land, though without forgetting the first and without essentially finding a central place in the second. I have been identified as an Armenian Diaspora writer because of my voluntary migration to Canada, but I could just as easily be identified as an Anglo-Indian Diaspora writer because, though I have been assimilated to a substantial degree by social and cultural Canadian circles, I remain peripheral to the centre, sometimes by choice, sometimes because of ethnicity and post-colonial culture. I don't really fit strict categories, although I grant the validity of Homi Bhabha's theory of hybridization as a compromise between "ethnicism" and post-colonial "westernism." My mother tongue came from England, as did many of my literary influences in boyhood and adolescence, but my social customs were a mix of English and Indian, and several of my passionate instincts are Armenian. I assented to being adopted by Canada, and have said Yes to much: Yes, to the sun, moon, and stars glowing over snow and ice and the years of my youth. Yes, to apartment-living, where neighbours often remain strangers. Yes, to apple and peach picking in summer orchards. Yes, to the best of ice-hockey, the Original Six, with Howe, the Richards, Plante, Beliveau, Crozier, Hull, till the sport became bloated with its own greed. Yes, to new texts, new art, new theatre. Yes, to plastic poppies, red with memories of sacrifice in wars that kept old and new empires alive. Yes, to the privileges granted by these empires, while hating myself at times

4

for this. Yes, to the literature I create, making and removing masks, poems which find words for memories to savour. Yes, to my duty to contest this country, while trying to make a mark on its shape, and find a small place in its story. Yes, to parts of me, parts I can keep or discard. Yes, to walking backwards in order to move forward.

Although there have been many moments when I allowed myself to be acted upon, I am usually an agent of my own changes. I have never considered myself a Fifth Business in Robertson Davies's sense of the term. I am neither Hero, nor Villain, and when I have served as Confidant, it has been because of discretion or loyalty, not neutrality. I am unable to achieve a denouement in my own life, much less than in any other's. I am guilty of failures in love, marriage, and personal relationships, and have elected to cover these failures in my poetry collection *Finger to Finger* (Frontenac House). I am assertive but not aggressive, except when faced with stupidity or wilful ignorance or perversity. That is when I lose my natural inclination to comedy or satire. I know what it means to suffer, what it means to be expatriated, what it means to battle stereotypes and prejudices, what it means to feel alone even inside a good relationship. Life is not copacetic. But I believe the best of my poetry are traces of what I have believed truly about myself and everything I contain within myself, including all that I have come from. I do not believe in Heaven, but I think (to use Richard Blanco's lyrical words) there is eternity "even in our ruin," because the traces of what we have believed must endure beyond our decay." In this way, I am an optimist … barely.

I know that this book expresses my deep-rooted disquietude at feeling out of place even in my adoptive country. The writer, however, cannot be separated from place, and (as Joy Harjo contends) "even placelessness becomes a place." My feeling of being out of place is in the heart, where poetry is born and the place where poetry ends. It is a deep feeling, something kicking and pulling from within me. I recall Harjo's lines: "I am memory alive/ not just a name/ but an intricate part/ of this web of motion." But like her, like most other poets or writers, I am centrifugal.

Memoirs and autobiographies, like photographs, are memento mori, memorials (good or bad) of what has already past or died. What has survived is my deep-rooted belief in the value of literate articulation. A value that surmounts the turmoil of an inner self. The themes of my life cannot be reconciled or harmonized mechanically or by simple volition, because life is motion, which means that various strange combinations rattle about, sometimes moving me forward, sometimes backward, creating contrapuntal forces without a central unifying theme. But this, ironically, is a freedom—a freedom to be dissonant, anomalous, and, best of all, a freedom to be creative while feeling out of place. I cannot predict the future; it is difficult enough to know the past. But the past is where a sense of place begins.

I began this book with themes of childhood and death, not out of any need to be simply dramatic, and not merely to show my fate in the hands of chance. I first conceived of my text as a memoir, but in the course of writing it, I realized that it is really a story of exile—not in the sense of being wrenched away from a family home; not in the sense of being forced to leave a country for political or economic reasons. My family was not forced to leave my birth-country. Our socio-economic status came with privileges. Immigration was a free choice, though some of its consequences were not. Reading some of Roberto Bolaño's essays on literature and exile made me realize that "all literature carries exile within it, whether the writer has to pick up and go at the age of twenty or has never left home." Bolaño alludes to Adam and Eve as "the first exiles on record," articulating from their example two radical questions: "Can it be that we're all exiles? Is it possible that all of us are wandering strange lands?"

As Bolaño indicates, Jonathan Swift, "master of exile," knew that exile was "the secret word for *journey*." In my case, it was no secret, my journey freighted with good reasons for its motive, and my destination Canada, my "strange" land where I continue to wander, not in a geographical sense, but mentally, psychically. I have always recognized my own restlessness that is linked not just to being an immigrant, but to a perspective on life that is an active questing—a risk to be many things or to have different selves. I am an exile by my accent (many Canadians having told me that I sound British), by early schooling (via the Cambridge School Certificate in colonial Bombay), by a refusal to be assimilated by any group (Armenian, Anglo-Indian, even Canadian). Becoming a writer has meant that I am an exile simply by venturing into literature, just as every reader (to quote Bolaño again) becomes an exile "simply by opening a book." In the best sense, then, "exile is a literary option, similar to the option of writing. No one forces you to write." Like most writers, I have entered the labyrinth voluntarily for several reasons: because I want to be understood for who I am, how and what I love; because I want the best of my work to be loved or, at least, appreciated; because I want some of what I have created to outlive me.

Paradoxically, I am not an exile in another sense; I can write no matter where I am, even while I dream. Books are my true homeland, even as they sit on my shelves or in my memory. Sharing some pieces of my self has enabled me to reach the true height of my self, without the exaggeration or fabrication of pure memoir. I have poked fun of myself, exposed some of my greatest embarrassments, and have never pretended to have been directly in, or passed through the eye of the storm. As the son of a genocide survivor, I am one of those whom Marianne Hirsch would identify as a living representative of post-memory: someone who has experienced the "*consequence* of traumatic recall but (unlike post traumatic stress disorder) at a generational remove." I turn to Maria Stepanova for further edification, where she points out in her book *In Memory of Memory* that post-memory, "Like language, like photography ... doesn't just show us the past, but changes the present, because the past is the key to everything that occurs daily in the present."

Consequently, my psychological and literary restlessness is probably better understood along the lines of Carl Phillips's distillation in *The Art of Daring*: "Restlessness carries us to penetration—we pierce the world as we knew it, the world as we've never known it pierces us, in turn." My own hybrid identity accounts in large part for this restlessness, but so does my literary ambition. I do believe that I am mainly outside the prevailing Canadian grain as a poet because for me, the sonic is far important than the cerebral. I do not subscribe to the view that to be experimental, a poem needs to be deliberately abstruse. Word games, anagrams, ellipses, deconstructed lyrics, et cetera are only some forms of experiment. They might be the latest technical fad; they are not necessarily or predominantly the best poetry. Again, I turn to Carl Phillips's words: "Unsatisfied with the given—the usual explanations, the usual goals for and trappings of a life—there are those who push past the given, are willing to enter into uncertainty—to take a risk—in order to get to something presumably superior and/or preferable to 'the old life'." Phillips makes it clear that he does not mean corporate ambitions; instead, he means "the quest for meaning, for heightened feeling, for expanded vision, even if that should mean that we arrive at what disturbs, leaving us more unsettled, less at rest than we had been." This view implicitly acknowledges that artistic growth cannot happen without disturbance. For a writer to ignore this reality would be tantamount to abandoning his sense of integrity—which is not to say that "we cannot regret the knowledge that we come into. One is human, after all."

In summing up this partial record of a rarely placid life, let me quote from my own poetry in *Against Forgetting*:

> Need pushes my mind over words,
> standing apart, singing in my chains,
> wounded by what I have seen.
>
> This self-portrait is a reflection
> once removed. Words the glass,
> unglazed, adhering to the face,
> soul trying to break through

words to mirror hint of smile,
peculiar slant of memory,
inclinations of surfaces,
enchantments of the self.

All is metaphor,
all is winding, leading to further windings,
all is changing slightly, profoundly.

The past is here.

ACKNOWLEDGEMENTS

As Palestinian writer Edward Said observed in his memoir *Out of Place*: "Along with language, it is geography—especially in the displaced form of departures, arrivals, farewells, exile, nostalgia, homesickness, belonging, and travel itself—that is at the core of my memories ..." By the time this book is published, I shall hopefully have survived almost eight decades, in two principal countries, and with many inheritances of loss and gain. I am thankful for my mixed heritage, though I wish the fact of being human had not meant coming to terms with forgetting many details of several experiences.

Autobiography is a valuable journey when it bridges the distance in time and place between life in the present and the past. Having always been a person of intense passion and some real vulnerability, I cannot pretend any cool detachment in reconstructing events of my life. However, I can truthfully claim that I have not spared myself embarrassing or ironic narratives, though I have only assembled significant pieces of my life here, leaving other significant pieces for my poetry or miscellaneous essays.

I confess that books are my true homeland, and, therefore, I thank every writer I have ever learned from, gloried in, or learned to imitate in some degree. In Canada, I have often (perhaps too often) turned to such figures as David and Rose Scollard, Allan Briesmaster, Elana Wolff, David Bateman, and Jeff Round for their valuable comments. I also thank Don Mills who was a most loyal supporter of my writing in Mississauga, when he was Director of Library Services, for appointing me the first critic-at-large at any Canadian public library in 2000.

I am deeply grateful to Guernica Editions in general, and to Michael Mirolla (my editor) in particular for allowing me to write this version of autobiography. I also thank the Ontario Arts Council for awarding me writing grants for the same project, and the Canada Council for its publishing programs for publishers.

ABOUT THE AUTHOR

Keith Garebian is an award-winning author of over a dozen books of non-fiction and ten of poetry. His authoritative biography, *William Hutt: Soldier Actor*, has been considered definitive, and his production histories of classic Broadway musicals have been brought him accolades in the U.S. Some of his theatre books have made course reference lists in Canada and the U.S., and his writing has been cited in scores of international books, dissertations, and essays. The only Canadian writer to have been awarded the prestigious William Saroyan Medal (Armenia), Garebian is also the only four-time winner of the Mississauga Arts Award for Writing. He was the first critic-at-large for any public Canadian library, a position created for him in Mississauga in 2000 in order to review books, theatre, and dance, which he did for three years. Ever since the start of his freelance writing career in July 1975, Garebian has been published in over a hundred different international newspapers, journals, magazines, and anthologies. He has won a Canada Council Senior Arts Grant, two Work-in-Progress Grants from the Ontario Arts Council (one for non-fiction and one for poetry), and dozens of OAC Recommender Grants. He was short-listed for the *Freefall* Poetry Award and the Gwendolyn MacEwen-*Exile* Poetry Award for Best Single Poem from a suite in 2015. The following year he was short-listed for the GritLit Poetry Award. Some of his poetry has been translated into French, Armenian, Romanian, Bulgarian, and

Hebrew. One of his poems was selected as Poem of the Month in 2009 by the Parliamentary Poet Laureate, and one of his Derek Jarman poems has been set to music for choir and string instruments by American composer Gregory Spears, debuting in Philadelphia, San Francisco, and New York in 2017–19 before being recorded on CD by Navona Records. Garebian has been a featured reader in Toronto, Oakville, Mississauga, Etobicoke, Scarborough, Hamilton, Barrie, Cobourg, Stratford, St. Catharines, Newmarket, Ottawa, Vancouver, Calgary, Edmonton, Armenia, and Romania. He has served as juror for many literary awards, including the Grand Prix de la Ville de Montreal, the City of Edmonton Book Award, and the Gerald Lampert and Raymond Souster Poetry Awards.

Printed in February 2023
by Gauvin Press,
Gatineau, Québec